Women Writers and Old Age in Great Britain,
1750–1850

Women Writers and Old Age
in Great Britain, 1750–1850

DEVONEY LOOSER

The Johns Hopkins University Press

Baltimore

2 4 6 8 9 7 5 3 1

The Johns Hopkins University Press

2715 North Charles Street

Baltimore, Maryland 21218-4363

www.press.jhu.edu

Library of Congress Cataloging-in-Publication Data

Looser, Devoney, 1967–.

Women writers and old age in Great Britain, 1750–1850 / Devoney Looser.

p.   cm.

Includes bibliographical references and index.

ISBN-13: 978-0-8018-8705-5 (acid-free paper)

ISBN-10: 0-8018-8705-4 (acid-free paper)

1. English literature—Women authors—History and criticism. 2. Older women—
Great Britain. 3. Women and literature—Great Britain—History—18th century.
4. Women and literature—Great Britain—History—19th century. 5. Old age—Social
aspects—Great Britain. 6. Edgeworth, Maria, 1767–1849—Criticism and interpretation.
7. Burney, Fanny, 1752–1840—Criticism and interpretation. 8. Barbauld,
Mrs. (Anna Letitia), 1743–1825—Criticism and interpretation. I. Title.

PR111.L67 2008

820.9′354—dc22

2008000586

A catalog record for this book is available from the British Library.

*Special discounts are available for bulk purchases of this book. For more information,
please contact Special Sales at 410-516-6936 or specialsales@press.jhu.edu.*

Would You Be Young Again?

Would you be young again?
So would not I
One tear to memory given,
Onward I'd hie.

—*Carolina Oliphant, Lady Nairne (1766–1845)*

CONTENTS

A decade ago I opened a copy of Victorian critic Jerom Murch's *Mrs. Barbauld and Her Contemporaries* (1877). Skimming the slim volume, I noticed that it concluded with a short section titled "How Long They Lived!" followed by a table of female author's names, listing the year in which they died and sorted by their ages at death. (Barbauld was squarely in the middle, at age 82.) Looking over this list, I thought, "These women lived awfully long lives. I wonder why nobody talks about that?" That moment, naive as it was, provided the genesis of this book. Now I see more to question in Murch's data. I learned that it was not so *very* strange for a woman to live a long life prior to the twentieth century. I, like many before me, had confused life expectancy with life span. It is true that life expectancy in Europe remained at around 35 years until 1800—less than half of what it is today in developed countries. But the age to which one might have been expected to live in eighteenth- and nineteenth-century Great Britain looks quite different when deaths in infancy and childhood are factored out. Life span (the maximum age that humans generally reached) was not all that different in past centuries. Even for those individuals who did not make it to the upper limits, living to what was considered old age was by no means extraordinary.

Although his conclusions were based on a handful of examples, Murch believed that women writers' long lives *were* remarkable, even when compared with the lives of literary men.[1] Still, Murch's chart is fascinating, indicative of an ability—or perhaps a willingness—to perceive aged authors as a group. As it turns out, Murch's was not a voice in the wilderness. In the mid-nineteenth century, claims about the long lives of previous generations of British literary women were made with frequency, viewed as sound scholarship, and used in some surprising ways. For example, a short periodical piece, "Modern Old Age," appeared in the London periodical *Once a Week* in 1863. The essay's anonymous author briefly analyzes the longevity of statesmen, military men, and philosophers, but at the end of the essay notes, "There is something remarkable in the longevity of our literary women in modern times, even if we do not look beyond our own country."[2] Oddly, the writer concludes that Hester Piozzi (1741–1821) and Mary Delany (1700–1788) "scarcely enter within the conditions," though both women authors lived into their eighties (584). Even more unexpectedly, as if to point out that some geniuses die young, the author concludes, "the still-lamented Jane Austen was under an early doom" (582). Then it is noted that "Miss Edgeworth was above eighty when she died; Joanna and Agnes Baillie were older still; and Mrs. Trollope died the other day at 84." (582). This paragraph on women writers and longevity was judged important enough to be excerpted and republished abroad in the *Scientific American*.[3] Throughout the Victorian era, there was a demand for stories about and explanations of longevity, and British women writers featured prominently in this literature.

Some decades before this piece was published, and before Edgeworth, Baillie, and Trollope had died, another writer created a Murch-like list, noting the names of celebrated eighteenth-century women writers who reached old age. That comment occurred in a review of R. R. Madden's *The Infirmities of Genius* (1833).[4] One portion of Madden's study attempted to calculate and account for the average age to which celebrated men lived, depending on their profession. He tried to account for the discrepancies in longevity discovered among practitioners, claiming that natural philosophers lived the longest lives and poets the shortest. His first reviewers were skeptical, and the *Quarterly Review* was especially damning. Its anonymous reviewer began "Here is a good subject sadly marred."[5]

Though it does a hatchet job on Madden's book, the *Quarterly* spends pages describing what the book might have been in more capable hands. In one colorful section, the reviewer criticizes Madden for overlooking celebrated women. It is strange to say, the reviewer notes, but "Mr. Madden, who mentions in his volumes some hundreds of writers, does not allude to one single female—unless, indeed, the name Radcliffe . . . is meant . . . for Mrs. Radcliffe the novelist" (52). The reviewer is skeptical that the cleverest women in the population are those who become writers but asserts that "the flagrant omission of Mr. Madden's tables has turned our attention to the longevity of many of the female authors of the last century" (53). The reviewer then constructs a new table of the most celebrated authors and their ages at death (some of which are in error): Lady Russell (87), Mrs. Rowe (63), Lady M. W. Montague (73), Mrs. Centlivre (44), Lady Hervey (70), Lady Suffolk (79), Mrs. Sheridan (47), Mrs. Cowley (66), Mrs. Macaulay (53), Mrs. Montagu (81), Mrs. Chapone (75), Mrs. Lennox (84), Mrs. Trimmer (69), Mrs. Hamilton (65), Mrs. Radcliffe (60), Mrs. Barbauld (83), Mrs. Delany (93), Mrs. Inchbald (68), Mrs. Piozzi (80), and Mrs. Hannah More (88).[6]

Despite the reviewer's acknowledgment that some of these women became authors involuntarily by the publication of their private letters, he or she concludes: "On the whole, we believe it will be found that eminent literary ladies are longlived." This is the case, the reviewer argues, because "the works on which their fame rests are generally the production of matured age" (53). As with the material from *Once a Week*, this reviewer's chart of "eminent literary ladies'" names and ages was considered significant enough to circulate further, reprinted in the *Medical and Chirurgical Review*.[7] No one took up the reviewer's challenge to tackle the subject of long-lived literary women in a better book than Madden's, and even Murch's book recapitulated rather than advanced knowledge on the subject. Still, anecdotes about the longevity of female authors from the recent past were published with regularity.

From today's scholarly perch, it is evident that Murch and his ilk were overstating the case about the extent to which British women writers enjoyed unusually long lives. If we were able to compile reliable information, it seems unlikely that we would find a significant tendency toward superlongevity among female authors, particularly if we controlled for class or financial status. Regardless of previous critics' exaggerations or errors, however, their studies show a shared *perception* that famous women writers lived long lives. These writers who reached advanced ages came to be considered interesting as a group and were believed to share certain personal qualities. For Murch, the lives of women writers in old age were "calm and gentle" (175). For Madden's reviewer, they were almost all of "immaculate private character" (53). Regardless of the ways in which they were criticized or condescended to individually, old women writers of the late eighteenth and early nineteenth centuries were almost always celebrated as a collective in the decades that followed. Reaching old age was not presented as something that long-lived female authors alone might appreciate; it was also understood as a condition for which Britons should rejoice. The people were encouraged to congratulate themselves for having provided the fertile soil that produced so many women writers of distinction and that nurtured those women into old age. To be able to boast long-lived eminent female authors was, at least for a time in the nineteenth century, a badge of national pride. This was something new indeed in

English literary history, although rarely pursued as a subject by twentieth-century scholars.[8] Longevity studies turned in a different, more scientific direction, and British women writers of the eighteenth and early nineteenth centuries no longer provided a patriotic rallying cry.

If the study of aged women writers in the past did not experience a flowering in the twentieth century, the study of the aged themselves did. In 1977, the Cambridge historian of aging Peter Laslett defined gerontology as "the study of aging as a process and of the old as a social group," noting that historical sociology was then the newest of the social sciences.[9] It would seem that the study of old age in the humanities got off the ground later. Labeling our work still remains a challenge, though Margaret Morganroth Gullette has suggested a shift from "literary gerontology" to "age studies," a term she coined to define "age more explicitly as a set of historical and cultural concepts (like gender or race) useful for investigating how a culture builds age constructions and reproduces them."[10] As she argues, "Age studies undoes the erasure of the cultural in the sphere of age and aging," much as feminist theory "denaturalized female/male difference."[11] It has been suggested that today's "feminists are beginning to examine age theory because feminists are themselves aging."[12] If so, we have thus far been most interested in our own lives and times.[13] For a while, I took to calling what I was trying to accomplish in this book literary historical gerontography, though that neologism seemed to confuse more than clarify. I still like the way it suggests that writing about lives with a focus on advanced age is a compensatory gesture, following what has so often been a slight to that life stage in traditional literary—and even feminist literary—biography.

In the years since I started working on this subject, I have been surprised at how many times I have been asked why a "young" (or middle-aged) person would choose to study the old. Though fewer and fewer academics today seem to raise an eyebrow at colleagues writing books about those not of their race, gender, class, sexuality, or nation, it seems that old age remains a subject assumed somehow unfit for the young. Or perhaps old age is perceived as an area of study of interest only to the old. Scholars themselves have tried to prove their credentials for writing about the old by stating their own ages, as when Laslett begins a book by revealing, "My first writing on the history of ageing . . . appeared when I was sixty-one and nearly all the rest of the work was done in my later sixties and early seventies."[14] I became so accustomed to getting questions about why I would choose to write this book before my own old age that my responses must have started to sound canned. Sometimes I offered my close questioners an academic answer—the one described at the beginning of this preface—charting an interest in the subject as it arose from reading in British women's writings and historiography. At that time, I had also been teaching William Wordsworth's poems, wondering about his allegedly becoming conservative (or even boring) in old age, in relation to Gloria Steinem's essay on why young women are more conservative.[15] The two subjects ignited the spark of this book.

At other times, when asked why I was writing about women writers in old age, I gave biographical answers. When I was ten years old, I would explain, my father's mother moved in with us. She was part of my nuclear family until she died, at the end of my first year in graduate school. Grandmother Looser and I had what is euphemistically called a "difficult relationship," and it was formative, prompting me to take an undergraduate literature course, "Grow Old Along with Me," from the amazing Barbara Andersen, at Augsburg College. We read Wendell Berry, May Sarton, and Elizabeth Jolley, among others, and twenty years later, I remember the course in vivid and appreciative detail. That indirectly led to my teaching an undergraduate course, "Stages and Transitions in Women's Lives," at the University of Wisconsin–Whitewater—an enriching experience. Finally, I would turn skeptical questions about my fitness for writing about this subject into a joke that usually fell flat: Gee, I sure hoped I would finish the book prior to my own dotage.

In addition to the skeptics, there were also those who immediately expressed enthusiasm for this project, often with greater knowledge than I had. One of the first to encourage me to write about eighteenth-century old age was Paula Backscheider. When she heard of my plan, she copied and sent me every piece of paper she had collected in a file on the subject, as she had once contemplated writing a book on it herself. I know I have not done justice to the capacious and learned study she once envisioned writing, but her generosity throughout this project has been unwavering and inspiring. Others, too, supported this project at an early stage and allowed it to flower. Judy Slagle chaired a session on old age at the American Society for Eighteenth-Century Studies in 1998 and was kind enough to include me on the panel. Many audiences at conferences and in classrooms indulged my interest and provided food for thought. The Jane Austen Society of Australia and the organizers and audience of their 2002 conference—particularly Susannah Fullerton, Penny Gay, Meg Hayward, and Helen Malcher—offered friendship and feedback. The James Smith Noel Collection at LSU-Shreveport twice provided a warm welcome, during their Women's Week Celebration and during the "Daring

Women of the Enlightenment" symposium. (I cannot thank enough the incomparable Bob Leitz, Helen Taylor, and Diane Boyd.) The Western Society for Eighteenth-Century Studies hosted me as a plenary speaker in 2006, at a meeting that organizers Hank Keithley and Skip Brack made congenial and fruitful.

Colleagues at several institutions encouraged the writing of this book. I ought rightly to list more of them, but it seems especially important to note the support of Dan Bivona, Jim Broaddus, Martin Camargo, Sandy Camargo, Elizabeth Chang, Anne Coldiron, Kevin Cope, Sharon Crowley, Pat Crown, Matt Gordon, Myrna Handley, Katie Heninger, Haskell Hinnant, Becky Hogan, Joe Hogan, Kitty Holland, Jake Jakaitis, Elizabeth Kim, Ted Koditschek, Trudy Lewis, Jackie Litt, Mark Lussier, Michelle Massé, Linda Maule, Harriet McNeal, Elsie Michie, Rick Moreland, Anne Myers, Pat Okker, Catherine Parke, Irv Peckham, Katy Powell, Malcolm Richardson, Joe Weixlmann, Sharon Weltman, Eric Wertheimer, Nancy West, Ed White, Jeff Williams, and Paul Young. Some colleagues read part or all of this manuscript, and I would like particularly to thank Rita Cavigioli, Noah Heringman, Emily Hipchen, and Bill Kerwin. Research Assistant Mike Redmond provided significant and helpful labor at Louisiana State University, as did Jennifer Albin, Jennifer Garlich, and Emily Wiggins at the University of Missouri–Columbia. I am also indebted to the students of two MU graduate seminars, "Eighteenth-Century British Women Writers and Literary Traditions" (winter 2005) and "Jane Austen Among Women" (winter 2007), for their incisive comments and good will.

I am profoundly grateful to a wider circle of colleagues elsewhere who offered their wisdom, including Andrew Baster, Martine Watson Brownley, Antoinette Burton, Susan Carlile, Tita Chico, Tom DiPiero, Elizabeth Eger, Bob Erickson, Margaret Ezell, Patsy Fowler, Linda Frost, Jane Gallop, Anne Goldgar, Jocelyn Harris, Deb Heller, Catherine Ingrassia, Laurie Kaplan, Christine Krueger, Tom Lockwood, April London, Teresa Mangum, Albert Rivero, George Rousseau, Peter Sabor, Norbert Schurer, Rajani Sudan, Kathy Woodward, and Howard Weinbrot. I honor the teachers who led me to this scholarly work, especially Ann Kaplan, Boyd Koehler, Cathie Nicholl, Ron Palosaari, Cliff Siskin, the late Michael Sprinker, and Rose Zimbardo. I am especially thankful to those without any institutional connection to me who graciously read parts of the manuscript, particularly Eve Tavor Bannet, Kate Davies, Laura Mandell, Bill McCarthy, Tom McLean, Rebecca Shapiro, and Orianne Smith. Patricia Meyer Spacks led an amazing seminar on Jane

Austen's *Emma* in 2003 at the National Humanities Center, in which I participated. Both the time Pat spent talking with me about this project and the experience at the NHC itself were wonderful. I am also grateful for the immensely helpful comments of Susan Lanser, who was the reader for the Johns Hopkins University Press, as well as to editor Michael Lonegro, copyeditor Barbara Lamb, and others, who believed in this project and worked to shape it and make it better.

This book was made possible by several research grants. The University of Missouri–Columbia Research Council provided a summer fellowship and much additional assistance, and the University of Missouri's Research Board provided a year's leave from teaching to travel and write. During that time, several libraries supported archival research. The Fletcher Jones Foundation Fellowship supported research at the Huntington Library, where I became indebted to Gayle Richardson. I benefited enormously from a King's College London Special Collections Fellowship and from the guidance of Katie Sambrook. Laura O'Keefe at the Pforzheimer Collection of the New York Public Library also went out of her way to offer expertise. My time as the Midwest Modern Language Association Fellow at the Newberry Library proved invaluable. The University of Kansas Spencer Library also provided a travel grant, and I was able to return there under the auspices of a Big 12 Fellowship. I am grateful to Karen Cook, Rick Clement, Bill Crowe, and the wonderful staff at the Spencer.

Quotations from the manuscripts of Jane Porter are reproduced by courtesy of Special Collections, Spencer Research Library, University of Kansas Libraries; by kind permission of the President and Council of the Royal College of Surgeons of England; by permission of the Manuscripts Division of the National Library of Scotland; from the Gilder Lehrman Collection at the New-York Historical Society, courtesy of the Gilder Lehrman Institute of American History (not to be reproduced without written permission); from the Jane Porter Papers, Huntington Library, San Marino, California; and from the British Library's Department of Manuscripts. Quotations from the manuscripts of Hester Lynch Piozzi are reproduced by courtesy of the Houghton Library, Harvard College Library. The image of Hester Lynch Piozzi from *Retrospection* is used with the permission of the James Smith Noel Collection, Louisiana State University in Shreveport.

Portions of the introduction first appeared in "What the Devil a Woman Lives for after 30: The Late Careers of Late Eighteenth-Century British Women Writers," published in the *Journal of Aging and Identity* (4.1 [1999]:

3–11). They are used with kind permission of Springer Science and Business Media. Portions of the introduction and chapter 1 appeared in "Women, Old Age, and the Eighteenth-Century Novel," in *The Companion to the Eighteenth-Century English Novel and Culture,* edited by Paula Backscheider and Catherine Ingrassia (Oxford: Blackwell, 2005), used by permission. An earlier version of chapter 2, " 'Those Historical Laurels which Once Graced My Brow are Now in Their Wane': Catharine Macaulay's Last Years and Legacy," first appeared in *Studies in Romanticism* (42 [summer 2003]), used by permission, with thanks to the Trustees of Boston University. Finally, portions of chapter 3 appeared in "Old Dogs and New Tricks: Austen's Female Elders," in *Sensibilities* (Journal of the Jane Austen Society of Australia) (25 [Dec. 2002]), also used by permission.

I save my final thanks for my family. Its two youngest members, Carl Anchor Justice and Lowell Williamson Justice, appeared during the writing of this book. I am extremely grateful to their caregivers—especially Libby Driscoll, Jessica Pike, Jesse Schulz, Amy Spindler, the teachers at Children's House Montessori, and the unparalleled Toni Crowell—for all they did to raise our children with us. My in-laws, Judy and Jack Justice, and the Gellert and Porter families, have been unfailingly supportive. My parents, Sharon and LeRoy Looser, joyfully took on childcare duties that made this book possible. My thanks, too, to my grandmother, Virginia Sarslow, a model courageous and colorful older dame. Final thanks must go to the Chief Justice, colleague, editor, and husband extraordinaire: George, you are generous.

Women Writers and Old Age in Great Britain,
1750–1850

Introduction

Women Writers and Old Age, 1750–1850

Jane Austen died at age 41. Her death in middle age, long decried as one of literature's notable tragedies, has led to some peculiar errors in grasping her position in literary history. In *A Room of One's Own* (1929), Virginia Woolf describes Austen as owing a debt to a foremother. Woolf argues passionately, "Jane Austen should have laid a wreath upon the grave of Fanny Burney."[1] This is an impossible admonition, as we ought to recognize. Austen died twenty years before such an offering could have been made. Burney, who published her first novel when Austen was two years old, lived until 1840 and to age 87. For years, however, many of us have read over and perhaps even sympathized with Woolf's wish without doing the math.[2] Maria Edgeworth, too, has been seen as a figure who "points forward to both Jane Austen and Sir Walter Scott," despite her substantial literary contributions long *after* the other two began (and stopped) publishing novels.[3] Most literary histories position Burney and Edgeworth as before, rather than after, Austen. In reality, they—like many of Austen's female contemporaries—were both.

Burney, Edgeworth, and dozens of other British women writers of this era enjoyed opportunities and faced obstacles that Jane Austen did not, as they pursued authorship into old age. These long-lived writers negotiated the literary marketplace early in their lives, during a time when women authors achieved greater visibility and, for some, greater respectability. Then, in their later years—as I argue in this book—these authors encountered a new set of complicated prejudices for which they were largely unprepared. Elderly women writers crafted many kinds of responses to these conditions, resulting in a myriad of experiences, choices, and outcomes. Nevertheless, little work has appeared to document the frequency and scope of these difficulties as faced by the first mass of published women writers who survived to advanced age. Indeed, there are no previous scholarly books on the subject, and only a handful of studies have been devoted to old women in the early modern period.[4]

The scholarship that has been published on the history of aging establishes that eighteenth- and nineteenth-century elderly persons were as different from each other in old age as in youth and middle age. Identity categories and experiences that differentiated individuals in early and mid-life persisted into old age. In eighteenth-century Great Britain, as Susannah R. Ottaway's pioneering work demonstrates, people experienced old age variously based on gender and class. The "decline of life" could be felt in incredibly stratified ways, with aged, elite men and males of the middling classes finding "an especially congenial context" in their later years.[5] Because retirement was optional and because there was no uniform stigmatization of the aged, rich old men might expect and be granted respect and authority. Aged men of moderate means would have had to struggle against downward mobility, but for women of the elite and middling classes, Ottaway argues, old age was more likely to be experienced as a period of loss—both in terms of property and law and in terms of the perceptions of physical decay.[6] The culture's fixation on a youthful physical ideal was especially directed toward women. "Men and women were deemed old based on very different criteria," as Teresa Mangum has argued about the later nineteenth century.[7]

Based on such conclusions, it seems that we have a good deal to learn by studying women writers apart from men in the context of eighteenth- and nineteenth-century old age. But just because men and women experienced old age differently does not mean that old men and old women *ought* to be studied separately. In each chapter of this book I bring in examples from the lives and careers of aged male authors, but I argue that we are often in a better position to identify heretofore unrecognized trends and cultural responses when we isolate women in studies of history, literature, and old age. Much work remains to be done to establish how ideologies of gender, class, and aging changed across the period, but initial research supports the claim that older female writers were judged more harshly than older male writers in early modern Great Britain. Just as a man's gender might go unremarked by those examining his writings, so might his age. For women, however, neither age nor gender was likely to go unnoticed, as the two categories combined to bring what we might now call sexist and ageist undercurrents to bear on their writings. Despite their significant differences from each other, women writers in old age ought to be considered as a group because they experienced similarly couched responses from critics and readers, who may or may not have been old themselves.

"Old woman" and "old woman author" called up quite different associations from "old man" and "old [male] author" in the eighteenth and nineteenth centuries. As one popular conduct book's narrator advised a daughter, "When you are old, no object of attainment remains to be pursued, except the practice of virtue."[8] This would seem to preclude pursuing authorship. To be sure, male writers also faced limiting stereotypes in old age, but they seem to have had access to more strongly developed and enabling roles, too, such as that of the revered sage. Eighteenth-century references to an "old sage" were almost always to men. Edward Burnaby Greene's poetical essay "The Youth and the Philosopher" (1772) is typical, admonishing readers to revere the joyful, peaceful, white-haired old sage as the "best of fathers—and of friends."[9] An elderly woman writing during this period could not expect that higher status and positive qualities would accrue with advanced years. If there was a tradition of forefathers and even foremothers on which some female writers (and their readers) could draw, there was no sense of "foregrandmothers."[10] In part, this is because of the way that literary history tended to erase or forget the accomplishments of previous generations of women. This is seen clearly in one of Elizabeth Barrett Browning's letters from 1845: "England has had many learned women . . . and yet where were the poetesses? . . . I look everywhere for Grandmothers and see none. It is not in the filial spirit I am deficient, I do assure you—witness my reverent love of the grandfathers!"[11] It is fascinating that Barrett Browning could not identify "Grandmothers" as she tried to imagine the history of women's poetry. Of course, she was not literally looking for old women writers in the past. But even her use of "grandmother," in addition to demonstrating that mainstream literary histories had not successfully handed down the names of many eighteenth-century women poets, suggests that she envisioned the accomplished older writers ("literary grandfathers" one could "revere") as men.[12]

If there was a danger in being forgotten as an aged woman writer, there was also a cost for being remembered. Some female authors took great pains to hide their ages, just as some hid their gender, through anonymous or pseudonymous publication. For a published author who laid claim to her past works, whether through their titles or through her own name, there was little opportunity to finesse chronological age—unless to portray herself as older than she actually was. *Fraser's Magazine* described this situation directly in a short biographical piece about the novelist Jane Porter (bap. 1776–1850), published

as part of its "Gallery of Illustrious Literary Characters." The 1835 essay, probably by William Maginn (1794–1842), was accompanied by a portrait of Porter,
then nearly 60. Of this portrait, probably by Daniel Maclise, Maginn comments:
"She wears the years well; but these publications [in her youth] are sad tell-tales.
Many a lady of Miss Porter's standing, if she had kept Miss Porter's good looks,
could well smuggle off ten or a dozen years from the account, if she had not
dabbled in the printer's work. Joe Miller informs us that a coal-porter having
inquired what the crime was for which he saw a man hanging at Tyburn-tree,
and being told that it was for forgery, exclaimed, 'Ay, that comes of knowing
how to read and write, my good fellow!' We are tempted to make a similar
exclamation when we find a lady rendering the footsteps of time traceable, by
manifesting her powers of penmanship."[13] To risk rendering the footsteps of
time traceable would seem a small price to pay for literary fame, but as this
droll anecdote implies, old women writers did so at their own peril. Old age
was presented as a woman's source of shame, something to be covered over,
and revealing it akin—in an associative sense—to a criminal act.

Regardless of how women writers of the era experienced the combination
of gender, authorship, and old age, all who lived beyond age 55 or 60 faced
the prospect of being judged for the united appropriateness of these characteristics, the parameters of which seem to have been narrower than those
faced by men. Wisdom was touted as a *desirable* quality for older women but
often as a fallback position. As poet Thomas Parnell (1679–1718) put it in "An
Elegy, To an Old Beauty" (widely reprinted throughout the century), "Why
really *Fifty Five* is something old." The poem encourages the old woman to
cultivate wisdom instead because with beauty gone, " 'tis easier to be wise."[14]
The figure of "grandmother wisdom," discussed by Robert Erickson, was one
avenue for that cultivation.[15] An old woman showcasing her knowledge relating
to marriage and childbirth—as long as it was on behalf of someone else—had
a long cultural history on which to draw to claim expertise (148, 6–7).

The connection of old womanhood to wisdom seems to have shifted across
the eighteenth century, although not all scholars agree about the nature of
the shift. "In [European] advice literature from the turn of the eighteenth
century," as Maria Van Tilburg argues, "the male gained wisdom at old age"
but "the female did not change with age."[16] In contrast to this position, Lois
Banner, in her landmark study, *In Full Flower: Aging Women, Power, and Sexuality* (1992), asserts that a "sharp break in the definition of women's nature
. . . occurred in the eighteenth century [that] . . . applied especially to aging
women."[17] Banner suggests that new family formations allowed a "definitional

Jane Porter

THE AUTHORESS OF 'THADDEUS OF WARSAW'.

Published by James Fraser, 215, Regent Street, London:

Portrait of Jane Porter, published in *Fraser's Magazine* (1835)

shift," producing a previously unavailable "modern 'grandmother' role for aging women" (17).[18] She spends little time on eighteenth- or nineteenth-century British lives or representations, however, and her hypotheses are not borne out in the materials about female authors that I have consulted. Terri L. Premo, too, finds that post-Revolutionary American aged women were able successfully to claim wisdom in a domestic context, possibly because of their memories and experiences in the war, though their reminiscing about and glorying in that knowledge also threatened to separate them from their descendants (115, 182). My work suggests that British women writers did not have a *necessary* connection to the once-available figures of the wise old woman or to the grandmother wisdom tradition, though, as we will see, some writers were more successful than others in reviving or reinventing the category to suit their own purposes.

Most twentieth-century literary critics have ignored or given short shrift to women's late lives in the early modern period, so it remains a challenge to draw together even bare facts about individual writers and their late works. Where they exist, biographies tend to consider old age the least interesting period of a subject's life, often treating it as a kind of epilogue. Books with titles such as *The Young Fanny Burney, Young Sam Johnson, Young Boswell,* and *Young Walter Scott* line our library shelves, but there are few companion volumes trumpeting these authors' lives as old men and women.[19] Not all of the challenges we face in gathering information about authors in old age are the result of neglect by critics. One obstacle may rest with the writers themselves, as the elderly are believed to have sometimes exaggerated their ages and "to have declared themselves at the decadal years to a great extent," as Peter Laslett has argued.[20] Ottaway describes this as "age heaping," the tendency to use round figures—ending in zero or five—when asked one's age (45). In addition to determining actual ages of lesser known authors, another obstacle in revisiting (or revising) our understandings of aged British women writers is that even for the most celebrated, late writings may be less accessible. Pulling together information about female authors and old age is challenging in that one often needs to rely either on questionable early sources or return to archival documents and rare editions.

Such work, despite these obstacles, is well worth our efforts, for many reasons. First, and perhaps foremost, continuing to ignore the later lives and writings of British women authors—even the most famous of them—skews our sense of literary history. Many writers whom we categorize as of the eighteenth century or Romantic era were active well into the nineteenth century.

As scholars of three different fields (eighteenth century, Romantic, and Victorian), we have tended to underdiscuss writers' late contributions when they straddle our traditional periods. Instead, we have grouped them as belonging to the era of their first publications. This may go some distance toward explaining why "Victorian" writer Frances Trollope (1779–1863) and "eighteenth-century" author Maria Edgeworth (1768–1849) are so difficult to imagine as near contemporaries. Considering the full life spans and careers of writers has the potential to refigure radically and productively our visions of literary history, whether in terms of periodization, authorial and generic trends, or the literary marketplace. We simply cannot understand the literary past with much nuance if we continue to pigeonhole authors into eras that their published and unpublished writings significantly postdate.

By studying women writers in old age, we may also discover additional explanations for phenomena that have formerly seemed to be individual vagaries. A theory that I work with in this book is that living to an advanced age may have had a generally negative effect on a woman writer's posthumous reputation. As my research into several key figures indicates, reviews of late writings were often derisive, as reviewers used the fact of a woman writer's old age to dismiss her work's relevance or quality. The best an older woman author could hope for was to become a "classic," and it was difficult to dwindle into a classic if you were still in the public eye or, worse still, had hopes of continuing to contribute to your stock of ideas. For a celebrated female author to continue to publish into old age was to risk lowering a once-high reputation, but ceasing publication was not necessarily a winning scenario, either. Where women writers did not (or could not) continue to publish into old age, gradual neglect or devaluation of their earlier contributions seems to have made posthumous notice that much less likely. A number of aged women writers saw their reputations and fame diminishing before their eyes, and a few fought to reverse the process. A number lived to see their earlier works branded classics, which had its own peculiar benefits and drawbacks. Of course, some long-lived women writing in the period did not seek print during their lifetimes. We might think of Dorothy Wordsworth (1771–1855), who published nothing, or Lady Louisa Stuart (1757–1851), who published very little. Though I do not consider cases like theirs here, the question of what happened to eighteenth- and nineteenth-century women writers' reputations when the bulk of their works were published posthumously is an interesting one.

The present volume opens up avenues in the territory sketched above, through a study of the lives, careers, writings, and receptions of a number of long-lived female authors. Using case studies of women writers who lived to advanced ages, I demonstrate what is at stake in exploring aging, gender, and authorship in tandem. I show some of the new readings, as well as critical and historical consequences, that might emerge if we attend to literary history through the lens of women's aging. We may discover, as I have already suggested, that the most significant thing these aged female authors had in common was the way they were treated by readers and critics—and even by posterity. I suspect we will locate more evidence of nascent forms of what Susan Sontag called "the double standard of aging" operating among authors in the early modern period.[21] Scholarship establishing the ways in which sex-based ideologies functioned during this era has rapidly advanced. Although scholarship on age-based ideologies is in a more fledgling state, as Kirk Combe and Kenneth Schmader conclude, "the elderly of pre-industrial Western societies" "both cognitively and sexually . . . suffered from the stigma of . . . callous myths" that may have been precursors to those we see today.[22]

In the remainder of this introduction, I review recent scholarship on the history of old age and draw together information from early modern sources in order to make sense of how "old" was defined from 1750–1850, a period of significant change for authorship and for conceptions of old age.[23] I describe dominant stereotypes and how they were stratified by gender as well as potentially experienced by aged authors. Next, I offer evidence to establish the variety of life circumstances and challenges that older British women writers of the period faced, comparing them to male contemporaries, and end with short descriptions of the book's chapters. Throughout the book, I argue for the importance of our recognizing the often hidden impact of women writers' old age on the history of British literature, on the level of both the individual and the group, synchronically and diachronically.

Charting the "Old" in Past Centuries

Recent historians and demographers have overturned many myths about the old in past centuries, including the idea that the elderly were few and far between and that they were once treated with universal reverence. As one scholar has put it, "we are at an exciting, if incomplete, stage of assembling both small and large stories about different times and places in the search for a more complete history of old age."[24] We now know that prior to the nineteenth century, "those who made it to 20 had . . . a good chance of living to their later fifties, or sixties, especially if they were female."[25] David

Troyansky notes that in the second half of the eighteenth century, "when one sets aside the large contingent of youth, one recognizes that those over 60 could represent 13, 15 or even 18 percent of all those over 20."[26] "There was no rarity value in being old" in the early modern period, as Lynn Botelho has argued.[27] Yet it has proven difficult to determine what to count as old, whether considered a matter of chronological age, bodily decay, or other factors. Most scholars agree that the term *old*, in actual usage, was fluid and had more to do with capabilities than with strict numerical benchmarks. In determining whether an individual qualified as old, emphasis was frequently placed on the ability to perform tasks. Distinctions were also drawn at this time between the *young old* (so-called green old age) and the *old old* or infirm old. These seem to have been conditional rather than chronological categories. Even so, numerical age remained an important marker.[28] William Gordon's *Plan of a Society for Making Provisions for Widows* (1772) proposes that members in the society be "not too far advanced in life" and sets an age limit of 60 for joining.[29]

Certain numbers took on special significance, such as the "grand climacteric" at age 63, an aging concept that circulated from the early seventeenth to the mid-nineteenth century. A climacteric was a life stage of either seven or nine years, and, according to the *Oxford English Dictionary*, the grand, or great, climacteric, which occurred at nine times seven, was viewed as particularly momentous, leading to "change in health and fortune" on a significant scale. The grand climacteric might be seen as a kind of gateway to old age, though some used decadal years as a shorthand for describing aging stages. Classical literature defined old age at 55 or 60 for men and at 45 to 50 for women.[30] Peter Stearns, following many recent scholars, defines the onset of old age in the early modern period as occurring between 55 and 60. Ottaway concurs that 60 is repeatedly invoked as the beginning of eighteenth-century old age. For the purposes of this study, *old age* will be understood to indicate a person's having reached the age of 60—except in the case of "old maids," who might have been considered old from age 30 or 40 onward.

Recent scholarship, especially the groundbreaking research published by historian Pat Thane, emphasizes that what it meant to be old has changed over time and that old people have never formed a single, simple category. Thane argues that competing discourses and representations of old age circulated simultaneously, but she questions whether gender ought to be understood as a significant separate factor in old age. Her studies of diaries, social surveys, and poor law records lead her to conclude that "for women as for men, old age was perceived more subjectively, in relation to social power and/ or physical activity, appearance, and capacity for work, rather than with some abstract conception of old age."[51] Elsewhere, she notes that "in all times older people (female and male) who retained economic or any other form of power, along with their faculties, could command, or enforce, respect" ("Social" 105). Although such generalizations may hold true for in-person contact—that is, that embodied factors and class outweighed gender in determining how older people were perceived and treated in person—there is at the same time evidence that "abstract conceptions of old age" were themselves rather powerful. These abstract conceptions were certainly used as filters for assessing aged authors, whose chronological ages may have been known but whose bodily condition or personal wealth were probably hidden from critics or readers. Authors (themselves of varying economic circumstances, though generally of the "middle ranks") were not simply able to command or enforce respect, despite the potential power of their access to print. Even so, I agree with Thane that "there is an ongoing dialectic between differing conceptions of what it is to be old" during any given period; this cultural dialectic is one that eighteenth- and nineteenth-century authors, male and female, attempted to manipulate for their own benefit ("Untiring Zest" 246).

Misconceptions have long circulated regarding the history of the study of old age. *The Oxford Book of Aging* mistakenly asserts, "As a separate topic of scientific inquiry, medical practice, philosophic speculation, personal meditation, or literary and artistic representation, aging is largely a creation of the last 150 years."[52] On the contrary, many earlier works attended to old age as a separate topic of inquiry. John Sinclair's four-volume *Code of Health and Longevity* (1804) included material from classical authors, pictures of the aged, and a list of approximately 2,000 titles on the topic, 309 of them published in Great Britain. Sinclair was most interested in methods of prolonging life, but his book, which enjoyed multiple editions, documents a society quite conscious of aging as a discrete topic of study.[53] Though his book contains a short section on sex and age, offering theories as to why women might live longer than men, Sinclair's book otherwise follows convention in that males generally provide the focus.[54] The era's old-age manuals noted that the very old—the centenarians— and the really creative among the elderly at any age were more likely to be male.[55] Although some women lived extraordinarily long lives, according to George Rousseau, they were "less prominent in the literature because male lives were more often recorded."[56] The potential for a pleasant, productive old age in previous centuries was overwhelmingly viewed as a masculine privilege.

The eighteenth century witnessed popular movements across Europe that sought to increase human longevity, and a rich literature illuminates these efforts. Longevity had long been a topic written about by men, implicitly to an audience of men. Books appeared in droves outlining the life stories of those who had reached extreme old age, presumably because these narratives held the keys to replicating their success. Fantastic elements were common to many of them. The most popular tales involved a man losing a head of gray hair at an advanced age only to have it replaced by shiny locks. Even more bizarre are the oft-repeated stories of the elderly losing their teeth and then sprouting several new ones or even entirely new sets. Though heredity was considered one factor in living to a very advanced age, evidenced by data collected about the ages to which an old person's parents lived, lifestyle was stressed as an element within one's control. As if to add insult to injury, one source warned, "those who are most anxious for longevity, are the least likely to attain it."[37]

Quacks and experts of all stripes dispensed advice. When their methods did not work, outlandish excuses were created for them. One "expert," a German named Christoph Wilhelm Hufeland (1762–1836), wrote a frequently republished eighteenth-century work, translated into English as *The Art of Prolonging Life* (1797).[38] His followers were prominent across Europe, calling themselves Hufelandists. When a well-known Hufelandist died at age 35, supporters said that he met an early demise because he followed to the letter the instructions of an early volume of *The Art of Prolonging Life* that contained printer's errors.[39] Another peculiar advice manual from the mid-eighteenth century indicated that the surest way to live a long life was to found a college for young women. This was considered beneficial because breathing in the exhaled air of the young—especially young virgins—was thought crucial to longevity.[40] The particles thrown into the air by the exhalations of the young were said to "bestow a kind of reflective youthfulness, which, by constant repetition, may for many years keep off and delay those infirmities, to which people of the same age are generally subject."[41] This source gives a new twist to the then-frequent admonition to the unwell that a "change of air" was the proper course of treatment. These suggested methods were not the norm, however, as most sources recommended what we might now call a balanced lifestyle or even an abstemious one in the quest for long life.

Eighteenth- and early nineteenth-century works on longevity also blamed the victim, implying that if you did not live to an advanced age, you did not deserve to do so. Throughout the period, reference was made to the writings of a sixteenth-century Italian philosopher of longevity, Luigi (or Lewis) Cornaro.

He wrote an extremely popular book of advice, proposing that the surest way to have a happy old age was to be sober and regular. Cornaro advanced an argument that many repeated into the Victorian period—that old age could be "the most pleasant and delightful stage of life."[42] Such arguments went back to the ancients, most notably to Cicero's *Cato; or, An Essay on Old Age.*[43] But Cornaro further suggested that wrinkles and gray hairs appearing on a person of less than 100 years old resulted from voluptuous living (16). Others implied, too, that unhappy or foreshortened old age was a personal—even a moral—shortcoming. William Godwin (1756–1836) believed that living long was a matter of mind over body. As he writes in his *Enquiry concerning Political Justice* (1793), "the term of human life may be prolonged, and that by the immediate operation of intellect, beyond any limits which we are able to assign."[44] Condorcet thereafter expressed similar views, seeing the human life span as increasing indefinitely as society progressed and human perfectability increased.[45] There were, to be sure, longevity skeptics like physician James MacKenzie (1682?–1761), who believed that "the greatest efforts of the human mind to extend a vigorous longevity much beyond fourscore, will generally prove ineffectual."[46] But a number of writers expressed the belief that living to 100 or even 500 could be a goal within reach, if one lived well.

We might think that a culture that discussed and dissected old age was experiencing growth in the proportion of the aged in its populace, but in fact, the percentage of elderly persons in the British population fell during the period. In the early eighteenth century, people over 60 made up approximately 10 percent of the population, a figure that dropped to about 7 percent by 1811 (Thane, *Old Age* 20). By the early nineteenth century, English women over 60 made up less than 8 percent of the female population and men over 60 approximately 7 percent of the male.[47] The percentages then remained fairly constant through most of the 1800s, perhaps as a result of high birth rates (3). But if the proportion of the old remained relatively static, the ability or willingness to perceive the old as a group changed dramatically. George Rousseau has argued that there was a "new awareness of their numbers" during this period, finding in Great Britain a fresh sense of "optimism—the sense that old age could be as blissful a time as youth."[48]

Whether such optimism was experienced in the same way by men and women is unclear. Women as a group fared slightly better in terms of reaching old age, but the ideologies of aging they faced have been understood as more cruel. Women "proved durable from a physiological standpoint in a culture which discouraged them from preparing for or accepting the results," according to Peter Stearns.[49] *The Female Mentor* (1798) provides further evidence. After quoting Oliver Goldsmith on the love of life as "increasing instead of being diminished by age," one of the female narrators comments, "I never could observe, that the longer we live, the more we expect to taste true felicity. Our sensations at the decline of life are less acute; our expectations of happiness, being frequently disappointed, are almost annihilated, and our pleasures more frequently arise from feeling other people happy, than from being happy ourselves."[50] It is tempting to read the "we" of *The Female Mentor* as a specifically female "we." Samuel Johnson, too, argued that old age was less happy for a woman than a man, writing that for "fine ladies" "age begins early, and very often lasts long," and that "joy vanishes from about them."[51]

The factors predicting whether one would live to advanced years were much disputed, with purported qualities changing dramatically from 1750 to 1850, particularly in regard to studiousness. This shift in qualities associated with reaching long life is one reason for marking out the parameters of this book. In the mid-eighteenth century, few would have thought it possible that writers, much less women writers, would be long lived. It was believed that the surest way to live a long life was to avoid study—or at the least to moderate it. The poor were said to enjoy powers of longevity that the wealthy had not yet mastered. Most sources held that readers and writers (or those with studious lifestyles) stood little chance of reaching old age. As one popular medical guide from 1768 concluded, "we see very frequently that those who are ignorant and stupid, enjoy a very sound and good State of Health, and live to a very advanced Age, whilst ingenious and studious Men of Letters are snatched away by immature Death: Instances of which occur every Day."[52] A century later, most of those who wrote on longevity declared exactly the opposite. One 1863 source put it this way: "Nothing is clearer than that a habitual activity of brain,—and especially of the intellectual organs of it,—is a leading condition of the most substantive kind of health. All the evidence in connection with longevity, gathered from every class, confirms this."[53] The gradual movement, over the course of a century, from one dominant belief about the learned and longevity to its opposite, coincides with the movement toward noticing and celebrating long-lived women writers as a group.

Directions to authors and scholars on how to maintain good health and to live long lives became more popular from the late eighteenth century onward. Intellectuals were no longer told to give up a life of mental activity in order to reach old age, though they were still encouraged to pursue exercise and a balanced diet. Advice varied, depending on the kind of work one did.

A penchant for statistics—however flawed—grew alongside the ever-popular lists and brief biographical descriptions of the aged. Males and females in old age were also somewhat more accurately compared. Some earlier sources had merely tallied up the number of centenarians recorded in encyclopedias of longevity and found that the men outnumbered the women, reaching the conclusion that men were therefore likely to live longer.[54] Because of a greater willingness to attend to gender in studies of old age, and because a new belief emerged that a life of letters could be long and rewarding rather than fore-shortened and miserable, celebrated women writers were more easily recognized for their longevity.

There were many ways in which prevalent cultural stereotypes of the old might have had an impact on the self-concepts or receptions of individual writers. *The Female Aegis* (1798) describes the common faults of old age as gay amusements (especially for women), avarice (especially for men), affectionate tendencies, querulousness, and peevishness.[55] Each of these "faults" had potential repercussions for aged authors. As the "gay amusements" comment shows, women's old age was often associated with all things trifling, whether harmlessly or perniciously so. Sir Walter Scott demonstrates such attitudes when he writes in his journal that nothing "relieves the mind so much from the sullens as trifling discussions about *antiquarian old-womanries*—It is like knitting a stocking, diverting the mind without occupying it."[56] Here Scott echoes the belief that antiquaries are faux intellectuals and that old women, by extension, ought to be lumped in with them. The *Oxford English Dictionary* uses Scott's phrase as its example for "old womanism" or "old womanry," meaning "the supposed characteristics of old women; querulousness." But Scott's usage seems also linked to "old wives' tales" and "old woman's tales" (or fables or stories), understandings of which held force across the eighteenth and nineteenth centuries. Then, as now, the phrase meant unlikely or erroneous stories. To narrate as an old woman, then, meant risking an imaginative coupling with old womanism or old wives' tales—in other words, with the false, the petty, the outlandish, or the peevish. (Needless to say, there is no corollary phrase for old men's tales or old husband's tales.)

Alongside trifling qualities and querulousness was garrulousness. The alleged garrulity of the old was much trumpeted, and references to garrulous old age abound in both fiction and poetry of the period, including works by Mary Wollstonecraft, Charlotte Smith, Matthew Lewis, and others.[57] The talkative, loquacious, or garrulous old woman—often of the working class—

was a stock character in eighteenth- and nineteenth-century British literature, where she was portrayed as both comic and annoying. (Garrulousness, though a particular danger of advanced age, was also imagined as a common failing of the old maid from middle age onward.) As a result of the garrulity stereotype, women writers who continued to "speak" through publications in their old age risked being perceived not only as saying things that were trifling or false but also as saying "too much." Some writers tried to forestall such criticism by addressing it head on. Hannah More thanked her readers for suffering through her multitude of works. In an 1819 preface to *Moral Sketches of Prevailing Opinions and Manners,* More writes of her authorship (in the third person): "In taking her final leave of her readers, may she [the author] be allowed to express her gratitude for their long and unwearied indulgence; for a patience which the too frequent demands made on it could not exhaust."[58] Old women writers were in danger of being viewed as garrulous because what came from their pens could be seen as frivolous *and* old-fashioned.

The news for elderly female authors was not all bad. More positive qualities, too, could adhere to old age. Aged wisdom, though more readily tied to men than to women, might be manipulated or drawn on by old female authors.[59] Virtue was another quality associated with old age in eighteenth-century Europe, as we saw earlier. In the Revolutionary period, La Fête de la Vieillesse (Festival of Old Age)—celebrated on the tenth of Fructidor (Aug. 27)—was also known as La Fête de la Virtue.[60] Virtue became associated with the old through two distinct lines of thinking, according to Sherri Klassen. First, old age was seen as a virtuous life stage because passions had been exhausted in youth, leaving only moderation and wisdom in their wake. Even those who had lived dissolute early lives were seen as having spent all of their criminal and intemperate impulses by the time they reached old age. Second, some believed that only the virtuous could survive into old age. Old age was, in other words, the reward for having lived a virtuous life (95). The English context, though in some ways less sanguine than the French, seems to have shared these assumptions.[61] The gendered dimensions of associating old age with virtue were predictably complicated, because putting old women on pedestals could also prove problematic.[62] Gaining a reputation as a virtuous old woman meant working to convince others that one was passive, resigned, amiable, pious, and retiring (Premo 108–9, 144). To speak of positive and negative stereotypes of gender and aging, then, is a complicated matter, as a great deal depended on who was deploying the stereotype and toward what end.

Sustaining Female Authorship in Late Life

Confronting old womanhood and authorship was not just an issue for a handful of exceptional writers. Between 1750 and 1850, Great Britain saw its first generations of professional women authors collectively advance to (and in some cases wane in) popular success.[63] "A hundred years after Aphra Behn [1640?–1689] and Delariviere Manley [ca. 1670–1724] chose authorship as their main occupation, many women had taken up the pen for money with varying degrees of success," as Cheryl Turner puts it.[64] This was a kind of revolution, Eve Tavor Bannet notes, as "between 1750 and the end of the century the sheer numbers of women writing novels, poems, conduct books, and tracts doubled each decade."[65] Determining which women writers ought to count as professional (which Turner defines as "those who received payment for their work" or "wrote expressly in response to financial hardship") and then calculating their average ages at death—when birth and death dates can be established—would be no easy feat (60). Janet Todd's *Dictionary of British and American Women Writers, 1660–1800*, includes approximately five hundred writers. Although not all of their birth or death dates can be identified, one quarter of these writers are known to have lived past 1800. Approximately 15 percent lived well past the turn of the century, dying after 1820. More than a dozen lived to 1850.[66] As a result, we might argue that a large number of "eighteenth-century women writers" should also be reckoned as of the nineteenth century, as a result of their long lives.

How did British women writers of the period fare in old age? How common was it to remain active in the world of letters? How many continued writing but ceased publication, either by choice or of necessity? What portion of them happily (or not so happily) retired into obscurity? Reliable answers to these questions are difficult to arrive at. Provisional ones might be gathered from a sample of women writers who were active during the period and who lived to advanced ages. Using information from two sources, Todd's *Dictionary* and Paul and June Schleuter's *Encyclopedia of British Women Writers*, I compiled information about two dozen women writers who lived more than seventy years and correlated their ages with their publication histories.[67] Collectively, the most prolific age for these writers was 50 years old, followed by a second slightly smaller peak at age 30. The average age at first publication was 29, with the youngest author publishing her first work at 15 (Maria Edgeworth) and the oldest at 45 (Hester Lynch Piozzi). The average age at publication of a last work was 75, with the youngest writer of a last published work found at 41 years old (Harriet Lee) and the oldest at 89 (Joanna Baillie). Although by the age of 70, numbers of published works for these writers fell to the levels seen during their twenties, many continued to find a mass audience during their later years.

These conclusions are based on a small and unrepresentative sample, and they are also based on the debatable premise that new publication and authorial productivity are linked. Nevertheless, what they suggest is that a good number of female authors were able to sustain literary careers well into old age. We already know this was the case for some European male authors. Frank Kafker's work on the great productivity of the (male) encyclopédistes in the late eighteenth century showed that 80 percent of the seventy-five contributors to the *Encyclopédie* produced their best work or continued to produce valuable writings after the age of 65.[68] The largest-scale quantitative study of this kind, Harvey Lehman's *Age and Achievement* (1953), concludes that "the creative years of women do not differ greatly from the creative years of men," but it reaches this conclusion from very little data.[69] Lehman's graph of the age versus production of miscellaneous literary works (2,250 of them by 543 British authors) is, however, provocative.[70] His sample, made up of canonical male authors whose work cuts across many centuries, does not show the mid-life drop in publication that my small sample of women writers generates, showing instead one peak in middle age but also showing a small upsurge in publication between the ages of 70 and 80 (86). Elsewhere, Lehman and Joseph B. Heidler conclude that "it would be absurd . . . to attempt to establish specific age limits for any particular type of creative writing. The fact of individual differences precludes this possibility."[71] At the same time, they criticize studies in which "an investigator merely lists a limited number of authors who have done excellent writing of a particular kind at some given age level" (301). The degree to which questions of gender, authorship, and old age can be or ought to be answered quantitatively remains an open question.

It is clear that very few writing—and publishing—women experienced their fame at a zenith in old age, though many men before them did. In the late seventeenth century, we might think of Thomas Hobbes (1588–1679) and Samuel Butler (1612–1680), both of whom published notable works in old age and received royal pensions to recognize their contributions, or of Izaak Walton (1593–1683), who added to his popular *Compleat Angler* (1653) throughout his sixties and seventies, seeing it through many editions. In the eighteenth century, the example of Samuel Johnson (1709–84) looms large, as he published his *Lives of the English Poets* (1779–81) while in his seventies. As biographer Robert DeMaria put it, "especially after publishing the celebrated *Lives,* Johnson enjoyed a higher degree of fame than he had ever known before."[72] Samuel Richardson (1689–1761) published his novel *Sir Charles Grandison* (1753–54) and William Cowper (1731–1800) his poem *The Castaway* (1799) in their sixties, though few contemporaries suggested that these works demonstrated lessening authorial powers based on age. In his sixties, the poet and clergyman George Crabbe (1754–1832) successfully negotiated with publisher John Murray to purchase his new manuscript, *Tales of the Hall* (1819), along with all of his copyrights, for £3,000—evidence that Murray thought much of the older man's likelihood for continued success with the public.[73] Francis Jeffrey had predicted in 1812 that Crabbe's reputation would continue to grow, but Murray ended up losing £2,500 on the gamble.[74]

Among some literary men themselves, there was a sense that old age brought *increased* powers of writing. As Sir Richard Bulstrode (1617–1711) wrote in an essay on old age, "I can with Truth affirm, that the Poems I have made since my Age of Seventy, have more of Force and Spirit, than those I had written some Years before."[75] Like Bulstrode, Richard Graves (1714–1804) advertised his increasing age rather than trying to hide it from the reading public. He published his collection *Senilities* (1801) at a time when that word meant "old age or the mental and physical infirmity due to old age," rather than exhibiting a loss of mental faculties.[76] Senility could signify young or green old age, rather than old-old or feeble old age, as the work of early nineteenth-century medical writer Sir Anthony Carlisle suggests: "The age of Sixty may, in general, be fixed upon as the commencement of Senility. About that period it commonly happens, that some signs of bodily infirmity begin to appear, and the skilful [sic] medical observer may then be frequently able to detect the first serious aberrations from health."[77]

In the preface to *Senilities,* Graves expresses anxiety about his book's reception, assuring readers that it is "positively" his "last time" of "performing" (ii). He also asks the "pardon of the Public for having so long trespassed on their patience" but says that despite his advanced age, many infirmities, and afflictive circumstances, he has pulled together pieces (some of which had been written years earlier) in a miscellaneous collection that he ventures to call humorous (ii–iii). Graves's doubts about whether his audience would find the literary productions of an old man to be funny show that issues of masculinity, authorship, and old age in this period deserve further study.

Graves must have been pleased enough with *Senilities*'s reception, however, because he went on to publish two more books. *The Invalid; with the Obvious*

Means of Enjoying Health and a Long Life, by a Nonagenarian (1804) was a work of autobiographical pro-longevity advice writing, highlighting its author's old age in a genre that saw few contributions from women. Graves's last work was *The Triflers* (1805), consisting of essays, anecdotes, and poems. Though published posthumously, the advertisement prefixed to *The Triflers* indicates that the "little Work was finished and delivered for Publication, a few weeks previous to the Author's Death."[78] Graves included others' poetic tributes to him in his old age, as well as his own gracious verse replies.

Even though "for a long time our image of the eighteenth century was dominated by males of advancing years," as Pat Rogers notes, rarely has old age itself been a category of analysis in our studies of the period.[79] Even in the case of canonical male writers, there has been a dearth of scholarship considering age qua age. Perhaps, as work in age studies develops, we will determine that there are shared authorial features or shared life experiences among eighteenth- and nineteenth-century aged authors. One possible shared quality of writing derives from what E. Ann Kaplan has called, in a contemporary context, "having-done-this-ness."[80] This phenomenon might be translated into the period 1750–1850 in a word used by Hester Lynch Piozzi: *retrospection*. The retrospective urge among British writers seems to have been strong. Piozzi's world history, *Retrospection* (1801), takes the term as a defining trope. Ann Martin Taylor (1757–1830) brought out her *Retrospection: A Tale* in 1821.[81] In the 1830s and 1840s, Jane Porter wrote copious "retrospective introductions" and "recollective prefaces" to her once-popular novels, making sense of her early work over and over again with each contextualization. Authors also undertook life writing or editing of their own or others' works as a way to make sense, retrospectively, of their careers.

Though not confined to this life stage, the retrospective lens was frequently employed in writings done in old age, by men and women alike, and it could be used to narrate a variety of emotional states. Some authors, like Piozzi and Edgeworth, turned the aged writer's (or narrator's, or character's) retrospective glances into central elements of new writing, using them as a platform to claim authority in fiction. Anna Letitia Barbauld looked back to writers of her youth for subjects to edit and reintroduce to the public in what seems a kind of selfless literary historical act. To have been through it—and to have looked back through it in writing—is a creative or narrative approach that many aged writers used, communicating self-awareness about the inherent differences of life in one's advanced years.[82] The "retrospective moment" remains a characteristic of twentieth-century women's writing in old age, according to

Phyllis Sternberg Perrakis, who identifies "a long look back as the woman of a certain age tries to assess where she has come from, assimilate the twists and turns along the way, and decipher a shape or pattern to the journey" (1).

Studying writers in old age also brings into focus the significant amount of cross-generational fertilization that was occurring in this group. Although we might be more likely to think of literary mentors of this era as old men providing assistance to young ones, this is but a part of the story.[83] Old women writers frequently forged and participated in friendships with males and females of the next generation, for a variety of reasons and with a host of effects. In her old age, Jane Porter befriended the American poet and essayist Nathaniel Parker Willis (1806–67) and English historian Agnes Strickland (1796–1874). It seems that Porter hoped one of them would serve as her biographer—a desire that came to nothing. She refers to them as crucially important people in her life (and in the case of Willis, as like a son to her), though her name barely registers in emerging scholarly work on either protégé. The relationship of Catharine Macaulay (1731–91) and Mary Wollstonecraft (1759–97) has only recently come to light. Many elderly women writers engaged in friendships with those of the rising generation, not just to pass on wisdom but perhaps also as a way to extend their own authorial powers and reputations. There is much more to learn about the workings of literary mentorship and how it was beneficial or detrimental not only to the junior but also to the senior members of these intergenerational partnerships.[84]

Studying cross-generational friendships ought not to lead us away from looking at interactions among old women writers themselves. The literary subculture during this era was circumscribed enough that many celebrated writers knew each other, had some contact with each other, or had overlapping experiences or interests into old age. Sometimes this overlap was incidental, for example, Royal Librarian James Stanier Clarke's contact with two women authors about the writing of a royal historical romance (see chap. 6), or the anonymous review of a last work that so incensed writer Catharine Macaulay written by an old friend of Anna Letitia Barbauld's (see chap. 2). At other times the overlap seems more purposeful, such as Jane West serving as a witness for Hannah More's will, or More's hosting Barbauld's visit just before her death.[85] There is much yet to learn about the social, intellectual, and professional networks of aged writers of both sexes.

Women writers themselves report a variety of attitudes toward and experiences of old age. Many—like Carolina Oliphant, Lady Nairne (1766–1845) —seemed to enjoy the prospect or even the reality of advanced years, as her poem in the epigraph to this book suggests. For others, late life involved un-welcome circumstances. Thanks to several decades of groundbreaking femi-nist literary scholarship, we now have studies examining the ways in which early modern women writers were treated and mistreated, understood and misunderstood, and accepted, ridiculed, or pigeonholed. Seldom, however, have we singled out the category of old age for examination alongside that of gender. Because stereotypes of women and old age in the past are ingrained and often invisible in literary histories (even feminist ones), they have be-come difficult to contest. Where early modern old age is concerned, we have far more questions than answers and a wealth of material yet to explore.

Aged authors' life circumstances offer stark contrasts. Some lived in finan-cially constrained but respectable conditions, while others sank into obscure penury. A few amassed great wealth. Charlotte Lennox, the one-time proté-gée of Samuel Johnson and author of the famed novel *The Female Quixote* (1752), died in dismal poverty. The archives of the Royal Literary Fund il-luminate her difficult state of affairs. Lennox was probably in her mid six-ties when she was first assisted by the fund in the early 1790s.[86] She received eleven grants over the course of as many years, several of which were more than £10 each, to assist her with living expenses or to send her ne'er-do-well son abroad to start a new life. In this level of support, she was more success-ful than any other female applicant to the Literary Fund during this period, as Jennie Batchelor has shown.[87] By the early 1800s, Lennox was no longer writing letters on her own behalf, and the grants were received through an agent, perhaps a caretaker. Lennox was in the end without family, friends, or resources, despite a literary career that spanned more than fifty years and that included the publication of many successful novels, translations, and plays, as well as a pioneering women's periodical. These achievements were not a buf-fer to increasingly dire personal circumstances.

A letter from 1802 speaks of Lennox as "in great distress for the common necessaries of life & is too ill & now too old to be able to assist herself in any way—she has not been able to go out of her lodging these three months."[88] A subsequent letter writer notes that her infirmities "have progressively in-creased" and that her "circumstances are greatly distressed." By July 1803, the Royal Literary Fund's committee decided to make her agent an allowance of a guinea a week for her maintenance, "in consequence of her advanced age & Infirmities" till their next ordinary meeting. In September, the report notes, "Mrs. Lennox is not worse in point of Health but has entirely lost her memory." Her condition further deteriorated through that fall, as one letter in

December reports that she "still continues very unwell having in addition to her former complaint a Bad Cough." The Committee elected to pay her maintenance until she died, which was shortly thereafter—on January 4, 1804.

If Lennox's case is among the more depressing stories of what a celebrated woman writer might face in old age, Hannah More's should be the opposite. More (1745–1833), the author of conduct books and of the series *Cheap Repository Tracts*, acknowledged in a letter that she was "almost ashamed" to "have made over £30,000 by my books."[89] This vast wealth made her subject to other late life dangers. In her eighties, having outlived her sister-companions, she was left alone to manage her home and many charities, confined as an invalid to her two upstairs rooms. When friends "discovered that her servants were taking advantage of her and that her finances were in disarray," "they moved her to Clifton." She lived there for five years, until her death at age 88.[90] Against the order of her doctors, More apparently continued to write into her last years, hiding the inkpot, pen, and paper under her bedclothes.[91]

Writing by old women of this era sometimes made it into print, but in other cases, once-successful female authors were unable to find publishers. Hester Piozzi's last full-length work designed for publication furthered her interest in the etymology of first names and was titled "Lyford Redivivus; or, A Granddame's Garrulity." In that work, Piozzi (1741–1821) signed herself merely "An Old Woman."[92] Her friend and agent Edward Mangin reports being impressed with the then 75-year-old Piozzi's "Lyford" as "learned," believing it to have "much information, ably compressed," promising an "excellent popular volume." Mangin presented extracts from the manuscript to a London publisher, but they "could not come to an arrangement."[93] Piozzi's employing the aforementioned stereotype of talkative old women in her title ("Granddame's Garrulity"), though probably cheeky, may also demonstrate anxiety about whether readers would be interested in hearing from her again. As if to prove her right, the work remains available only in manuscript.

Other writers published considerable numbers of works in old age. Frances Trollope (1779–1863) was the author of thirty-four novels and several works of travel writing. She did not begin publishing until late middle age, broke and looking for a way to support her family—conditions that led many educated women from all age groups to the writing life. Her son, the novelist Anthony Trollope, described his mother's writing career in his *Autobiography:* "She continued writing up to 1856, when she was seventy-six years old,—and had at that time produced 114 volumes, of which the first was not written till she was fifty." He concludes, "Her career offers great encouragement to those who have not begun early in life, but are still ambitious to do something before they depart hence" (28).[94] In her very last years, living comfortably with family in Florence, she had gone deaf and lost mental acuity. (Her son would later publish a dystopic satirical novel about forced euthanasia of the elderly, *The Fixed Period* [1882], which has become an important text in Victorian studies of old age.)

Some aged women writers apparently did not seek new publishing opportunities. Among that group were those who continued copious literary efforts or private life writing and those few who seem to have laid down their pens for good. Though Harriet Lee (1757/58–1851) stopped publishing in the 1820s, "an album of her later poems and stories is preserved in the British Library," and "the verses it contains, many addressed to or written in memory of relatives and friends, are full of the sorrow of having survived all her loved ones," according to April Alliston.[95] In late life, Clara Reeve (1729–1807) declined to publish a new edition of her book *The Progress of Romance* (1785), declaring, "I have written 21 Volumes, beside pamphlets," but "after seventy years of age, an old woman is good for little, writing for the press is out of question." She apparently had several drawers full of material and could not decide whether to save or burn it, but "referring to the proverb that a prophet is not respected in her own country, thought it would 'all go to the flames.' "[96] Significant work on Lee, Reeve, and other writers with similar late life trajectories remains to be done.

Some aged women authors undertook little in the way of new writing but tried to reap profits from the republication of their once-popular works. Changing copyright laws—and unscrupulous publishing practices—made their attempts a challenge. Jane Porter and Sydney Owenson, Lady Morgan (ca. 1776–1859) both wrangled with publishers over copyrights. Through her lawyers, Porter reached an agreement with publisher Richard Bentley (1794–1871) in her attempt to regain the copyright of her most successful novels. These novels were eventually brought out in new, illustrated editions, which she revised, for which she wrote new prefaces and for which she was modestly paid. Lady Morgan was not so fortunate in her dealings. In 1855, Bentley's former partner, Henry Colburn (1784/85–1855), acting as an agent for another publisher of reprints, approached Lady Morgan, who had been his first high-profile author forty years earlier. He "wanted her to sign over the copyright for one of her novels," but "when he left, the near-blind" Lady Morgan "found out that he had secretly substituted a form which assigned control of *all* her literary property."[97] Fortunately, Morgan had a different kind of financial security, one that (as we shall see in chap. 6) Porter desperately sought but never received—a pension in honor of her literary achievements.

Writing for publication (or republication) was not the only way in which a once-celebrated woman writer stayed in the public eye. Stories circulated about old women writers' appearances at gala events, whether celebrating or making sport of their "decline of life." The entry on Amelia Opie (1769–1853) in the *Dictionary of National Biography* notes that in 1851, at the age of 82, Opie visited the Great Exhibition. While there, she met Mary Berry (1763–1852), and Opie is said to have playfully proposed that the two of them challenge each other to a chair race. For her part, Hester Piozzi, on what she called her eightieth birthday, threw herself an attention-grabbing, grand party. Some six hundred friends gathered with her at the Lower Assembly Rooms in Bath for a lavish concert, ball, and supper, where she allegedly danced with astonishing elasticity. Piozzi's late-night dancing and card playing has served as a focal point either to commemorate or to ridicule her last years.[98] Though Piozzi made fun of the extent to which she had become a spectacle in old age, dubbing herself "one of the antiquities of Bath" for tourists to gawk at, she repeatedly sought the spotlight.

Other renowned writers continued to receive visitors but demonstrated greater conventional feminine delicacy, advertising to the world that they were withdrawing from public life. Joanna Baillie (1762–1851), the famed playwright and poet, is among those who declared themselves "in retirement." Baillie later revised this to describe herself as living "in strict seclusion."[99] This was one effective way in which to discourage visitors who desired a look at an aging literary relic. It was also more acceptable in terms of mid-nineteenth-century mores. The public seems to have found choices such as Baillie's to be admirable and those like Piozzi's ridiculous. Piozzi, for her part, applauded her contemporary Sophia Lee's (1750–1824) refusing visitors, writing, "Why should She let the People in to visit her as it is called? She knows they come for Curiosity—not from Affection."[100] It is behavior like Baillie's and Lee's that led to Victorian critic Jerom Murch's laudatory description of "calm and gentle" old age. Even more admirably, Baillie filled her time with philanthropic work, visiting the poor and sick into her seventies and giving money to charity. It is difficult to tell how much impact these activities had on Baillie's continuing to draw a readership in her old age, but we would be unwise to discount it entirely. Literary celebrities of the eighteenth and nineteenth centuries had no image consultants, but many seemed to understand the benefit of such efforts and to engage in that work on their own behalf. In

Baillie's case, her public relations efforts seem to have succeeded; like a small number of other aged female contemporaries, she had a hand in editing her complete works in her late eighties, living to see its publication in 1851.[101]

If publications and public appearances varied widely among women writers in old age, so did attitudes about the aging process. Some of them were sanguine about the approach of or the appearance of old age, and others were sour. And, of course, some were both, depending on their audience or circumstances. The aforementioned balladeer and poet Lady Nairne appears to have felt comfortable with old age long before she reached it. She wrote under the name Mrs. Bogan of Bogan, and even her publisher did not know her true identity, because "she disguised herself as an old gentlewoman when she held interviews with him."[102] Nairne's poetic answer to the question "Would You Be Young Again?" is a decided no. She agreed to have her songs collected and published anonymously just before her death, but when they reached print a year later, they were attributed to her, with the approval of her sister.

It is hard to imagine a more opposite attitude toward old age than Lady Morgan's. Secretive about her age, Morgan published an autobiography in what was probably her eighties. She was offended by a reviewer's comment that she had lived through the love, admiration, and malignity of three generations of men. She responded in a verse manuscript, writing with acidity,

> My life is not dated by years
> For Time has drawn lightly his Plough
> and they say scarce a furrow appears,
> To reveal what I ne'er will avow.

Ultimately, she rails at the reviewers:

> Then talk not to me of "my age."
> I appeal, from the phrase to the fact,
> That I'm sold in your own brilliant page
> I'm still young in fair Fancy, & Tact.[103]

On her deathbed, she is alleged to have said, "Put just a touch of rouge on my cheeks; one might as well look one's best at the last."[104] Whether true or not, this scene is in keeping with the persona she worked diligently to create and maintain in her late life.

Morgan may have had reasons other than vanity for wanting to hide her age. When an identifiably older woman published a book-length work during this period, the fact of her age rarely passed without comment, as we saw in the case of Jane Porter in *Fraser's Magazine*. Works dealing with love and romance posed a peculiar catch-22 for the aged female writer. If an older female author pretended to youthfulness or to special knowledge about romance, she could be seen as sexually suspect. As Katharine Kittredge writes, "The older woman may be blameless, but she knows too much to ever again be innocent."[105] Proper older women were supposed to be asexual, and a sexualized older woman might be perceived as grotesque. An older woman, because beyond her reproductive years, is "more readily seen as superfluous" or as "less than a true woman," which "partially explains the 'unnatural' sexuality so often attributed to her" in eighteenth-century literary stereotypes, according to critic Irene Pines (205). On the other hand, if an older woman author did not seem in touch with youth, her writings ran the risk of being labeled as outdated or unfashionable—a problem particularly in the genre of the novel, which often endorsed presentism in its content and moral lessons. Many novels published in the eighteenth century "had apparently been written by 'Young Ladies,'" as Cheryl Turner shows (94). An older woman writer who trafficked in romance (whether in writing or in life) could be belittled from multiple vantage points.

The most famous example of the complications of writing romantic fiction in old age occurs in a review of Frances Burney's last novel, *The Wanderer* (1814), published when she was in her early sixties. Burney (1752–1840) was called by a reviewer "an old coquette author who endeavours, by the wild tawdriness and laborious gaiety of her attire, to compensate for the loss of the natural charms of freshness, novelty, and youth."[106] The body of the novel and the body of the aging female author are found similarly repugnant and false fronted, as *The Wanderer* is deemed "*Evelina* [the title and heroine of Burney's famous first novel] grown old; the vivacity, the bloom, the elegance, 'the purple light of love' are vanished, the eyes are there, but they are dim; the cheek, but it is furrowed; the lips, but they are withered" (125). The reviewer implies that Burney, as an old woman, is incapable of writing a novel of freshness, elegance, or vivacity. These qualities, it would seem, were the exclusive purview of younger women writers of fiction.

Not all aged women writers received harsh treatment. Those who found the greatest respect in late life and immediately afterward generally rested on the laurels of morally upright works or wrote about old age itself in pious terms. For instance, Barbauld's most famous poem during much of the nineteenth century was "Life," a seemingly simple, happy ode about saying goodbye to the world. The last stanza of the poem reads,

Life! we have been long together,
Through pleasant and through cloudy weather;
'Tis hard to part when friends are dear;
Perhaps 'twill cost a sigh, a tear;—
Then steal away, give little warning,
Choose thine own time;
Say not Good-night, but in some brighter clime
Bid me Good-morning!

About this poem Wordsworth is reported to have commented, "I am not in the habit of grudging people their good things, but I wish I had written those lines."[107] Burney is also said to have repeated the lines to herself at bedtime in her old age. But in this positive commentary on a woman writing in old age, there is also condescension. Despite the attention it attracted, "Life" also led to odd constructions of Barbauld's poetic career (chap. 5).

The chapters of this book examine in detail some of these stories and others from late careers in order to return women writers' old age to our histories and to provide a more nuanced account of literary history itself, one that focuses on an author's complete oeuvre, regardless of whether it crosses traditional period lines. Chapter 1 considers the era's two most celebrated women writers who lived to advanced ages, Burney and Maria Edgeworth (1768–1849). Both were lionized in their early careers, gaining great popularity and critical acclaim. I compare the two, showing that they were both appreciated (and sometimes subtly depreciated) as "classics," despite their continuing to produce new work in late life. As early as 1823, Edgeworth was being referred to as the "Great Forgotten," and Burney's last published novel received the above-mentioned vituperative review. Through readings of Edgeworth's *Helen* (1834) and Burney's *The Wanderer* (1814), as well as an exploration of each novel's reception, I argue that Edgeworth performed the role of "old woman novelist" far more conventionally than did Burney, which in the short term contributed to the former's greater success as a late-life author. I examine each writer's ability to speak to changing literary fashions and to anticipate the treatment an aged woman author might expect to face.

The eighteenth century's most famous British woman historian, Catharine Macaulay, provides the focus for chapter 2. I use unpublished manuscript materials (unavailable to her first biographer) to show how Macaulay was devastated by her changing status as an author in old age. Concentrating on an angry sixteen-page letter that Macaulay wrote in response to a tepid review,

I argue that she was trying to shape what she feared would be her lackluster posthumous reputation. Although her life extended only a short time into what would have then been considered old age, I argue that because of Macaulay's attempt to resuscitate what she calls her "waning" laurels, she emerges as an important figure for studies of women's authorship, reception, and old age in the period. Macaulay successfully anticipated, but unsuccessfully tried to stave off, the rancor and dismissal that would ultimately mar her late life and posthumous reputation; she invoked her gender and her age (whether ironically or seriously) to try to soften the blows.

In chapter 3, I first consider the underexamined question of Jane Austen's attitudes toward the old, as they are revealed in her letters and fiction. Though Austen died in middle age, she is famously associated with a peculiar category of "old" in her culture—that of the "old maid." I look to her representations of old maids (particularly in *Emma* [1816]), arguing that, contrary to what we might expect to find, Austen repeats most of the mildly negative stereotyping in which her culture indulged when describing old maids. I examine the ways in which old maids were discussed in the late eighteenth century, using William Hayley's *A Philosophical, Historical, and Moral Essay on Old Maids* (1785). I show that, like Hayley, Austen did not challenge dominant representational trends. Though her surviving comments about being single in midlife suggest that she herself was happy with her identity, she does not in her fiction forge an imaginative alliance with or mount a defense of the group of old women to which she has been so closely linked. This chapter serves to remind us that belonging to an identity category (whether "old" or "old maid") need not mean serving as its representative or publicly sympathizing with its cultural conditions.

Chapter 4 takes on some of the voluminous materials documenting Hester Lynch Piozzi's late life, looking at Piozzi's last published writings (both the world history *Retrospection* [1801] and the broadside "Old England to Her Daughters" [1803]) and her unpublished late writings and private letters. These texts demonstrate Piozzi's acute awareness of what it meant to write as an old woman and to face the potential loss of a mass audience. I show that the once-maligned and misunderstood friendship of the aged Piozzi and the young actor William Augustus Conway served as a vehicle through which Piozzi tried to ensure that she would be memorialized. Piozzi may have hoped Conway would extend her literary powers into the next generation, during a period when she was unable to find a receptive reading public. Rather than seeing that as a desperate act, I argue that we ought to see it as a resourceful one. Resourceful or not, however, the relationship backfired. Long after both of them had died, Conway kept Piozzi's name before the public, but in none of the ways she might have hoped.

In chapter 5, I first look at Anna Letitia Barbauld's important editorial and literary critical projects—including introductions and biographies—in order to argue for this labor as a central contribution of her later years. Rather than seeing it as work she did because she could not pursue more challenging writing (as most nineteenth-century commentators intimated and as many of today's literary critics repeat), I view her labor as an attempt to make a different kind of contribution to literary history. In bringing back authors of the previous generation to the public eye, I speculate that Barbauld was doing for others what she may have hoped would be done for her in the next—reviving almost forgotten texts for a readership that needed to be nudged toward them. The second part of the chapter considers Barbauld's last published work— her prophetic poem, *Eighteen Hundred and Eleven* (1812), which imagines a future London in ruins. As with Burney's last novel, Barbauld's last long published poem received a damning review. Just as he had done with Burney, reviewer John Wilson Croker focused on Barbauld's sex and age in order to demean her accomplishments. A great deal of work has been done in the past ten years to look at the reasons why *Eighteen Hundred and Eleven* failed and to examine Barbauld's posthumous reception. Few scholars, however, have investigated the possibility that old age may have played a role, concentrating instead on gender, religious non-conformity, or political beliefs. My chapter deepens this work to incorporate the factor of her old age into our speculations.

Jane Porter (bap. 1776–1850) provides the focus for an exploration of women writers and money in later life, in chapter 6. I use unpublished manuscripts to illuminate the artistic and financial choices Porter made in the latter half of her more than fifty-year literary career. I focus on her heretofore unknown attempts to secure a royal pension by writing a novel about the king's ancestors, *Duke Christian of Luneburg* (1824). Porter self-consciously undertook this project with the hope that it would produce a financial safety net in her old age. Rather than continuing to rely on the reading public to make her living, Porter aimed for a preferment. In contrast to the handful of female contemporaries whose bids for government or royal pensions were successful (notably the aforementioned Lady Morgan, as well as Elizabeth Hamilton [1758–1816], and Anne MacVicar Grant [1755–1838]), Porter never received the pension she assiduously sought. Her old age was in some ways desperate, as she wrote begging letters to powerful people, looking for shelter and economic support. In straitened circumstances and occasionally in poor health, she remained vigilant in her efforts to republish her novels, fighting to regain copyrights. I show the ways in which the aged Porter strove to maintain the dignity of and recapture the literary celebrity of her youth.

In the book's conclusion, I return to the questions raised in this introduction to reflect on what is altered when we look at literary history through the lens of women's aging. I discuss avenues for further research in this area, arguing for the importance of our undertaking it in order to see the full range of writings and writers active in a given era. We have a great deal to learn about the self-concepts and activities of women writers later in their lives, whether they were able to publish and find access to readers, continued to write but were unable to secure publication, or chose to take on other challenges. We also have a great deal of work to do to reconstruct how these writers were received as they grew older and what, if anything, such responses did to reinforce or revolutionize ideologies about gender and age in British culture. When taken together, these case studies open up territory to refigure our perceptions of and knowledge about what kinds of writing were being done, by whom, and with what degree of success, over the course of a tumultuous hundred-year period in cultural, literary, and political history.

CHAPTER ONE

Past the Period of Choosing to Write a "Love-tale"?

Frances Burney's and Maria Edgeworth's Late Fiction

It would be a perverse biographer who sat down to compose a portrait from which [Maria Edgeworth's] charm and humour in old age are deliberately omitted.

—*Marilyn Butler*, Maria Edgeworth

It is melancholy to think that the whole fame of Madame D'Arblay rests on what she did during the early half of her life, and that everything which she published during the forty-three years which preceded her death, lowered her reputation.

—*Thomas Babington Macaulay*, Critical and Miscellaneous Essays

To the world, Maria Edgeworth (1768–1849) and Frances Burney (1752–1840) in old age seemed to be enduring periods of silence, inactivity, or stagnation. Each then went on to publish new fiction. Their novels appeared after a long hiatus—for Burney, from 1796 to 1814, and for Edgeworth, from 1817 to 1834. (During this time, their previously published novels continued to appear in new editions or reprintings, keeping their names before the reading public.) But the differences in Burney's and Edgeworth's writing in later life—and the differences in how they were written about—are just as instructive as their similarities. Whereas Burney pushed the envelope for expectations of women's aging, Edgeworth toed the line. In the short run, Burney endured punishing reactions from critics, while Edgeworth was celebrated or politely condescended to. In the long run, however, the late works of each were put aside by readers. What I entertain in this chapter is the possibility that publishing novels in old age itself played a significant, if not central, role in the fate of these authors' works. Burney, whose writings deviated from properly feminine representations of old age, was repeatedly chastised or rebuked for overstepping or ignoring these invisible boundaries. Edgeworth, with her more conventional performance of female old age, within and outside of her late fiction, was treated with less rancor. Contrasting these authors' late novels tells us much about the ways and means (and pros and cons) of navigating authorship, gender, and old age during this period.

A comparative focus on the late fiction of each novelist does not, of course, tell the full story of their writings in old age. The memoirs that each woman had a hand in writing, editing, and arranging for her late father would provide another rich avenue for comparison. Burney's publishing her father's *Memoirs* (1832) has recently been called "achieving a double coup of reiterating her deserved position as the most fêted living novelist and puffing herself within the *Memoirs* of a supposedly oppressive father."[1] Edgeworth's last published fiction, *Orlandino* (1848), might allow us further opportunities for reassessing her late career. Sometimes referred to as a short story, it is a 175-page book, the first volume in William Chambers's one-shilling Library for Young People. Billed as "a story of Self-Denial," *Orlandino* follows a young runaway alcoholic circus performer, who suffers through delirium tremens in the course of his reformation. Writing off this text as insubstantial propaganda for children sells it far too short.

Looking at nonpublishing, as well as publishing, in the late careers of Burney and Edgeworth is also instructive. We might think of the decision Edgeworth made, two years before she died, not to be involved in a new edition of her tales and novels, as planned by the publishers Simkins and Marshall. Edgeworth was asked to supply prefaces and background materials, similar to those Jane Porter was producing at the time for her own once-famous works and to what Sir Walter Scott had provided for his own "magnum opus" some twenty years earlier. Edgeworth refused, turning down the opportunity to reintroduce her novels, explaining to the publishers that, "in truth I have nothing to say of them but what my dear father has said for me in his prefaces to each of them as they came out. These sufficiently explain the moral design; they require no national explanations, and I have nothing personal to add. As a woman, my life, wholly domestic, cannot afford anything interesting to the public: I am like the 'needy knifegrinder'—I have no story to tell" (qtd. in Butler 9). Despite Edgeworth's (heartfelt? feigned? formulaic?) self-perception, there are indeed interesting stories to be told about her old age. Placing these stories alongside those of Burney's late life and writings offers us opportunities for reflection on cultural conditions of aging, gender, and authorship.

Burney's interest in old age as a literary subject dates back to the writings of her youth. Even in her earliest publication, Burney paid close attention to women and aging, although in ways that are sometimes difficult to interpret. In her first novel, *Evelina* (1778), the libertine Lord Merton quips, "I don't know what the devil a woman lives for after thirty; she is only in the other folks' way."[2] Lord Merton is a detestable character whose statements are of questionable use, but the novel also includes a notorious scene of illegal betting by Merton and another man on a footrace between two old women. The women—chosen because they are over 80 and strong—fall from overexertion, are plied with wine, and complain of injury. One ultimately slips and falls so badly that the other is declared the winner. A contemporary found that reading the account of the race "excited a roar of laughter," and critic Earl R. Anderson called it one of the novel's "most delightful incidents."[3] Most recent critics have expressed horror. Elizabeth Bergen Brophy judged the footrace "completely gratuitous," and Richard Freedman called the scene "cruel and grotesque" because described in "mindless, lip-smacking detail."[4] As Kristina Straub argues, "The race becomes a spectator event, a source of amusement analogous to the entertainment provided by foolish old women throughout eighteenth-century English literature."[5] Burney's good characters deplore the race, so the novel would seem to expose the evils of exploiting the old, but there is an established pattern in Burney's fiction of using the pain endured by older women to provoke readers' laughter. (*Evelina*'s Madame Duval is another example.) As a young female author, Burney obviously grasped the cruel treatment old women were subject to in comic fiction, but whether she set out to endorse or undermine such representations is less clear.

Later in her life and posthumously, Burney was herself subjected to representations that paralleled those she used in her novels. Her last years were regarded as a footnote, rather than a vibrant period worthy of attention, and the initial posthumous treatments she received tended to disregard her final decades. In the first edition of Burney's journals and letters (1842–46), edited by her niece Charlotte Barrett, old age is sketchily represented. The publisher may be at fault, as it is said that he came to fear the expense of bringing out the voluminous work, but Burney's last years are accorded just a handful of pages in that edition.[6] (In the journals and letters published more than a century later, material from age 60 to her death spans more than six volumes—

several thousand pages of text.)[7] Barrett's first compressed edition claims that from 1835 to 1838, Burney's "letters were now very few," stressing instead the thing "elegantly said" about Burney—"she lived to be a classic."[8] Living to be a classic was perhaps the most desirable end constructed for an aged woman writer during the period, though it implied graceful, polite retirement—a constriction that Burney often refused to accept and that Edgeworth worked to embrace in life and fiction, as we shall see.

Frances Burney's *The Wanderer* as *Evelina* Grown Old?

Burney's novel-writing career spanned nearly forty years. Her late fiction was overlooked, if not actively demolished, by contemporaries, a pattern followed posthumously by a century and a half of critics. Thomas Babington Macaulay, in his famous essay on Burney written shortly after her death, asserts that "the world saw and heard little of Madame D'Arblay during the last forty years of her life, and . . . that little did not add to her fame."[9] He locates in Burney's last works "no trace of dotage" but finds it "melancholy to think that . . . everything published during the last forty-three years . . . lowered her reputation" (5: 60). He spends several pages describing her decline, concluding "That her later works were complete failures is a fact too notorious to be dissembled" (66). Macaulay praises *Evelina* as the first female-authored tale that lived or deserved to live. He also names two women writers who have surpassed Burney, her "successors" Edgeworth and Jane Austen: "In truth, we owe to her, not only Evelina, Cecilia, and Camilla, but also Mansfield Park and the Absentee" (67). Macaulay omits direct mention of Burney's last novel, *The Wanderer* (1814), and editor Barrett, too, ends the journals and letters by praising Burney as "the Author of Evelina, Cecilia, and Camilla," as if *The Wanderer* did not exist.[10]

For years, few challenged these assertions. As Rose Marie Cutting puts it, "Later students of Fanny Burney, even partisans, usually scrutinize [*The Wanderer*] for evidence of her literary decline."[11] Joyce Hemlow and George Sherburn see Burney's career as a novelist ending after *Evelina* and *Cecilia*, with her last two novels viewed as so inferior that they are better understood as outside the genre, as essentially "conduct books—dull, and badly written" (qtd. in Thaddeus 3–4). Hemlow writes, "every reference to *The Wanderer* must serve to poke it further into the shadows."[12] It was not until the 1970s that Burney's last novel began to receive consideration as an accomplished work of fiction. Though many theories have been proposed to explain why this novel "failed," and though no single reason provides sufficient explanatory power, one factor that has remained unexplored is how it was packaged (by Burney and her critics) as the work of an aging female author. This packaging seems worthy of our consideration, as we attempt to construct a more complete picture of the work and its position in Burney's career, not to mention in literary history.

Burney declares in the preface to *The Wanderer* that she writes as an older woman. She is "past the period of chusing to write, or desiring to read, a merely romantic love-tale, or a story of improbable wonders."[13] A year earlier, Burney made a similar statement in a letter to her brother. She asked that *The Wanderer* be called a work, because, as she puts it, "I am passed the time to endure being supposed to write a Love-tale."[14] In her letter even more so than in her preface ("being supposed to" versus "chusing to write"), Burney recognized that the connection of old women and romance is not one her culture found palatable. In the preface, she elaborates not only on what she has left behind with age but on what she wishes to retain. If she ever had it, she hopes she still has "the power of interesting the affections, while still awake to them herself, through the many loved agents of sensibility, that still hold in their pristine energy her conjugal, maternal, fraternal, friendly and . . . filial feelings" (9). Although her first statement disavows the idea that an old woman—Burney was, at this time, in her early sixties—should write a narrative of romantic love, her second undercuts it. She tells readers that she remains "awake" to her "affections," not only as a mother, sister, daughter, and friend but also as a wife. An old woman who sought to interest the affections (particularly conjugal ones) was more likely to be the butt of a joke or an object of derision. Burney was taking a risk in highlighting her own romantic life, moving beyond what was generally permissible for old women.

Despite Burney's pronouncements, *The Wanderer* is, among other things, a love tale. It centers on an unnamed young woman—the Incognita, the Wanderer, L.S., or Ellis—later revealed as Juliet Granville, an Englishwoman not formally recognized by her aristocratic father. Raised in France, she becomes the victim of revolutionary corruption and is forced to flee her adopted country. When she arrives in England, she finds her purse gone and tries to convince others that she is respectable, despite her financial need and her refusal to offer any details about her "female difficulties" (the novel's subtitle). She is helped and harmed by a cast of characters, several of whom assume she is sexually available. She witnesses the world's benign and more serious evils— selfishness, criminal acts, and suicide attempts by a lovelorn protofeminist "rival," among them. Juliet also discovers the good, when she miraculously locates her French childhood friend in England; finds out that another beneficent friend is actually a sister; and is finally free to renounce a forced sham marriage in order to wed the hero. Though innocent, Juliet is not an innocent. She is worldly and has seen the world, perhaps more than a woman of her age and station "ought"—a far more mature character than the naive, sheltered Evelina.

The Wanderer is not centrally concerned with old age, despite Burney's touting the book as written by an older woman. Most of the older female characters, like the aptly named Mrs. Ireton, are unsympathetic. Ireton is described by another character as in her fourth stage of existence, having passed through petted childhood, adored youth, forgotten and supplanted maturity, to reach "old age, without stores to amuse, or powers to instruct" (543). The man who thus characterizes her is an "old bachelor" of 75, Sir Jaspar Herrington (632, 532). He is a comic, likeable character, although he does make an unwanted proposal of marriage to Juliet. Later, he acknowledges that he could be her "great grandfather" (542). There is sparse commentary in the novel on old age. When it does appear, it is notable.

The novel's heroine is youthful, but one character speculates that her age, like her insistence that she is honest and virtuous, is a sham. While Juliet is applying to be Mrs. Ireton's humble companion, the old woman accuses her of *pretending* to be a young woman. Juliet refuses to reveal details about her background. The curious Mrs. Ireton, rebuffed, reaches a boiling point and accuses Juliet of being supernaturally youthful looking because she has kept "the same face" since she first saw her: "Pray, if I may presume so far, how old are you?—But I beg pardon for so indiscreet a question. I did not reflect upon what I was saying. Very possibly your age may be indefinable. You may be a person of another century. A wandering Jewess. I never heard that the old Jew had a wife, or a mother, who partook of his longevity; but very likely I may now have the pleasure of seeing one of his family under my own roof? That red and white, that you lay on so happily, may just as well hide the wrinkles of two or three grand climacterics, as of only a poor single sixty or seventy years of age" (485–86).[15]

Of course, it is Mrs. Ireton who is "a person of another century"—as her creator may also be said to be. But the climacteric is the more significant part of this paragraph. As the editors of *The Wanderer* note, the climacteric is "a critical moment in human life, occurring every seven years" (940). The grand climacteric refers to one's sixty-third year (seven times nine). When *The Wan-*

derer was published, Burney was nearing her own grand climacteric, so that supposed life stage may take on special meaning.[16] Mrs. Ireton, however, sarcastically speculates that Juliet may be 126 or 189 years old (940). In addition, Mrs. Ireton associates old age with vanity (laying on red and white makeup so happily), with witchcraft or the supernatural, and with hiding its true number. In this description, she gives voice to then-prevalent stereotypes about the elderly. To further highlight Juliet's connection to the aged, she is also mistaken for an old woman by her uncle, Admiral Powel (836). The novel's characters themselves lay the groundwork for the tongue-in-cheek speculation that heroine Juliet is as old as (or even older than) Burney then was.[17]

Mrs. Ireton's reference to the grand climacteric is not the novel's only mention of that phenomenon. It is cited, too, by Sir Jaspar, who lightheartedly reports that he will not fight a duel with one of Juliet's abusers. The young man dismissed Sir Jaspar's challenge as coming from a superannuated goose, past his grand climactic, who "ought not to meddle in affairs of which they had lost even the memory" (504). Sir Jaspar teases Juliet about his would-be gallantry, encouraging her to indulge his "garrulity of age" (504). This time, a sympathetic character echoes another set of stereotypes about the old—that they are foolish, half-senile, and loquacious. The only quality Sir Jaspar jokingly assigns to himself is garrulity, understood as a negative consequence of old age. In Burney's novel, Sir Jaspar's "garrulity of age" is endorsed as a quality to be pandered to, though an approval of garrulity may not perhaps be surprising in a novel that runs to five volumes and approximately 2,000 pages—long even by the standard of long novels of the day.

It may be making too much out of several obscure passages of text (as well as potentially blaming the victim) to suggest that *The Wanderer*'s discourse on aging unwittingly paved the way for the vituperative notice Burney received from critics. There were other works published at this time that made elderly women central, such as Mrs. Carver's *The Old Woman: A Novel* (1800), a Gothic novel featuring a horrid female ghost who turns out to be the benign, heroic grandmother of the heroine.[18] But Burney's novel, though it did not focus on old age, was already being scrutinized for the negative signs of aging. From calling attention to her own affectionate old age in the preface, to indicating that her worldly heroine might be suspected of false youth, to repeatedly citing the grand climacteric, to suggesting that we should indulge garrulity in old age, Burney's novel—indeed Burney herself—courted associations with negative stereotypes of aging. The infamous notice in the *Quarterly Review* by the acerbic John Wilson Croker capitalized on and ridiculed these associations, rather than finding in them an occasion for leniency or chivalry.

Croker's arch-nemesis, Thomas Babbington Macaulay, thought that one of the "scandals of Croker's literary life" was his "ferocious insults to women."[19] If Croker's review of Burney (and, as we shall see in chap. 5, of Anna Letitia Barbauld) indicates a pattern, he seems to have had a pronounced mean streak where *elderly* women writers were concerned.[20] It is worth revisiting his review of *The Wanderer* at length. From the first line, Croker makes much of Burney's age: "None of our female novelists (not even Miss Edgeworth) ever attained so early and so high a reputation as Miss Burney, or, as we must now call her, Madame D'Arblay. . . . We regret to say, that the Wanderer, which might be expected to finish and crown her literary labours, is not only inferior to its sister-works, but cannot, in our judgment, claim any very decided superiority over the thousand-and-one volumes with which the Minerva Press inundates the shelves of circulating libraries."[21] Croker finds the novel inadequate on several levels, the most notorious of which invoke the rhetoric of old age. The novel is "feeble" (124). It has a "total want of vigour, vivacity, and originality." Because it is by Burney, for whom expectations are high, it is especially disappointing: "During the thirty years which have elapsed since the publication of Cecilia, she has been gradually descending from the elevation which the vigour of her youth had attained." The novel is called a "lame and impotent conclusion" to her career, although Burney nowhere calls it her last. *The Wanderer* has no splendor, cannot dazzle, is not beguiling and is "increased in size and deformity exactly in the same degree that the beauties have vanished" (125).

Croker, damning the novel as repetitive and superannuated, leads up to this oft-quoted tour-de-force censure: "The Wanderer has the identical features of Evelina—but of Evelina grown old; the vivacity, the bloom, the elegance, 'the purple light of love' are vanished, the eyes are there, but they are dim; the cheek, but it is furrowed; the lips, but they are withered. . . . We have completed the portrait of an old coquette author who endeavours, by the wild tawdriness and laborious gaiety of her attire, to compensate for the loss of the natural charms of freshness, novelty, and youth" (125–26). A more pointed demonstration of the dangers of publishing a novel as an old woman would be difficult to locate. Female novelists, Croker suggests, had best not age or best not show their ages. The power of their fiction fades, as does its beauty. The more that female authors try to deny the loss of bloom in their works, the more ridiculous they become, as the aging woman novelist's body of work is like her own body.[22] The wanderer in Croker's comment could also refer to Juliet—a heroine who has "grown old." Croker, echoing the voice of Mrs. Ireton, suggests that both heroine Juliet and author Burney are painted, aged harridans. To pretend to youth was one of the greatest "sins" an old woman could commit, as Croker echoes dominant ideologies at this time.

Croker's review reveals a near obsession with old women. His description of the novel's plot begins (as the novel does not) with a description of elderly women: "Two cautious, selfish, ill-tempered, ill-mannered old ladies" introduce his summary (126). Croker twice more in his review refers to old women and holds a mock funeral for previous Burney heroines: "We have now done with this novel, on which we should not have been justified in saying so much, but that we conceived ourselves in duty bound to attend the lifeless remains of our old and dear friends Evelina and Cecilia to their last abode" (129). He rebukes Burney for implicitly capitulating to Napoleon, pronouncing *The Wanderer* dead on arrival and Burney's career over.

This review is telling about the treatment an aging woman author might endure. Seeing it alongside several other notices of the novel demonstrates that the review was more than the anonymous vendetta of a notoriously caustic critic. William Hazlitt, writing in the *Edinburgh Review*, also finds *The Wanderer* to have little power: "We are sorry to be compelled to speak so disadvantageously of the work of an excellent and favourite writer; and the more so as we perceive no decay of talent, but a perversion of it. There is the same admirable spirit in the dialogues, and particularly in the characters of Mrs. Ireton, Sir Jasper Herrington, and Mr. Giles Arbe. . . . But these do not fill a hundred pages of the work; and there is nothing else good in it."[23] Hazlitt moves away from the direct mention of aging that Croker employs, though he raises it elliptically by alluding to the possibility of decay. Instead, Hazlitt implicates Burney's perversion of powers in the novel's "failure." In short, echoing Burney's Sir Jaspar, Hazlitt finds the novel unfortunately garrulous; it includes just 100 pages of valuable material, while the rest is judged wild, chimerical, and perverse. Charges of garrulity were leveled by several other reviewers. One suggests that the work is "unnaturally lengthened" and could have accomplished in three volumes what it did in five.[24] Another wants it reduced by half.[25] Yet another argues that five volumes could have been compressed into one and that "Madame D'Arblay has forgotten throughout too many of the pages that length of description should have some relation to the importance of the events related."[26]

Garrulity is not the only weakness critics identify, as Burney's age itself potentially limits her powers. The *British Critic*'s reviewer notes that public expectation is exceptionally high for a novel from an "old favourite," heightened by her "long silence" (374). The *Monthly Review*'s William Taylor emphasized that Burney was over the hill: "Since the modest entrance of Evelina into the world, the sparkling triumphs of Cecilia, and the delicate embarrassments of Camilla, many years have elapsed, fertile not only in political but in moral revolutions. A new generation has grown up in the salons of Great Britain . . . an alteration insensibly progressive has effected considerable change in our idea of the gentleman and the lady. Whether a corresponding modification of the canon of propriety, or internal rule of excellence, has taken place in the mind of Madame D'Arblay, during her long residence in France, may be liable to question: but we are glad to see depicted again such society as our matrons remember."[27] Though Taylor finds *The Wanderer* "truly varied, original, and interesting" (413), he, too, asks whether a "matron" can write an effective novel. The *Anti-Jacobin Review* wondered whether ten years in France "had the effect of incapacitating this lady from fixing the attention or exciting the interests, of an English reader" and says that the novel "falls very far short" in its "powers of attraction" (347). For the *British Critic*'s reviewer, *The Wanderer* demonstrates that Burney's powers have declined because of her "long residence in France," during which she has "forgotten the common elegancies of her native tongue" (376)—implying that France corrupted her or possibly contributed to her senescence.

Reviewers concluded that the book was out of touch. Because of its protofeminist character, Elinor Joddrel, the *British Critic* declares *The Wanderer* to be hopelessly out of date: "The revolutionary spirit . . . is, fortunately for a bleeding world, now no longer in existence: few of our female readers can remember the *egalité* mania" (385). Female readers, the reviewer assumes, are young, and Burney's age compels her to create an old-fashioned heroine. The *Gentleman's Magazine*, in its positive review, also highlights the antiquated features of Elinor, despite viewing her as useful to "serve as an historical antidote to any lurking remnants of poisonous doctrine."[28] Burney's fascinating character is reduced to a kind of historical remnant.

Burney explained that her novel was set in the 1790s and was composed beginning in 1802, a fact critics used to question whether "old" material could make successful new fiction. The *European Magazine*'s reviewer thinks it is "doubtful whether the public will consider the subject sufficiently *modern*, though managed with the skill of a Burney."[29] The *Anti-Jacobin Review* believes Burney could not avoid "anachronism"; furthermore, "her farmer's sons and daughters are such as they were in *Evelina*'s days, but such as are not to be found as present. Madame D'Arblay does not seem to be aware of the change which has taken place . . . since she first began to write novels" (352–53). Taylor's review sums up the general assessment: "It is not enough that pictures of the *past* are executed with vital fidelity; they must be re-garded with the eye of the *present*" (413).

Burney's most supportive critics questioned whether she had an eye for the present or whether she could only repeat pictures of the past. As her first critics saw it, Burney's writing in old age did not lead to wisdom, affection, and truth, but to painting, decay, and falsehood. In his work on aging and Jonathan Swift, Brian Connery argues that "the construction of the literary 'author' Swift has proven remarkably adaptable to those who wish to find in his later years . . . confirmation of their own views of the relation between middle adulthood and old age."[30] Perhaps we have the same phenomenon at work in Burney studies, with her late novel's critical reception and her later years being used mutually to confirm expected weakness. As we have seen, *The Wanderer* was for years downplayed in (if not omitted from) discussions of the history of the novel and of Burney's career.[31] Early, negative responses to Burney's attempting authorship in old age may be one factor that helped to set that process in motion.

Maria Edgeworth: "The Voice of Old Experience"

Maria Edgeworth's last novel, *Helen* (1834), "written in her sixties, long after her father's death, is so interesting because old age seems to have set her free to be, and write about herself," according to novelist Maggie Gee.[32] Find-ing in *Helen* evidence of "a new maturity," biographer Marilyn Butler makes a similar claim, identifying a "strengthening of confidence that came in her sixties from years of self-reliance."[33] Studies of the career of Edgeworth have been dominated by "the image of a daughter so timid that she has nothing to say for herself in her father's presence, so utterly devoted to him and his ideas that he speaks for her and through her," as Caroline Gonda said.[34] Ma-ria's father, Richard Lovell Edgeworth, was a noted inventor and educator, and with him, she coauthored several books. Married four times and father of twenty-two children, he took an active role in his eldest daughter's career. After his death, Maria Edgeworth (like Frances Burney after her) completed her father's memoirs—itself an important project of her late life. Critics con-tinue to argue over whether her father's influence over her and her authorship was benign or malignant—whether she needed his guidance in order to be able to write or whether her writing was shackled by his interfering hand. Regardless of how the debates about Richard Edgeworth's influence are settled, we know from Maria Edgeworth herself that *Helen* was not an easy novel to write. She claims she was "more anxious far (and for good reasons) about this book than any I ever sent into the world" because she did not want to "have lowered what my father took such pains to raise for me"—that is, his standards (qtd. in Butler 463). Burney's last novel took risks in its rhetoric of gender and old age, as we have seen. Edgeworth's last novel, published almost twenty years after her father's death, appears by comparison far more careful and "age appropriate."

The novel begins as heroine Helen Stanley gives up her small fortune to repay her recently deceased guardian uncle's business debts. She joins the household of a lifelong friend, the former Lady Cecilia Davenant, now wife to General Clarendon.[35] Lady Cecilia's mother, Lady Davenant, is staying at Clarendon Park until she joins her husband, named ambassador to Petersburg. Helen greatly values (and is greatly valued by) Lady Davenant, even more so than Cecilia.[36] Cecilia is enthusiastic and coquettish, but her mother has "a sort of deep high character" of which Helen is in awe (13). Lady Davenant has flaws, too, including an early, meddling interest in politics that led her to be nearly a stranger to her daughter. These three imperfect but likable women form the heart of the story, and their strengths and weaknesses play out in a drama propelled forward by Cecilia.

Before her marriage to him, Cecilia swore to the upright, gruff General that he was her first love. When her earlier love letters to another man, since deceased, resurface, Cecilia persuades Helen to take responsibility for them, at least until Lady Davenant leaves the country. Cecilia promises that she will afterward tell all to the General, but she is worried that the truth would jeopardize her mother's health. What starts as a series of white lies to keep a friend's mother in good spirits balloons as the novel proceeds. Cecilia's promised confession is repeatedly postponed until the material consequences increase exponentially. Helen's engagement to the novel's generous and idealistic hero, Granville Beauclerc, is called off; the love letters are bowdlerized, published, narrowly circulated, and suppressed; and the General refuses to shelter Helen any longer. Helen goes to live with the General's sister, who suspects Cecilia's deception. Ultimately, Cecilia is caught in another web of lies and is estranged from her husband. Then she confesses. Helen is put back in the good graces of the General and the matrimonial path of her hero. The novel ends with

the returned Lady Davenant, on her deathbed, witnessing her dying wish fulfilled—that Helen and Granville marry and that her daughter and son-in-law
be reconciled, since all of the trouble arose out of a mother's early neglect.

Unlike *The Wanderer*'s elliptical treatment of the subject, *Helen* includes
a great deal of commentary on old age. Much of it comes from Lady Davenant, who calls herself the "voice of old experience" (46). She confesses to
Helen her early mistakes, revealing a disappointed love from her youth. She
says, "My identity is so much changed that I can look back upon this now,
and tell it all to you calmly" (59). She presents herself as long past the age
of inspiring (or being inspired by) passion, although the novel does not un-
derestimate the magnitude of her errors. As Butler puts it, "Lady Davenant
is the first of Maria's magisterial parent-figures to be subjected in her turn to
impartial criticism" (477–78). Cliona Ó Gallchoir argues, "Lady Davenant
could ... be said to represent a 'progression' in terms of Edgeworth's portrayal
of older women," though she is ultimately relegated "to peripheral significance" because she disappears during "the most dramatic scenes."[37] Though
Ó Gallchoir is certainly right about Lady Davenant's peripheral status during
the novel's narration of Cecilia's most serious bungling (as her mother must
be), I argue that Lady Davenant functions, throughout the novel, as a figure
of perfectly acknowledged female imperfection and hard-won aged wisdom.

Despite her early errors, Lady Davenant is presented as a model older
woman not only in her just self-criticisms but also in her love for the young.
She is not jealous of their powers, though she is sometimes amused by their
idealism. In an argument with her favorite, the hero Granville, she disabuses
him of his sense of the new, bringing him "presently to see that he had been
merely saying old things in new words" (93). She deems him "a resurrection-
ist of obsolete heresies, which had been gone over and over again at various
long-past periods, and over and over again abandoned by the common sense of
mankind" (93). She manages this transformation by "slow degrees," showing
him that his systems are "old to older eyes" (93). Lady Davenant demonstrates that the voice of old experience need not be grating (or merely garrulous) to the ears of the young.

She is an equal-opportunity critic of youth and age. When brought a book
by the idealistic Beauclerc, she proclaims, "As we advance in life, it becomes
more and more difficult to find in any book the sort of enchanting, entrancing
interest which we enjoyed when life, and books, and we ourselves were new"
(126). She says it is vain to try to determine "whether the fault is most in
modern books, or in our ancient selves" (126). This is because the imagination

cools and weakens with age, as the old become "too much engrossed by the real business and cares of life, to have feeling or time for factitious or imaginary interests," though she avers, "while they last, the imaginative interests are as real as any others" (126). Lady Davenant believes the old have an excess of care in the world's affairs and the young too great a desire to escape them through books of imagination. On her deathbed, she again contrasts youth and age, finding weaknesses in both. The weaknesses she assigns to age—too little enthusiasm, benevolence, and confidence in self and others (in other words, taciturnity, greed, and skepticism)—seem not to be those of her own character (463–64). She locates imperfections and strengths in young and old alike, making her seem a reliable, rather than a one-sided or prejudiced, source for information and aphorisms about aging.

It is unclear how directly Lady Davenant's commentary should be allied with Edgeworth's, but Lady Davenant is not the novel's only repository of wisdom on old age. The novel's narrator reflects: "There is a precious moment for young people . . . a time, before the passions are awakened, when the understanding, with all the life of nature . . . is at once eager to observe and able to judge, for a brief space blessed with the double advantages of youth and age. This time once gone is lost irreparably; and how often it is lost—in premature vanity, or premature dissipation!" (106). The named advantages of old age—to observe and judge without awakened passions—resemble a novel's desirable, impartial narrator. Old age and novel narrating would seem to go together in this formulation. In each case, a moral message may be conveyed from a disembodied or disinterested position. In that sense, the old would seem the *best* situated to write dispassionate novels about regulating passion. *Helen*, by implication, heads off criticism that novel writing—writing about love and romance—does not belong in the hands of the old. Burney's attempt to forestall criticism of *The Wanderer* and old age was not nearly as effective, because it tried to link old age and passion rather than to distance these qualities.

Edgeworth was also more successful than Burney in showing the advantages of expressing in fiction the knowledge of the past coupled with that of the present. *Helen*'s narrator reflects on past trends, emphasizing the differences between now and then: "Formerly in England, as still in every other country but England, a marked difference was made in the style of dress in the country and in town" (177). And, "formerly, overdressing in the country was reprobated as quite vulgar; but now, even persons of birth and fashion are guilty of this want of taste and sense" (177). As the narrator's perceptions of the history of fashion and manners demonstrates, an "old" narrator has an advantage over a young one in that, if convincingly objective, she can offer access to what is now *and* what was then. She can offer viewpoints that are by turns forward thinking and retrospective.

Setting her novel in the present and carefully highlighting cultural differences between past and present, Edgeworth avoids the charge that her novel is old-fashioned. One late nineteenth-century critic agreed, seeing Edgeworth as having kept up with the times. Emily Lawless takes the unusual step among critics of placing *Helen* in the later time period, where it belongs: "In reading [*Helen*] we are aware that the eighteenth century has at last dropped out of sight, and that we are well out upon the nineteenth, not indeed as yet 'Victorian,' but in a sort of midway epoch" (194). Such a reading is facilitated by the novel's carefully drawn distinctions between past and present, youth and age.

If Edgeworth is more skilled than Burney in maintaining her novel's appearance of being newfangled, she also seems savvier in her treatment of garrulity. As we have seen, Burney's aged character requests indulgence for his stereotypical garrulity, and Burney's novel was a five-volume production. Edgeworth's novel also includes a garrulous unnamed old woman, featured in a handful of scenes with Granville and Helen. Though she is indulged, the old woman occasions kind treatment because of her poverty. She allows Granville and Helen to demonstrate their respect for the poor aged. The old woman says to them, "Well, well! I'm old and foolish. I'm old and foolish, and I should not talk" (84). The narrator reports, "But still she talked on, and as this seemed her only comfort, they would not check her garrulity" (85). For Edgeworth, garrulity is not to be indulged for its own sake—or even for the sake of age—but because it is charitable. Talking too much is the "only comfort" of a poor, aging woman. *Helen* does not ask readers to indulge novelistic garrulity either. Edgeworth and others worked to make her novel a radically shorter book. She had "resolved to keep *Helen* down to two volumes" and relied on her sisters to "cut back the narrative to the requisite length" (Butler 460). It was publisher Bentley who later decided to make it three volumes (464). Edgeworth felt that "Good books & precious stones are made by compression" (qtd. at 460 n. 3). One critic, expressing a minority opinion, finds that *Helen* exhibits "sprawling formlessness . . . that makes one almost wish for Mr. Edgeworth's supervisory cutting," but by these various methods Edgeworth mainly escaped the negative associations of authorship, old age, and garrulity that continued to circulate twenty years after *The Wanderer* was published.[38] Burney's last novel seemed to sanction garrulity over truth, while Edgeworth championed truth over garrulity.

Garrulity is not the only stereotype of old age that Edgeworth and Burney addressed in different ways. Whereas Burney's novel stressed the necessity of keeping secrets through her mature, youthful heroine, Edgeworth's stressed the importance of telling secrets as a result of the costs paid by her heroine's and friend's deceptions. Burney's older female characters in *The Wanderer* are unrepentant harpies, while Edgeworth's most visible older female character in *Helen* demonstrates appropriate feminine strength, regretting her earlier ambitions outside the domestic sphere. Edgeworth's novel, in form and content, demonstrates a "good" old woman's aging; Burney's flirts with the "bad." Of course, this does not make one a good and the other a bad novel. On the contrary, Burney's has much to interest readers, as does Edgeworth's, and the literary merits of both novels deserve renewed investigation. But perceived quality (as judged by then-prevailing aesthetic tastes) was not the only factor that influenced reception; the ways in which authors negotiated (or anticipated) how old age would play to readers could make a significant difference in the immediate, if not long-term, receptions of their works.

Critics were more generous in their assessments of *Helen*, although it received far less notice than did *The Wanderer*. *Helen* was financially successful, bringing Edgeworth an estimated £1,100 (Butler 464).[39] Gauging precisely how popular the book was is more difficult. Samuel Taylor Coleridge noted in a letter that *Helen* was making "noise" and exciting "great interest," but according to Marilyn Butler, *Helen* was not a runaway success (478–79). Earlier, Bertha Coolidge Slade concluded otherwise, considering *Helen* "not only well received and widely read, but one of Miss Edgeworth's most popular books."[40] Slade stresses that the novel was translated into Swedish, Danish, and French, and "probably went through more different English editions than any other of her books" (199). Lawless also believes that *Helen*, "at the time it was written, was possibly the most successful of all her novels."[41] Late nineteenth-century critic Helen Zimmern would have it both ways: "Concerning *Helen* contemporary public opinion was much divided; some regarded it as a falling-off in power, others as an advance, but all agreed there was a change."[42] If imitation is the highest form of flattery, then Elizabeth Gaskell's drawing on *Helen* in crafting her *Wives and Daughters* (1866) is further evidence of Edgeworth's late-life literary powers.[43]

Helen's initial critical success is as hard to judge as its popular success. One major notice appeared in a British periodical, written by Edgeworth's friend and agent (and Sir Walter Scott's son-in-law) John Gibson Lockhart. Lockhart's anonymous review reassures readers that Edgeworth's talents have not lessened with age: "If any of our readers had ever listened to the envious whispers, so indefatigably circulated among certain circles, to the effect that Miss Edgeworth's vein of creative fancy had been buried with her father— Helen will undeceive them."[44] After praising the work, he compares it to her earlier books, emphasizing that her age indeed has had an impact on her latest production: "As writers of a reflective and introspective turn advance in the walk of life, they are likely to detach their imagination more and more from the broad and blazing contrasts which delight the eye and heart of youth; and it is no wonder that the interest of this tale, put forth after an interval of, we believe, nearly twenty years, should be of a more sober cast than Miss Edgeworth chose to dwell upon in some earlier works" (483). Because of its author's age, *Helen* is a more "detached" and "sober" work, and Lockhart believes those are its principal strengths. The novel is "already in everybody's hands," so Lockhart does not make extracts. In contrast to Croker, who declares Burney's career as a novelist at an end, Lockhart wishes Edgeworth to publish more. He ends with a plea to her to complete and make public two novels that he understands she had begun "some years ago" (484).

Additional, favorable reviews appeared in North America, perhaps because there "literary fashions were slower to change" (Butler 478). Still, Edgeworth is talked about as if she were a relic. She is described as an author whom one is surprised to find still living:

> We know not when we have been more delighted, either as reviewers or as men, with any occurrence in the literary world, than with the opportunity of giving another welcome to Miss Edgeworth, the friend of our earlier years. And yet we must confess that our pleasure was mingled with many fears; for it was possible, that the recollection of the interest her writings used to inspire, might be stronger than the reality; there was a chance, too, that during her long silence she might have lost something of her power. . . . But whatever sentiments prevailed in our minds—whether hopes or fears,—we believe . . . the fears were uncalled for, and the hopes have been exceeded. We remember her as the morning star, whose radiance was lost for a time in the excessive brightness of the sun [i.e., Sir Walter Scott]; now we see her reappearing more beautiful than ever as the planet of evening, after that sun has left the sky.[45]

The reviewer, the Reverend W. O. Peabody, outlines the history of Edgeworth's published works and compares them to Scott's and to eighteenth-century novelists such as Samuel Richardson and Tobias Smollett.[46] When finally arriving at *Helen*, Peabody again uses the language of age and aging to assess its value. He says that often authors "serve up old incidents and characters in new forms, while the reader, instead of being glad to meet his old acquaintance again, is vexed to see them endeavoring to hide their respectable antiquity under a youthful dress" (181). This seems very much like the criticism Croker made of Burney. Though many others before her have done so, Edgeworth, according to Peabody, is not pretending to youth. She is acting her age, and he is grateful that she has proved "that the light within has not grown pale with age," but in saying so he implies that (women?) authors generally do worsen with age—a backhand compliment indeed (181). As Frances R. Botkin has put it, "Unlike Edgeworth's earlier works, *Helen* left little impression on critics," though the novel "engages the reader with its skill, fluidity, and emotional impact."[47]

In the short run, Burney's "badness" and Edgeworth's "goodness" as old women authors and narrators appear to have played a significant role in their late novel's critical receptions. This may be because, as Margaret Ezell has argued, "the nineteenth-century valorization of 'the feminine' in its histories of women's writings . . . led to the dismissal or the reduction of the reputation of most of the women writing before the Victorians."[48] In the long run, however, even those authors who benefited from the Victorian valorization of the feminine may have fallen into an undifferentiated mass as their old age itself (rather than its acceptable or unacceptable qualities) predominated in evaluating their later works. As early as 1823, Maria Edgeworth was being referred to as "the great forgotten."[49] Her six-volume set of works from that time is dubbed the work of an "old favorite," and she is again classed with Richardson, Henry Fielding, and Smollett, in a historical sketch of novel reading and readers. Her "little works" of 1800 to 1810 are appreciated as those produced "precisely at the time of life when the faculties possess their maturest vigor" (384). It is then bemoaned that she has "withdrawn from" the world of literature (389). When this review was written, Edgeworth was in her fifties, had published several novels and children's stories in the previous decade, and would live another twenty-five years, and yet by this assessment she was already a valuable antique.

After Edgeworth's death, *Helen*, like *The Wanderer*, was either glossed over in accounts of her authorship or pointed out as an unusual work of value by an elderly woman. Zimmern (1883) gives extensive treatment to *Helen*, recuperating it *because of* Edgeworth's age: "Too often when men and women go on writing far into their latter years we are apt to wish that, like Prospero, they had buried their want before it had lost its power. This is not the case with Miss Edgeworth" (260). She concludes that "a writer who can learn from criticism and experience, who can adopt a new method of writing when past the age of sixty, is a remarkable writer indeed" (266–67). Later editions of *Helen* also focus on Edgeworth's old age. In an 1893 edition, a one-page note begins, "Seventeen years elapsed between the publication of *Harrington* and *Ormond* . . . and the issue of *Helen*." The rest of the note describes how Edgeworth published little from 1820 to her death.[50] A more extensive introduction by Anne Thackeray Ritchie begins a 1903 edition, which touts *Helen* as a work that "Mrs. Gaskell used to say she thought one of the best of all English novels"; Ritchie's introduction quickly moves to a discussion of old age: "Age had not dimmed the author's brightness of intellect nor divided her from the interests of the generations which had followed upon her own. When Miss Edgeworth was getting to be quite an old woman, long after her father's death, after ten years of silence, she once more began to write a novel."[51] The rest of Ritchie's essay focuses on Edgeworth's grieving at family members' deaths and on describing her old age. The most notable thing about *Helen* became its author's age at composition.

When not celebrated as the work of an elderly woman, *Helen* has generally been ignored. In a forty-page review of Edgeworth's *Memoirs* (1867) that describes nearly all of her major writings, *Helen* receives nary a mention.[52] In her 1959 study, *The Great Maria*, Elisabeth Inglis-Jones moves from a chapter titled "1831–1833" to one called "Epilogue," a common biographical model when dealing with a female author's old age.[53] Although some twentieth-century critics have given *Helen* its due, Mark D. Hawthorne's assessment (1976) is more typical: "I have discussed Miss Edgeworth's career only from 1795 to 1817, thus omitting the very fine novel *Helen*, published in 1834. Since the intellectual and artistic structure of this final novel shows no remarkable advance over *Ormond*, the novel in which she finally reconciled her father's assumptions and her own beliefs, a discussion of it would be anticlimactic."[54] For most critics, the old age of an eighteenth- and nineteenth-century female author has been described as a time of preparing for death or resting on her laurels, not for producing original literary work. Female authorship in old age has too often been seen as an anticlimax.

The treatment that Edgeworth's and Burney's novels faced may be attributable to many factors, but it is important to add old age to that list. Even when age is taken into account, differences emerge in each novel's reception. These may be due not to something intrinsic in Burney or Edgeworth but to changes in book-reviewing practices from 1814 to 1834, with Burney facing ageist criticism that became less venomous two decades later. The differences in their treatment may have been caused by changes in literary fashion—an explanation several critics have embraced. Butler notes that "Maria's name must have seemed quaintly old-fashioned beside those of Bulwer Lytton, the Countess of Blessington, Lady Charlotte Bury, and Mrs. Gore" (479). For Butler, Edgeworth "belongs to a more primitive stage of the novel's development" (480). Embedded in Butler's vocabulary, however, is the suggestion that old age may have played a part in what she identifies as *Helen*'s lackluster showing. Edgeworth's novelistic techniques were of a "primitive" sort compared to those used by others published in the 1830s. This does not seem to give credence to the idea that authors can adapt to changes in literary trends in old age. But even if we determine that Edgeworth could not "keep up" (a conclusion I am skeptical of), and even if readers in the 1830s might devalue a novel perceived to deviate from current trends, such judgments make little sense a century or two hence. Surely Edgeworth and Burney belong to all of the years during which they wrote and published, rather than to a particular stage of the novel's development. There is much to lose when we group authors only or even principally in the era demarcated by their youthful writings.

Toward the end of Edgeworth's *Castle Rackrent* (1800), Sir Condy Rackrent decides that he has "a great fancy to see my own funeral afore I die."[55] He longs to hear all of the things that his mourners will say about him at his staged wake but ends up disappointed. He is of a "sad order in the midst of it all, not finding there had been such a great talk about himself after his death as he had always expected to hear."[56] Edgeworth and Burney may well have experienced the reception of their late novels as Sir Condy did his mock funeral.[57] Despite material evidence of their continued authorial vigor, both writers were repeatedly declared forgotten or measured for faded powers. Both Edgeworth and Burney, like Catharine Macaulay before them, witnessed the mounting devaluation of their late lives and writings. As we will see in the next chapter, Macaulay attempted to fight back publicly when she saw the wheels of this process being set in motion. Perhaps, given the continuing high regard expressed for their earlier novels throughout their late lives, Burney and Edgeworth did not take action because they saw they had much more to lose.

CHAPTER TWO

Catharine Macaulay's
Waning Laurels

Every age has its particular character, Hortensia. Love, chivalry,
and romance, are the leading features of one; gravity, hypocrisy,
and a puritannical preciseness, of another; but what shall we
say of the times in which we live, where the motley garb of
folly confounds by its variety, and where show and ornament in
all cases, take the lead of solid excellence.

— *Catharine Macaulay*, Letters on Education *(1790)*

In *A Vindication of the Rights of Woman* (1792), Mary Wollstonecraft (1759–
97) generously praises the late Catharine Macaulay Graham (1731–91). Wollstonecraft calls Macaulay the woman of the greatest abilities ever produced by
Great Britain and then expresses her grief: "When I first thought of writing
these strictures I anticipated Mrs. Macaulay's approbation, with a little of the
sanguine ardour, which it has been the business of my life to depress; but soon
heard with the sickly qualm of disappointed hope; and the still seriousness of
regret—that she was no more!"[1] Angry that there has not been "sufficient respect . . . paid to her memory," Wollstonecraft expresses confidence that where
Macaulay is concerned, "posterity . . . will be more just" (105). Recent critics
have made much of Wollstonecraft's prediction for Macaulay's reputation,
particularly because posterity has for so long been unjust.[2]

In this chapter, I look at an unenthusiastic review of Macaulay's last published full-length work, *Letters on Education* (1790)—and her enraged unpublished response to it—for what it can tell us about the conditions facing
women writers who put forward new work in late life. Macaulay's unpublished response shows how clearly she understood what it meant to be devalued as an aging woman writer and how she linked her own aging to her

history making. In an angry letter to the *Monthly Review,* Macaulay seems to be fighting for her earthly afterlife, having witnessed her stature as an author crumbling. She redeployed the rhetoric of female old age and used her characteristic political verve to defy the mistreatment she believed she was facing. Her battle, as we now know, was not won. Turning in the latter part of the chapter to the unflattering and even preposterous stories that circulated about her after her death, I show how Macaulay successfully anticipated, but unsuccessfully tried to stave off, the rancor and dismissal that would mar her posthumous reputation. Macaulay apparently saw her aging body mirroring her allegedly outmoded history, as she fought in the final year of her life to recapture the respect she had once enjoyed.

Wollstonecraft, though she also faced virulent treatment, has found justice from posterity. Her complete works were published a decade ago, and it is difficult to open any anthology or encyclopedia of the period without locating extended reference to her life and writings.[3] Macaulay's re-emergence has been more belated, even though the two women had much in common.[4] Both espoused radical politics, both successively published angry responses to Edmund Burke and treatises considering women's education, and both led lives that engendered public scandal. Wollstonecraft's life is famously filled with daring, disastrous, and heroic events, tragically cut short. Macaulay's, which also had its share of notoriety, seems in comparison more stable and less pitiful, as she lived much longer, though just to the cusp of what was then considered old age. Yet Macaulay began to experience what it was like to be received as an aging woman writer, a phenomenon markedly different from the frisson of celebrity and infamy she had experienced as the young "English Clio."

Early in her career as a writer, Macaulay began a history of England that would reach more than 3,500 pages—an impressive accomplishment. Macaulay herself reached 60 years of age, dying on 22 June 1791 after "a long and very painful illness."[5] She was frequently in poor health, though apparently never poor. Her first marriage was seemingly happy, and her husband supported her writing. Some years after his death, she surrounded herself with a band of toadies whose fulsome actions on her behalf made her look foolish in turn. Among this group, she met her second husband, defying convention and expectations to remarry at 47, an age that the *Times* already considered her "*decline* of *life.*"[6] Her choice was William Graham, a 21-year-old surgeon's mate and younger brother of her quack doctor. Despite the union's occasioning vengeful public ridicule, it was, by all indications, a good match. Still, it has proved difficult for critics to package Macaulay's choices as heroic, even where her politics are so considered. Her march toward death was, if anything, the uneventful end to what some would have us believe was a farcical middle age.

It may be that Macaulay's re-emergence to critical acclaim has been slower than Wollstonecraft's because the former's life is less easily romanticized. It is also possible that Macaulay has not fared as well because she wrote in genres that have traveled poorly across the centuries. Macaulay "lacked but one claim to a central position" in the period, according to Margaret Kirkham: "she was not a novelist."[7] Nor was she a poet. Her historiography has rarely been lauded for its literary merit or its formal innovation.[8] Additionally, she did not survive into the 1790s. Had she lived through more of that decade, perhaps her political views—though they would have brought her a great deal of trouble—might also have placed her in circles now celebrated and scrutinized by scholars of British Romanticism. She may well have been able to create and assume the role of wise granddame. Macaulay certainly functioned as a kind of foremother for Wollstonecraft, as we have seen.

Several important essays have been published considering the immense influence of Macaulay on Wollstonecraft, most of which examine their respective positions on women's rights.[9] The emergence of two formerly unknown letters between Wollstonecraft and Macaulay definitively establishes what many suspected—that the two women were in contact.[10] Wollstonecraft also favorably reviewed *Letters on Education*.[11] These connections themselves suggest Macaulay's importance to the world of letters in her later years. But as new evidence illustrates, at the end of her life, Macaulay felt (or believed others perceived) that her authorial powers were slipping away; she despaired of her ability to maintain an audience. Her response was characteristic: defiant self-defense, rather than passive acceptance. Macaulay's late writings, and her rejoinder to their reception, do not demonstrate the "calm and gentle" old age that Victorian critic Jerom Murch believed characterized the era's elderly women writers.[12] Indeed, the aged Macaulay was, as we now know, quite the opposite—strident and forceful—on at least one notable occasion.

Gathering materials to make sense of Macaulay's later life and writings has, until recently, been quite difficult. When Bridget Hill published the first biography of Macaulay, *The Republican Virago* (1992), she failed to locate family papers, speculating that any surviving documents were burned in an estate fire in the early twentieth century.[13] She finds that Macaulay's "movements in the last ten years [of her life] are obscure" ("Links" 178). Three years after the biography appeared, Hill describes being "appalled" to learn that a number of Macaulay-related documents had recently been sold at auction.

Subsequently, the Gilder Lehrman Collection advertised that it acquired the Catharine Macaulay Papers, consisting of some 190 pieces, including letters to and from John Adams, Horace Walpole, and Mercy Otis Warren, as well as dozens of letters to and from Macaulay's second husband and her only daughter, Catherine.[14] These documents put us in a much better position to understand Macaulay's concerns and challenges during the last years of her life, so that her old age need no longer be shadowed in obscurity.

Macaulay's final publications were *Letters on Education* (1790) and *Observations on the Reflections of the Right Hon. Edmund Burke, on the Revolution in France* (1790).[15] She may have planned "to resume . . . on a political subject," but Burke's *Reflections* "persuaded her to devote all her dwindling energies to a spirited reply" (Hill, *Republican* 128–29). *Observations on the Reflections* takes its cue from other English responses to the French Revolution, but it can also be seen as a continuation of Macaulay's earlier work.[16] In it, as in her other texts, she argues that the Glorious Revolution of 1688 was incomplete and warns against the dangers of the national debt (e.g., "the larger the debt, the *greater* will be the *degree* of evil" [33]). Her primary aim is to refute Burke and to insist that one cannot rush to judgment about the French Revolution. She argues that history is not relevant as an interpretive guide in the case of the current uprising in France: "We cannot venture to establish an opinion on the state of a country not yet recovered from the convulsive struggles which every important revolution must occasion. We can gain no light from history; for history furnishes *no example* of any government in a large empire, which, in the strictest sense of the word, has secured to the citizen the *full* enjoyment of his rights" (*Observations* 42). Despite identifying this lack of historical precedent from which to judge the Revolution, Macaulay has hope for the future of France. In a darker moment, she predicts that if municipalities abuse their power, it will lead to "utter destruction," and if the army gains control, its members will unwittingly become enslaved themselves (42, 43). She concludes that, regardless of what the French do, the only legitimate government is in "the will of the people" (45).

When examining the final stages of Macaulay's authorial career, however, the *Letters on Education* is arguably the more important text. As Jonathan Wordsworth has claimed, it is "the last of [Macaulay's] considered writings on which she hoped that her reputation would be based" (49).[17] Her obituary in the *Gentleman's Magazine* wrongly lists *Letters on Education* as her "last publication."[18] The *Letters on Education* is a bizarre and fascinating book, divided into three parts of twenty-five, thirteen, and thirty-eight letters on diverse subjects. More successfully executed than her previous epistolary work, *History of England from the Revolution to the Present Time, in a Series of Letters to a Friend* (1778), the *Letters on Education* uses a fictional correspondent, Hortensia, as its addressee. The text employs a conventional framework, but it is jarringly disconnected and seems rushed throughout its nearly 500 pages. *Letters on Education* ranges far beyond its titular subject to offer a patchy how-to guide for contemporary life.

Macaulay's book features a greater number of personal asides than is typical of her earlier works.[19] When discussing the care of infants, she digresses to include her philosophy of talking about oneself:

> I would rather have had an American savage for my nurse, than those to whose care my infancy was committed. Many a time has my pen been wrested from my hand by the tyranny of a headach; many a time have I deplored the influence of early habits; perceived mistakes which it was impossible for me to remedy, and lamented infirmities acquired before I enjoyed the privilege of a voluntary agency. But away with this egotism! one can never have a worse subject to discuss than dear self, for we are ever more interested in it than the person to whom we address our discourse; and I have often laughed at the ridiculous situation which I have observed myself and others to be in, when relating with a passionate vehemence a succession of afflicting evils to hearers, who could hardly force such a seeming attention as is consistent with common politeness. So much more weight have the slightest circumstances which concern ourselves, than the most important ones which can effect others; that I would advise the person who seeks for pity and relief from the sympathy of friends, to be very brief in his tale of woe; to deal in generals as to himself, and to dwell on those particulars in which his hearer has a personal concern. (30)

Macaulay presents this advice to keep mum about one's own troubles as something learned from previous experience, but she rarely belabors her own stories in her writings. Her surviving correspondence presents occasional tales of personal woe (primarily about her health), but it is more often politically focused. Her published writings delve into first-person material even more rarely. It took a great deal, apparently, to rouse Macaulay to righteous anger and passion in writing of her personal affairs, though she freely expresses such emotion in her political writings.

Like other epistolary books on conduct and philosophy, *Letters on Education* considers education, childrearing, happiness, religion, and a host of virtues and vices. Her book, however, is—as she recognizes—"novel" in its arguments (iii). She writes that "the organs of sense are the same in both sexes" and titles this argument with Rousseau, "No characteristic Difference in Sex" (203). Her innovations are even more notable on questions of everyday habits. Macaulay recommends limiting animal products in one's diet (38), though feeding infants pure gravy of meat (32). Children should be allowed to go to church only occasionally to "reward [them] for well doing" (96). As an alternative, their Sundays should be spent doing needlework and reading in the morning and listening to music in the afternoon (95). She would keep the Bible out of the hands of the young until they are 21, because introducing it too early produces infidels and fanatics (91–92, 135–38). She touts the merits of needlework for girls (65) and encourages handicrafts as hobbies for boys (65), but she would educate them together. She favors small class sizes (20). She repeatedly discusses ways to inculcate kindness to animals (120–25). She believes that children should go barefoot until the age of six (43) and that public nurseries should be provided for infants of all ranks, paid for by graduated taxes (17).

Her rambling practical idealism is coupled with a grave concern for present corrupting tendencies. She notes that though she engages in a "vindication of female nature," she is not an "apologist" for the "conduct of women" (214). She disparages coquetry but concludes that men abuse power more often than women (215). She criticizes the use of cosmetics among old women (41). She expresses concern throughout the *Letters on Education* that religious principles are increasingly being discarded (321). As a result, she is prone to make suggestions that limit temptation, such as the proposal that theatrical performances be held only in the morning in order to prevent the scenes of "license and debauchery, which regularly follow the close of those entertainments" (314). She would have members of the gentry trade in the time and expense spent on tours of the Continent for acts of domestic charity (291).

She also uses the *Letters* as a platform to respond to past criticisms. She responds to James Boswell's anecdote about her argument with Samuel Johnson over political distinctions, which had implied that she was a hypocrite. In her three-page rebuttal, she reports that Johnson questioned her, "Why . . . do you not ask your servant to sit down with us, instead of suffering him to wait?" (167). She reports—as Boswell does not—that she replied to Johnson, "You seem to mistake the whole bent of my reasoning; I was not arguing against that inequality of property which must more or less take place in all societies, and which actually occasions the difference that now exists between me and my servant; I was speaking only of political distinctions: a difference which actually does not exist between us, for I know of no distinctions of that kind which any of the commoners of England possess. Was my servant obliged to serve me without a pecuniary consideration, by virtue of any political privilege annexed to my station, there would be some propriety in your remark" (168). Macaulay ostensibly presents this story to demonstrate the evils of sophistry and to show that "Doctor Johnson would argue loosely and inaccurately when he thought he had a feeble antagonist; and that victory, not truth, was too often the thing sought after." She also takes pains to establish that "the opposition of opinion between us passed off with great good humour on both sides." Macaulay attempts to right the record about this personal interaction, but it is, of course, Boswell's version that continues to be repeated.

Not all of *Letters on Education* was new work. The last third of the text recasts her earlier *Treatise on the Immutability of Moral Truth* (1783), which deals with religious and metaphysical subjects.[20] Macaulay acknowledges the use of this material in her preface to the *Letters*, though she maintains that she "has endeavored to correct the faults" that writer Samuel Badcock (1747–88) pointed to in his private, halfheartedly complimentary, and posthumously published letter on her work (viii). Badcock wrote to a friend that Macaulay's work was good, especially since ladies are not adapted to abstract speculations.[21] By correcting the "faults" noticed by Badcock, and in asides such as the one on Boswell's Johnson, Macaulay seems to be trying to pave the way for the book's (and her own) favorable reception. Despite her efforts, if they were such, the *Letters on Education* received mixed notice.

The *Analytical Review*, in its detailed essay by Wollstonecraft, was largely positive.[22] Wollstonecraft occasionally disagreed with Macaulay, notably on the ease with which people of fortune could find suitable caretakers for their children and on the number of literary works the young could reasonably be expected to read (243, 245). But Wollstonecraft warmly recommends the work to parents and finds that it "adds new lustre to Mrs. M's character as an historian and a moralist" (254). The review concludes by stating that the book "displays a degree of sound reason and profound thought which either through defective organs, or a mistaken education, seldom appears in female productions." In April 1791, the *European Magazine* reviewed *Letters on Education*, primarily quoting from and summarizing its contents. The review was continued in the July issue, dated some weeks after Macaulay's death.[23] Praise for the book did not appear until the continuation of the review. There, *Letters on Education* is called "elegant and instructive," though the reviewer laments that "limits" prevent "particularising the beauties it contains" (48).

Macaulay, perhaps unaware of the positive assessment forthcoming in the *European Magazine,* was apparently shocked by the treatment she received elsewhere. The public soon learned of Macaulay's displeasure with the *Monthly Review.* Several months after its review of *Letters on Education* appeared, a notice was published in the correspondence section of the periodical. Editor Ralph Griffiths writes, "We are sorry to learn, by an angry, and rather impolite, letter from Mrs. Macaulay Graham, that this lady is dissatisfied with our criticism on her 'Letters on Education.' "[24] Griffiths reports that "after the fullest and most deliberate consideration, we expressed our unbiassed sentiments . . . on revisal, we find nothing to retract" (119). His response is both mocking and defensive:

> If we pointed out some particulars in the work, which did not accord with our judgment;—if we could not agree with this ingenious speculator, concerning the method of treating infants, the utility of amusing modes of instruction, the propriety of her plan of study, the expediency of transferring theatrical entertainments from the evening to the morning, and some other subjects;— why should a mere difference in opinion be treated as a ground of offence? In expressing our disapprobation . . . we only hazarded an opinion contrary to that of the author. We ventured, indeed, to question the advantage of keeping young persons ignorant of the scriptures, during the period when habits and principles are formed: but it was by no means our intention to insinuate a doubt concerning the writer's friendly disposition toward the interests of morality and religion. Whether Mrs. M. G.'s opinions, or ours, are most consonant to truth, and what degree of applause is due to her speculations on education, it remains with the public to determine. (119)

After turning to the public as his arbiter, Griffiths apologizes for hurting Macaulay's feelings: "Our only reason for bringing the subject of these letters again before our readers, is, to express our regret, that our duty to the public should have obliged us in any degree to hurt the feelings of a female writer; of whose abilities as an historian, we have often expressed our unequivocal admiration." He concludes that Macaulay is a woman of "great intellectual energy, united with the purest philanthropy." But as a conduct book or philosophical author, he implies, she is something less than admirable.

Macaulay Writes Back: An Unpublished Protest against the *Monthly Review*

Until recently, we could only speculate on the contents of Macaulay's "angry, and rather impolite, letter" to the *Monthly Review*. We are now in a position to judge her side of the argument, as well as Griffiths's characterization. The Macaulay Papers contain a draft of her letter to Griffiths.[25] The letter, if it resembles what she ultimately sent, warrants the label "angry." That Macaulay would have been unsatisfied with Griffiths's chivalrous published apology may be surmised. Whether her letter deserves the label "impolite" depends on one's sense of the fairness of book-reviewing practices in late eighteenth-century British periodicals, among other things. Macaulay wrote an astounding and moving 16-page response to Griffiths regarding the review of her book, ignoring her own advice to stay away from long tales of woe about oneself. Her letter is by turns sincere, sarcastic, self-pitying, and enraged. She writes that she has never responded to a review before but was prompted to by the unfair treatment she received from the *Monthly:* "Sir, I have never before troubled any Reviewer with my animadversions. But your Review of my Letters on education, is so uncandid and unfair it contains so many misrepresentations and is sketched over in so slovenly a manner it compels me . . . to show you that in this instance at least; you have taken upon you an office . . . which you have not in any measure fulfilled" (GLC 1794.47). Macaulay's criticisms can be summarized as follows: (1) that the reviewer was ill-chosen and ill-prepared to assess her work; (2) that he repeatedly misrepresents or misconstrues her meanings; (3) that the reviewer is not chivalrous enough and that his chivalry is little more than irony; and (4) that the *Monthly Review* practices favoritism in its reviews. Macaulay demands either "a new Review" or the publication of her letter "as a fair criticism." She got neither.

Macaulay's cross letter to Griffiths must be read in the context of her long, distinguished career as an author. She had published her first book, the initial volume of her history of England, some thirty years before, to great acclaim. That celebration took a turn in the late 1770s when, as a widow, she and her young daughter moved in with her aging mentor, a rector. There is no record of Macaulay objecting when this rector, Dr. Wilson, put up a statue of her in his church, an act that drew loud complaints. She also participated in a birthday party in her honor, in which she was placed on a throne—a ridiculous position for an avowed Republican, according to her detractors. As one caustic critic put it, her numerous band of "Poets, Patriots, Puppies, Pimps, presented their respective homages to this extraordinary idol."[26] Even Bluestocking Elizabeth Carter, who had been friendly to Macaulay earlier in their lives, gave a harsh assessment in a private letter to Elizabeth Montagu: "It is really painful to observe, that with parts and talents which under the direction of happier principles, would have made a very distinguished and respectable figure, [Macaulay] has contrived to render herself so consummately ridiculous, by a total want of all sober sense. Surely nothing ever equaled that farcical parade of foolery with which she suffered herself to be flattered, and almost worshipped. . . . I think one never heard of any body, above the degree of an idiot, who took pleasure in being so dressed out with the very rags and ribbons of vanity, like a queen in a puppet show."[27] Gossip about and satires on her personal life mounted in the periodicals. Of course, shifts in the political winds did nothing to help her reputation either.

In 1783, the *European Magazine* concluded that Macaulay had "experienced more of the extremes of adulation and obloquy than any one of her own sex in the literary world" and that "perhaps there never was an instance, where the personal conduct of an author so much influenced the public opinion of their writings."[28] During the 1780s, she and Graham traveled, and she struggled with increasingly fragile health, living "retired from the world" ("Account" 334). There were those who nevertheless continued to celebrate her. In his *Strictures on Female Education* (1787), the Rev. John Bennett writes that he would "wish not to deny the fame of a [Macaulay] Graham" while maintaining that "female literature, in this country, is swelled beyond its natural dimensions."[29] Particularly in the last fifteen years of her life, Macaulay was subjected to halfhearted compliments and abuse, as recent work has shown.[30] This commentary was in direct contrast to the "entirely unprecedented" "scale and nature of . . . adulation" she enjoyed in the 1760s and 1770s (Davies, *CM* 40). Earlier in her life, Macaulay had come "to represent the ideal of public virtue which Britain, in the years preceding the war with America, seemed so obviously to lack," as Kate Davies argues (43). But by the late 1780s and early 1790s, Macaulay's own confidence in inhabiting this role and her audience's apotheosis of her in it had significantly eroded.

Although Macaulay appears to have done little to address the public criticisms of her personal life that she was subjected to in later years, in her *Letters on Education* she made one rejoinder of sorts. It implicitly addresses an incident from the period of her "farcical parade of foolery." Without naming any names, she discusses the practice of placing statues in churches, an act she informs readers that she is against, except under special circumstances: "In order, Hortensia, to impress the more strongly on the people's minds the superiority of benevolence, to that of any other virtue; No statue, bust, or monument, should be permitted a place in the church, but of those citizens who have been especially useful in the mitigating the woes attendant on animal life; or who have been the authors of any invention, by which the happiness of man, or brute, may be rationally improved" (336).[31] This principle on church monuments is given a prominent place in the book. It makes up the section that ends Part Two, the last in the *Letters* of entirely new material. Though her comment could be seen as a subtle disapproval of Wilson's putting up a statue of her in his church, believing it to be so would depend on seeing Macaulay as someone who was *not* the author of an invention by which the happiness of man or animal might be improved. Do these strictures apply to Wilson's Macaulay statue or not? If Macaulay's historiography could not be described as contributing to the happiness of man or animal, surely her *Letters on Education* could.

Set against this backdrop of criticism and response, Macaulay's letter to Griffiths emerges as the straw that broke the author's back. Absent of this context, it may seem to be a disproportionate reaction, but I believe Macaulay was fighting to shape her posthumous reputation in the face of evidence that it would not measure up to her expectations. The *Monthly Review* could make or break an author's or a work's reputation, as James Fieser argues. Fieser quotes William Cowper, whose playful anxiety about his upcoming review is telling: "All these [i.e., watchmakers, carpenters, bakers] read the *Monthly Review*, and all these will set me down for a dunce, if those terrible critics show them the example. But oh! wherever else I am accounted dull, dear Mr. Griffiths, let me pass for a genius at Olney!"[32] A 1796 reviewer presents the *Monthly* as answering "a double purpose; its pages being not only read in order to learn what is passing in the literary world at the moment of their appearance, but often consulted in times long subsequent, as a regular history of literature" (qtd. in Fieser 647). Macaulay's high level of frustration with the *Monthly*'s reviewer (now known to be Unitarian minister and author William Enfield [1741–97]) is evident throughout her letter to Griffiths and is more understandable when seen as the result of a long-building resentment.[33]

Her angry missive is like the *Letters on Education* itself in that it gives the appearance of thoughtful organization (using numbered sections and points) but occasionally proves difficult to follow. Macaulay's letter catalogs what she believes are Enfield's errors and misconceptions. For example, she is aggravated because he mistakes her tongue-in-cheek comments about aristocratic mothers' breastfeeding as an apology for their neglect of children. Describing the reviewer's errors is de rigueur in this kind of letter to the editor, but what is more surprising is the way that Macaulay repeatedly calls into question her own capabilities and authority as a female author, something that she did very rarely in her publishing career. At several points she makes apologies for her shortcomings with obvious irony, but at others she is more equivocal. She rails at the reviewer, wondering at his blaming her for ideas that have been taken from Fenelon, Locke, Rousseau, and Genlis, as well as from her own experience. She also complains that Enfield has been unduly hard on her shortcomings as a classical scholar and a learned woman:

> Indeed [the reviewer's] critical rod is laid on with an unsparing hand for he has found out my weak part, he has found out that I have not read all Plato's works; nor am acquainted with their forms; he has found out that Aristotle's philosophy is forgotten and that mathematics are wrong placed. Now to give him a full triumph Sir I will acknowledge that I am no classical scholar that my education in this respect, has been more deficient than most of the female writers in this country and indeed Sir, if you had experienced the unremitting industry, and even labor necessary to the task of cultivating one's own mind . . . without a guide, you would pity us poor unlearned women, and encourage us in our laudable endeavors, to fill up that void in the mind which has been made by prejudice, ignorance, and inattention. (GLC 1794.47)

She writes that it is from "a full sense of the many inconveniences that I have my self struggled with that I recommend a learned education to women." Macaulay's complaints about Enfield's lack of chivalry ("Sir, pity us poor unlearned women") seem highly sarcastic, but there are moments at which it is difficult to construe her level of seriousness. "Laudable endeavors," for instance, seems wholly serious.

Macaulay expresses her discontent with what she sees as the false chivalry of the *Monthly*'s reviewer, who concludes his remarks by stating that Macaulay's talents are not well spent on a work of philosophy: "Mrs. Macaulay Graham excels more in the character of an historian, than in that of a philosopher. The present work will, we apprehend, add little to the wreathe of honour which already graces the brow of this literary heroine."[34] In her response, Macaulay, who was familiar with such lukewarm praise, expresses disgust:

> Your critic is pleased to say Sir that in the moral part of education I am more successful. . . . But lest I should be too much flattered with this little sweetning

of the preceding bitter, and the public led in some mistake as to the degree to which they are to rate my letters, he closes his review with an opinion that Mrs. Macaulay Graham excels more in the character of an historian than in that of a philosopher, and that he apprehends the present work will add little to the wreath of honor which already graces her brow. I have confessed to you Sir that I am an unlearned woman tho ready to pick up a little knowledge wherever I can find it now will you or yr critic be so good as to inform me what the meaning of the word philosophy is, for I protest to you that I was ignorant enough to fancy that the science of morals and the knowledge of the human mind formed the most useful branch of it. As to the compliment which seems to be implied in the last sentence of yr review alas I fear there is an ironical meaning couched in it. (GLC 1794.47)

Macaulay ironically calls herself an "unlearned woman" and then accuses the reviewer himself of irony in complimenting her as a historian. Was the reviewer questioning her right to claim achievement in that genre, too?

She follows up this section with two sad and stunning rhetorical questions: "Do not you know Sir that those historical laurels which once graced my brow are now in their wane. Do not you know that the principles and notions with which that history is replete are now exposed as antiquated absurdities" (GLC 1794.47). It is difficult to determine how seriously we should take Macaulay's comments here or decide who precisely is the target of her sarcasm. Is she accusing the *Monthly* of being ignorant of her fallen historical reputation or of hypocrisy in not acknowledging it? Does she worry that her authorial powers are on the wane or simply recognize that others believe so? Does she think that contemporary historians have left her methods and conclusions behind? Is all of this just irony?

I view Macaulay as exhibiting something more than righteous sarcasm. In this letter, she reveals serious concerns about her damaged reputation as an aging woman historian. Her letter cites the successful reception of the work of John Louis De Lolme (1741–1806), which she mockingly states has exposed her own history as wrongheaded. De Lolme, whose conservative notions of constitutional governance opposed Macaulay's, became a favorite political author of John Adams. De Lolme's work "was cited by both supporters and opponents of the 1787 federal constitution."[55] Macaulay's comparing her history to De Lolme's may reflect her disenchantment with American politics as well as her disappointing standing in Great Britain. Macaulay writes,

Do not you know that Mr. de Lolme has since that history [Macaulay's] was published condescended to enlighten [the?] country on the grand subject of

politics and shewn them the excellencies inherent in the British constitution. . . .
What do you suppose in this state of public opinion my readers (if any I have)
must think of my political abilities, and historical talents. . . . What will they
think of my democratic spirit which would at least put the Democratic branch
of our constitution on an equal footing with the other branches; . . . shame on
all such reveries, they are only Sir for the reading of school girls and deserve
to be committed to the lining of Trunks or other more ignoble purposes! (GLC
1794.47)

Macaulay and De Lolme represented opposing constitutional and historical
views, but they also had opposite historical methods. Macaulay painstakingly
worked to construct arguments from primary documents, while De Lolme
had "a cavalier attitude to research," and "the historical aspects of his analysis" were "full of errors" (Macdonnell). Nevertheless, De Lolme was "fêted
by the London political establishment" (ibid.) while Macaulay suggests that
she may have no readers left, save schoolgirls and those seeking paper to line
trunks. Macaulay's implying that her notions represented "reveries" in comparison to those of the fashionable De Lolme may be interrelated; her ideas
had come to be seen as representative of an old-fashioned idealism. Had she
lived a few more years into the French Revolutionary period, her radical republicanism might once again have seemed au courant. In 1790, however, her
rhetorical questions show frank concern, as well as angry irony, about the ways
in which she and her writings were being dismissed as out of touch and out
of date.

Macaulay's sense of herself as a "waning" writer may have been highly
personal as well as political, tied to her realization that her long-term illness
was taking its final toll. During the 1780s, she had considered writing a history of the American Revolution, a project that she apparently discontinued
because of poor health (Hill, "Daughter" 42). But she obviously did not stop
writing altogether, turning from history to philosophy. From the tone of the
letter to Griffiths, she seems to have been shocked that she could get no better reception for her contribution to a more feminized genre, the philosophical conduct book, than she did in masculine historiography. Even if the world
thought that her *historical* laurels were on the wane, one might read her as saying, must her authorship in another genre also be seen as superannuated? Her
use of the metaphors of aging and ageism ("waning," "antiquated") suggests
that she was well aware that her ideas were not being received as aged wisdom.

She puts this awareness even more directly before Griffiths later in the letter, writing: "Now Sir as this is the sad condition of my Historical laurels, it is I think a little severe if not ill natured of you and your critic to damp in this manner the hopes of a disappointed woman, who has toiled so long in vain over the Historic page; in her attempt to gain a little sprig of laurel in the harmless province of morals and to tell her that her pretensions to philosophy have yet a less foundation then her pretensions to the character of being a good Historian" (GLC 1794.47). This passage is most unusual, as Macaulay did not make many apologies for her sex.[36] Before the newly discovered materials surfaced, Bridget Hill wrote that "after the appearance of [Macaulay's] first volume [of history] . . . [she] did not ask for leniency on account of her sex" (*Republican* 132). But Macaulay here asks for leniency not only as a woman but also as a writer of "waning," "antiquated" works, as a "woman who has toiled so long"—in short, she asks for better treatment because she is an aged female author. She makes a claim to the very chivalry she says she abhors in the review, but her version offers greater leniency on the basis of sex *and* age. Her rhetoric suggests that we ought to put old women writers on a pedestal, to give their "harmless" works a "little sprig of laurel"—if we take her comments at face value. Whether mocking, serious, or some combination thereof, her letter shows that sex and age were central to how she imagined herself—and how she expected others to imagine her—as a writer.

The rest of the letter resumes the tone of vitality and courage that scholars of Macaulay rightly associate with her. She is disgruntled that more paper could not have been given over to describing some of her "ingenious and liberal observations" (GLC 1794.47). She worries that readers, swayed by the dismissive review, will not take up her volume to find out for themselves if the reviewer is on the mark. She notes the ways in which the *Monthly Review* attempts to manipulate the reading public: "But myself and many of yr readers Sir when . . . not at all interested in your partialities cannot help observing that you have yr favorite authors whose works on the first publication are immediately advertised in yr Review in the engaging style of panegyric. To those favorite authors you are neither sparing of yr trouble nor yr paper, the public attention is kept up thro two or three Reviews; and all yr powers are exerted in a display of the beauties to be found in their works." In her complaint that Griffiths's periodical has its "favorite authors," who are "immediately advertised" and rewarded with generous and generously sized reviews, the example that rushes into her mind is "Mr. Badcock's letter to the Revd Dr. White." Then, in a tour de force, she likens the reviewing practices of the *Monthly Review* to a corrupt government.[37] She sums up, "we cannot help sighing to find that the Republic of letters is not free from those corruptions which disgrace most political systems."

Badcock is the aforementioned letter writer who halfheartedly complimented Macaulay's work, whom she cited in the Preface to her *Letters on Education.* Her singling him out in her letter to Griffiths may seem somewhat idiosyncratic, but he was in some ways a safe example, having died two years earlier. Badcock was someone whose "services were in constant demand by the conductors of the critical papers" and whose "most famous . . . contributions appeared in the *Monthly Review.*"[38] He reviewed more than 650 works between 1779 and 1787, the most famous of those in the *Monthly*, and, to Editor Griffiths's chagrin, dropped hints and made disclosures about his authorship of some of them.[39] Badcock as a reviewer "ranks among the best known names of the [eighteenth] century."[40] As we saw earlier, Macaulay had tried to change parts of her *Letters* to address Badcock's criticisms, perhaps in the hope of eliciting generous treatment. After his death, Badcock's name was frequently before the public when a friend, Dr. Robert Gabriel, published a pamphlet alleging that Badcock had ghostwritten Dr. Joseph White's Bampton lectures on the effects of Christianity and Islam (Courtney, *DNB*). This pamphlet would seem to be the work that Macaulay mentions in her letter to Griffiths, as it contains correspondence between Badcock and White.[41] The pamphlet prompted a rejoinder from White, and these and other pamphlets were "widely reviewed, achieving maximum exposure for both sides" (ibid.). Is it possible that Macaulay was envious of the extent of the coverage, or was she merely frustrated at what she saw as the *Monthly*'s double standard in giving some works extensive positive reviews?

Another, more speculative reason we might entertain as to why Macaulay mentions Badcock in the Preface and again in her letter to Griffiths is that he may have embodied for her those things *she* desired to become after her death—a regretted loss, a literary insider, even a kind of founding father. Because of the scandal of the Bampton lectures, biographical notices and republications of Badcock's poems "proliferated in periodicals in 1790–1792" (Courtney, *DNB*). Macaulay, perhaps following the Badcock affair and watching his stock rise while fearing her own work would not be given its due and would fall away, lashed out at the *Monthly*'s tepid review. In her letter to Griffiths she anticipates (correctly, as it turns out) harsh treatment by the republic of letters, returning to the rhetoric of the political arguments on which she had built her reputation. She purports to expose injustice and corruption in the reviewing process, as perpetrated on the people by the powerful few.

Her letter dwells on her own "tale of woe," but she concludes by enlarging it, generalizing her own story into one that is emblematic of corrupt reviewing practices and the politics of powerful periodicals.

It would be wrong to characterize *Letters on Education* as an immediate critical or popular failure, despite Macaulay's fears. In the months and years following its publication and then her death, the *Letters* enjoyed a fair amount of press.[42] In addition to the reviews, there were some reprintings and extended published remarks on the work. The *Aberdeen Magazine* reprinted without comment two of the *Letters* sections, "On the Idea of a Sexual Difference in the Human Character" and "Various Interesting Observations on Women."[43] There were brief notices as well, such as the reference to the *Letters* as "excellent" and by an "ingenious female author" in a 1793 book of sermons, or the inclusion of Macaulay in a listing of "Men of Learning and Genius."[44] Clara Reeve's *Plans of Education* (1792) compares itself to Macaulay's *Letters on Education*. Reeve, praising her predecessor's book, also distances her own from the qualities that had prompted criticism from Macaulay's reviewers: "I have seen Mrs. Macauly [sic] Graham's Letters on Education, in which there are many fine things, and many serious truths; but it does not interfere with my design, which is to simplify my subjects; and my method of treating them, to reduce them to the standard of common sense, and within the limits of practicability."[45] Reeve touts her "plain reasoning" (viii), implying that Macaulay's *Letters* were not simple, not commonsensical, and not practical.

Even where Macaulay's work was more directly criticized, it was seriously engaged. The author of *Literary and Critical Remarks, on Sundry Eminent Divines and Philosophers of the Last and Present Age* (1794) considered Macaulay important enough to include an ample seventy pages of commentary on her *Letters on Education*, incorporating a good deal of summary and quotation.[46] The remarks indicate appreciation of Macaulay's aims, sincerity, and candidness and conclude that she is a "rational sound Christian" (289). Still, the author finds much to criticize. The most persistent criticism is of Macaulay's alleged contradictions, and it is often rendered in sexist terms. Citing Pope on women having no character at all, the author determines that Macaulay's character is "as fickle as the hue of the chameleon" (275). Her intellectual capabilities are frequently called into question, as when she is labeled a "poor gentlewoman" unable to "write a quarter of a page without contradiction or ambiguity" (276). The author's prejudice against Macaulay seems a theological one, finding her not high church enough and too attached to Locke (285, 303, 331–32).

But despite frequent invocations of her as ingenious and ingenuous, the author's conclusions echo those of the *Monthly Review*. Macaulay might be said to have " 'dived into the depth of science' to walk in the mud"; her "female shoulders sometimes totter under the Herculean weight of philosophy" (340–41). The author of *Literary and Critical Remarks* also finds occasion to dredge up Macaulay's negative reviews. The author concludes that because of "the reception [Macaulay's work] has met with since its emersion, [it] might have as well remained in its well" (341). The *Literary and Critical Remarks* damned the *Letters on Education* with faint praise, as well as with outright hostility. It would seem to substantiate Macaulay's fears about the damage that the *Monthly Review*'s notice could inflict.

Macaulay's letter to Griffiths shows that she anticipated comments like those in *Literary and Critical Remarks*, but she could not have guessed that there was far worse treatment in store. Her statement that her laurels were on the wane is too soft an expression for what she endured posthumously at the hands of one prominent and highly persistent critic. Her wish for "a little sprig of laurel in the harmless province of morals" was extinguished as her name surfaced repeatedly in the periodicals for alleged wrongdoing. Even after death, Macaulay was embroiled in scandal, as a charge circulated against her that, if true, would have made her claim to moralize (and her alleged store of life wisdom) seem laughable.

Posthumous Scandal: Macaulay's Unsettled Reputation

For reasons probably more political than personal, Isaac D'Israeli (1766–1848) made an accusation against Macaulay that unleashed a fury of published letters. In his *Dissertation on Anecdotes* (1793), D'Israeli reported that Macaulay was a "dilapidator of manuscripts" who had defaced seventeenth-century state letters while working in the British Museum in 1764.[47] D'Israeli ultimately acknowledged that the rumor was "impossible to authenticate," but he also maintained that Macaulay made it a practice in her historical researches, when she came to any material unfavorable to her political leanings, to destroy the page of the manuscript (*Curiosities* 446). He offered anecdotal "proof" of just one incident, based on an ambiguous notation made in a collection of papers she had consulted at the museum, from which he claimed four leaves were missing. It was a brief mention in a long book, but the story took on a life of its own.

Reviewers of D'Israeli's book gave prominence to the short anecdote. The conservative *British Critic* not surprisingly deemed D'Israeli's anecdote "too remarkable to be omitted" and reprinted it in its 180-word entirety.[48] The *Gentleman's Magazine*'s review (attributed to leading reviewer Richard Gough) not only approved of D'Israeli's work; it reinforced his accusations against Macaulay by calling for greater policing at the British Museum: "Those who frequent that national repository will perhaps agree, with us, that it cannot be too well watched."[49] D'Israeli's later work was branded by one reviewer as "very partial or exaggerated," but most reviewers seemed to take the gossip about Macaulay at face value.[50]

One suspects it would have been a shock to Macaulay that *this* was the great question debated about her reputation in the years after her death: Not, was she a good historian; not, did she deserve claim to some small status as a philosophical moralist; rather, had she become a thief in middle age? Did the 1764 notation by a librarian indicate that Macaulay had returned Harleian ms 7379 with missing leaves or that its leaves were missing prior to her having consulted it? D'Israeli quoted the lines in question as follows: " 'Upon Examination of the Book, November 12, 1764, these four last Leaves were torn out,' C. Morton." "Mem. Nov. 12th, sent down to Mrs. Macaulay."[51] D'Israeli alleged that this kind of notation was unprecedented and claimed that it proved that Macaulay had removed the pages. Letters flew in the *British Critic*, the *Gentleman's Magazine*, and the *Monthly Review*. Correspondence was exchanged in print between D'Israeli and Macaulay's widower, who had by then emerged from divinity school as Dr. William Graham. The *British Critic* claimed it "received more than one Remonstrance" on the subject of the accusations against Macaulay.[52]

Widower Graham said he had called upon Morton, the British Museum's former Keeper of the Manuscripts, who was then an old man. Graham wanted Morton to refute the charge of Macaulay's dilapidations. This service was duly rendered, although Morton's reported use of the word "rather" (in "it rather appears to me") came under dispute.[53] Graham later wrote to D'Israeli (through the periodical press), "What your motive could be in making so wanton and malicious an attack on the memory of a most worthy and amiable woman, three years after her death, I am at a loss to conceive."[54] Her death should be a protection from such vituperative comments, Graham suggests. He asks for better treatment for a woman no longer alive, just as Macaulay before him sought it for an aged female author.[55]

D'Israeli refused to stoop (or rise?) to chivalry and would not let his charge die quietly. In the backmatter of his *An Essay on the Manners and Genius of the Literary Character* (1795), he included a page that he titled an "Advertisement."[56] The page was devoted entirely to the Macaulay debacle. D'Israeli had not stopped writing about the charge: "I take this opportunity of declaring, that having been repeatedly attacked in the most illiberal manner by WILLIAM GRAHAM, respecting an Anecdote of Mrs. MACAULEY'S mutilation of a Harleian MS. that no just reason has yet been assigned to afford me the pleasure of retracting this accusation against a Lady of her eminent talents" (225). Simultaneously asserting the anecdote as fact, as well as accusation, he did not give an inch: "At present, the mysterious note of DR. MORTON remains unexplained, yet if it is allowed to have any meaning, it must convey a charge against the Historian, and as such will no doubt be received by impartial posterity."

He accuses Graham of mutilating Morton's original note when he quoted from it in the periodicals. D'Israeli suggests that the husband and wife practiced similar methods when he claims, "Mr. G. had the ingenuity to give it only in the state which was most adapted to his purpose" (225). D'Israeli says he has not based his evidence on the "floating reports" of thirty years but on textual evidence: Morton's note. D'Israeli describes his own motives as pure: "I was induced to notice this singular occurrence, not by design, but by accident; with no other view than that of literary instruction, and for no other party than that of truth." Confident that he would be proven right by subsequent generations, D'Israeli does concede, "I cannot *prove* this circumstance, for I was not born when it took place." D'Israeli points out the generational differences between him and Macaulay, claiming for himself both the vigor of youth and the good judgment of posterity.

Youth and age would continue to play a role in D'Israeli's defense (or offense?). Decades afterward, D'Israeli was still stewing in print about the accusation against Macaulay. In his second series of *Curiosities of Literature* (1823), he appends the following footnote to his anecdote:

It is now about twenty-seven years ago that I first published this anecdote, at the same time that I had received information that our female historian and dilapidator had acted in this manner more than once. Such a rumour, however, it was impossible to authenticate at that distance of time, but it was at least notorious at the British Museum. The Rev. William Graham, the surviving husband of Mrs. Macaulay, intemperately called on Dr. Morton, in a very advanced period of his life, to declare, that "it appeared to him that the note does not contain any evidence that the leaves were torn out by Mrs. Macaulay." It was more apparent to the unprejudiced, that the doctor must have singularly lost the use of his memory, when he could not explain his own official note, which, perhaps, at the time he was compelled to insert. (139)

Implying that Morton's defense of Macaulay was due to senility, D'Israeli dismisses the word of the only person who offered firsthand testimony. He also does what he earlier claimed was unnecessary—used "floating reports" to buttress his case. Remarkably, thirty years after the initial kerfuffle, D'Israeli continued to rehash his assertions of Macaulay's culpability. D'Israeli's virulence alone was enough to keep Macaulay in the public eye—negatively—for decades.

D'Israeli also impugned Macaulay in his other published works, though there he maintained that she had been "forgotten."[57] Most notable among these is his reference to her in his *Commentaries on the Life and Reign of Charles the First, King of England* (1828), in which he dubs her "a person of high passions, which were displayed in the extravagant incidents of her life."[58] He allows that "a masculine genius invigorated her historical compositions" but says that her "levelling reveries, which at the time had the delusion of novelty, and perhaps her sex, created about her a party of political enthusiasts" (1: xxi). In a final damning pen stroke, he concludes, "She beheld a statue raised to herself, but she lived to see it pulled down for ever; and her unquoted name has long been deserted by every historical writer." This is a strange statement, given that D'Israeli himself had had such an investment in quoting her name (in order to disparage it) for so long after her death. But D'Israeli, too, believed that Macaulay outlived her own good reputation. In this comment, at least, he and she would seem to be in agreement. As her letter to Griffiths demonstrates, it was a phenomenon she perceived happening before her eyes.

Attempts to recuperate Macaulay's posthumous reputation were also made. Mary Hays's *Female Biography; or, Memoirs of Illustrious and Celebrated Women . . . Alphabetically Arranged* (1803) describes (through information provided by her acknowledged informant, William Graham's sister) the mistreatment that Macaulay endured: "The author was attacked by petty and personal scurrilities, to which it was believed her sex would render her vulnerable. Her talents and powers could not be denied; her beauty was therefore called in question, as if it was at all concerned with the subject."[59] Hays offers a moving account of Macaulay's last years. It describes her declining health and makes the case that Macaulay's "prospects grew brighter with her progress toward the grave: she anticipated the period when her spirit . . . should no longer be impeded in its aspirations and researches."[60] Given Macaulay's responses to her last reviewers, this rhetoric about Macaulay's bright prospects while ruminating on her own death may take on a more somber cast.

Hays's sympathetic account paved the way for others. Anna Letitia Barbauld's essay, "On Education," refers to a gentleman in his library who has collected books on education, "all that were worthy of notice, from Xenophon to Locke, and from Locke to Catharine Macauley."[61] In the *Memoirs of Mrs. Frances Sheridan* (1824), Alicia Lefanu offers a short anecdote about the meeting between her grandmother Sheridan and Macaulay, during which they praised each other's work. After telling this story, Lefanu considers Macaulay's reputation in its positive and negative strains. She expresses doubt about the accounts of Macaulay provided by both Hays and Boswell, skeptical of charms described by the former and of the levity and extravagance claimed by the latter. After rehearsing the charges against Macaulay of vanity and coquetry, however, Lefanu defends her: "But let us be just to the memory of a very uncommon female, who rose above the disadvantages and deficiencies of education, at a time that literature was not cultivated among women as it is at present. Small could not be the industry and perseverance of a woman, who, under these circumstances, was able to raise herself to rank with the historians of her country; nor was the merit inconsiderable of that person, who was admired by Cowper, and quoted with approbation by Mr. Fox."[62] Thirty years after the *Vindication* was published, Lefanu's call to be just to Macaulay's memory echoes Wollstonecraft's, coupled with the very rhetoric that Macaulay used in her letter to Griffiths. Was this the way in which Macaulay in her old age felt she deserved to be remembered—for her industry and exceptionalism?

To say, as many have, that Macaulay was forgotten by the end of the eighteenth century is an overstatement, though she was remembered in odd ways. Her late life in particular comes in for some strange characterizations. In his *Traditions and Recollections* (1826), Richard Polwhele has occasion to recollect Macaulay several times, including a 1778 letter from her praising his poetry.[63] Someone—whether Polwhele, editor, or publisher—considered Macaulay's letter important enough to use her name in his work's title, among its "distinguished characters" whose correspondence is printed therein. Polwhele was a one-time supporter of Macaulay's who contributed to her infamous birthday party odes, but a note in his text (by him? by his editor?) gets the details of Macaulay's late life completely wrong: "It is well known that Mrs. Macaulay was afterwards married to Dr. Graham (who, in the introduction to the six odes, presents his acknowledgments to Dr. Wilson, 'through her agreeable medium'); and that, with Dr. Graham (and other champions of democracy) she emigrated to America and died there" (1: 43). Macaulay did not marry the Dr. (James) Graham mentioned in the six odes—who was her "doctor," though perhaps more showman than medical man.[64] She married his younger brother. Macaulay visited but never emigrated to America; she most certainly did not die there. But this "well known" version of events makes for moving fiction—a fitting and dramatic end that is in its own way more glorious than Macaulay's self-reported waning-away laurels and certainly more glamorous than the picture painted of her by D'Israeli.

If Macaulay's life was misremembered (or if only its scandal was recollected), her histories continued to receive sparing and even positive notice.[65] A largely complimentary review of Godwin's *History of the Commonwealth* (1824) published in the *London Review* takes Godwin to task because he "overlooks the fact that [parliamentary journals] are continually referred to by Macaulay"—that she had previously conducted this sort of historical research. Godwin's argument is compared to that of "Mrs. Macaulay," who did not "live quite long enough" to see the wide sentiments in regard to liberty that Godwin has been able to witness.[66] Eugene Lawrence's *Lives of the British Historians* (1855) includes a scant two pages on Macaulay in its two extensive volumes, but she is the only woman so represented. He concludes, "the name of the author is hardly remembered, except among historical inquirers."[67]

Over the next century and a half, Catharine Macaulay became the historian whom historians liked to remember had been forgotten. Alice Stopford Green's *Woman's Place in the World of Letters* (1897) lists history as the only pre-nineteenth-century genre in which female writers excelled, and she mentions just two contributors to it: Lucy Hutchinson and Catharine Macaulay.[68] Doris Mary Stenton wrote that "within a generation of her death," Macaulay "had become little more than a half remembered name."[69] So many, for so many years, lamented the state of her reputation.[70] In her last years, as we have seen, Macaulay expressed anxiety or perhaps anger that her renown as an author was slipping away. She may have had her own situation in mind when she wrote in an aside in the *Letters on Education*, "all persons of declining age feel the truth of Solomon's reflection, that their days have been spent in a fruitless vexation of the spirit" (77). We might call this an expression of retrospective dissatisfaction or regret. Considering what Macaulay's reputation once was, her status as an author had fallen dramatically in old age, and fruitless vanity or not, she was vexed enough to write a long letter outlining what she saw as the large and small wrongs against her. Her words might be seen as acts of self-promotion and historical preservation—or perhaps of self-preservation and historical promotion. For Macaulay, the scene of history and sense of self were closely intertwined.

In her letter to Griffiths, Macaulay suggests that she sees her alleged mistreatment by the reviewer as a systemic, not a personal, problem. Whether this was clever rhetoric or genuine perception is difficult to decide. The mixed hostile and recuperative treatment she faced after her death does little to clear up the question, other than to suggest that more than paranoia was at work in the anxious expressions about her late reputation. Macaulay was unequivocally a trailblazer among women writers, due to her extraordinary celebrity and her historical achievements; at the end of her life, she again blazed a trail by attempting to use her identity as an elderly female author to shape her late-life reception and potentially her critical afterlife, too. She took umbrage at the lack of veneration shown her and her work, and she must have understood that that lack of respect did not bode well for how her works would be received thereafter. Though Macaulay has not yet received the redress she sought from Griffiths—the publication of her "angry letter" in full—this chapter provides the possibility of her late life authorial machinations finding a fuller hearing than she has, as yet, received. Moreover, it demonstrates one older woman writer's refusal to do what her culture expected: to go away quietly.

CHAPTER THREE

What Is Old in Jane Austen?

> But, alas, I am afraid that every benevolent person, who begins
> a work to befriend any part of his species, must be surprised, as
> he advances, with unexpected difficulties.
>
> —*William Hayley,* A Philosophical, Historical, and
> Moral Essay on Old Maids *(1785)*

Jane Austen (1775–1817) may not seem an obvious candidate for a study of
old age, especially because one of the biographical details most remembered
about her is that she led a life cut short. Nineteenth-century critics clearly
thought of her in relation to her long-lived contemporaries, as they used her
in contrast to them; for a time, Austen served as the exception that proved the
rule of British women writers living to old age.[1] Though this critical practice
did not survive into the twentieth century, other misconceptions just as limiting took its place. Virginia Woolf wrote, as we have seen, that "Jane Austen
should have laid a wreath upon the grave of Fanny Burney," even though
Austen died more than twenty years before Burney.[2] A good number of Austen's contemporaries lived twice as long as she did. As a result of our neglect
of this fact, we have yet to place Austen squarely in relation to them. For this
reason alone, Austen is worthy of consideration in a study of British women
writers in old age.

There are other, perhaps more compelling, reasons. Chief among them is
that Austen, despite her death in middle age, has long been labeled a peculiar
kind of old: the "old maid." Austen is perhaps the most famous British author
described so prominently as a spinster. The limiting ways in which Austen
has come down to us have been beautifully documented by Emily Auerbach
in *Searching for Jane Austen* (2004). Auerbach has collected two centuries of
comments on our obsession with and judgments about Austen's supposedly

narrow life and her status as an "old maid." Virginia Woolf's complaints about being annoyed by those who talk about Austen "as if she were a niminy priminy [sic] spinster" "ring true," according to Auerbach, as "the phrase 'never married' appears over and over again" in accounts of the novelist's life.[3]

Austen's reputation as a polite, happy Christian spinster who went to an early grave has provided a restrictive framework through which her works have been interpreted. Through this framework, first established by Henry Austen's posthumous memoir of his sister, Jane Austen became known to many as the good spinster-author.[4] When critics have not followed Austen's brother's lead in apotheosizing her as a virtuous old maid, they have often used negative stereotypes of spinsters to write her off. For example, D. H. Lawrence famously referred to Jane Austen as "English in the bad, mean snobbish sense of the word," simultaneously dismissing her as "this old maid" and "thoroughly unpleasant."[5] John Halperin's controversial biography used Austen's "failure" to marry to explain what he saw as the anger and rage exhibited in her life and writings.[6] The legend of Austen's "thwarted love," as Hermione Lee puts it, "satisfies conventional habits of explaining the life of a spinster or old maid" and "can also fuel a negative view of a resentful, bitter, caustic Jane Austen."[7] Whether marshaling stereotypes good or bad, and for better or for worse, Austen as old maid has carried and continues to carry enormous explanatory power.

Although positive and negative stereotypes of spinsterhood have been employed prominently in Austen criticism, studying Austen in concert with the *history* of old maids has been a relatively recent critical trend. Despite a body of work that considers everything from white soup to gleaning nuts, relatively little Austen scholarship has sought to make sense of old maids, or, more broadly, women and aging in her fiction. In this chapter, I first investigate remarks on old age and aging in Austen's novels, in order to gauge her explicit and implicit attitudes toward age as they conform to or deviate from dominant representations. Next, I return to the subcategory of old in Austen's writings that has most resonated with her life—the "old maid," looking in particular at the controversial characterizations of the type presented in *Emma* (1816).

We might wish that, as an old maid herself, Austen had become a champion of them in her mature fiction. It is my contention in this chapter that she did not do so in *Emma*. Austen, I argue, echoed stereotypical treatments of old maidism in this novel, even if she did not accept these limiting views in her own life. Her young heroines may rightly be labeled feminist, in comparison to other representations during her era, but that progressive impulse did not extend to all of her female characters, as Austen appears not to have chosen to overturn dominant representations of old maids. Making sense of her most visible old maid, *Emma*'s Miss Bates, my argument points to the perhaps all-too-obvious conclusion that there were as many ways to be an old maid writer as to be an old woman writer in the period. Austen's way, at least as it is presented in *Emma*, involved a willingness to conform to, rather than to overturn, prevalent stereotypes.

Not Young: The Life Course in Austen's Fiction

Among Austen's family members, death in middle age was unusual. "Most of the other members of her family survived well into their 70s or 80s," as Jan Fergus notes; Austen's often-ailing mother was 87 when she died, and her sister Cassandra lived to be 72.[8] Austen did not experience the so-called winter of her life, as they did, but a glance at her novels demonstrates that she did not ignore old women in her fiction. Indeed, Austen demonstrates an awareness of the challenges facing the elderly in her culture and presents these issues in her writings. Her fiction includes characters who display, notice, and are acutely affected by the aging process, and she generally indicts those who engage in the most exaggerated and harmful stereotyping of the old.

Undoubtedly, Austen's novels center on the young rather than on the old. As Claire Lamont has put it, "What is surprising about Austen's novels is how few old people there are in them."[9] For every use of "old" in Austen's fiction, there are three uses of the word "young." According to *The Concordance of the Works of Jane Austen*, there are 355 uses of the words *old, older*, and *oldest* in her writings, and 954 of the words *young, younger*, and *youngest*.[10] The phrase "not young" is sometimes preferred to "old." To pay too close attention to old age and aging is usually a character flaw, as when *Northanger Abbey*'s hideous suitor, John Thorpe, uses the word *old* with great frequency. He employs it as an adjective to describe Catherine's guardian "old Allen," as well as fellows, songs, and places. In that novel, there are repeated references to "ancient" places and to the "age" in which the characters live, but there are few direct comments on old age.

The elderly most often populate Austen's fiction in a way structurally similar to the way her servants do—as faceless backdrops, rather than as comic grotesques. Descriptions of the old and the servant class also overlap, as there are references to "old superannuated servants."[11] Many of them, when referred to by name or position, are called "good old," or sometimes "poor old," such as Dorothy, the "ancient housekeeper" in *Northanger Abbey* or the "poor old coachman" in *Mansfield Park* (158).[12] Austen also wrote wonderful one-liners satirizing her culture's lack of generosity toward old age, like *Sense and Sensibility*'s reprehensible Fanny Dashwood's caustic observation that "people always live for ever when there is an annuity to be paid to them" (10).

Qualities of youth and age are frequently used as comparisons, jokes, and elements of exposition. In *Sense and Sensibility*, Mrs. Jennings is described as "a good humoured, merry, fat, elderly woman who talked a great deal" (34). Austen here links old age and garrulity, a stereotype discussed in previous chapters, but she does so in a character who largely redeems herself by novel's end. Mrs. Jennings, as a garrulous old woman, is undoubtedly a mixed character, and largely sympathetic, rather than a one-dimensional comic or annoying stereotype. Other characters are more difficult to place in terms of age. We might think of *Pride and Prejudice*'s Lady Catherine de Bourgh as "old," perhaps because of her power and gravitas, but she is not so labeled. Instead, she is described as "a tall, large woman, with strongly-marked features, which might once have been handsome."[13] Putting this description in the past tense suggests a character well into middle age. Mrs. Jenkinson, who lives with her, is dubbed an "old lady" (158).

The word *old* in Austen's novels is, as these examples demonstrate, a fluid term. This fluidity is in keeping with eighteenth-century conversations about age and aging. Despite this fluidity, Austen's work simultaneously suggests 55 as an expected age for the end of life, such as when it is supposed that *Sense and Sensibility*'s Colonel Brandon, at 35, "may live twenty years longer" (37). A short epistolary piece from Austen's juvenilia, *Love and Freindship*, also homes in on the significance of age 55. The piece begins by implying that old women are not free from misfortunes. Isabel writes to her friend Laura on her 55th birthday, arguing, "If a woman may ever be said to be in safety from the determined Perseverance of disagreeable Lovers and the cruel Persecutions of obstinate Fathers, surely it must be at such a time of Life."[14] Laura responds that she "cannot agree with you in supposing that I shall never again be exposed to Misfortunes as unmerited as those I have already experienced" (2). Laura is a melodramatic, exaggerated, and humorous character, typical of the raucous women featured in the juvenilia, but there is alongside the thick irony of this piece an attention to debates about the relative happiness of old women and the continuing variety and color possible in their lives.

Age is shown to be a matter of attitude, as well as number, in other Austen novels. In *Mansfield Park*, there is a description of a young person acting old.

Heroine Fanny Price is asked to play "a very proper, little old woman" in the private theatricals, to be dressed in "a brown gown, and a white apron, and a mob cap," with "a few wrinkles, and a little of the crowfoot at the corner of your eyes" (146). Fanny does not want to act any part, though the fact that her friends and cousins select her for the least glamorous (and least sexualized) role is central to establishing her character and theirs. Old women were seen by that set as proper, brown, wrinkled, and wearing appropriately dowdy headgear. *Sense and Sensibility*'s Marianne Dashwood's skewed judgments on age are demonstrated through her first impression of Colonel Brandon's "forlorn condition" as an "exceedingly ancient" "old bachelor" at 35. She makes reference to his complaints of rheumatism as "the commonest infirmity of declining life," to which her mother replies that Marianne must find it "a miracle that [her mother's] life has been extended to the advanced age of forty" (37). In Austen's early epistolary work, *Lady Susan*, the unscrupulous main character chastises her friend Alicia Johnson for marrying a man "just old enough to be formal, ungovernable & to have the Gout—too old to be agreeable, & too young to die!"[15] Negative and limiting perceptions of the old reveal character flaws in each instance.

Persuasion's Sir Walter Elliot is obsessed with age and especially horrified at the signs of aging in those around him. He is troubled at "the wreck of the good looks of every body" but himself and his daughter Elizabeth, because "he could plainly see how old all the rest of his family and acquaintance were growing" (6). He is also disgusted at the premature aging of sailors and tells a story of one Admiral Baldwin, who was a "deplorable looking person" with a "face the colour of mahogany, rough and rugged to the last degree, all lines and wrinkles, nine grey hairs of a side, and nothing but a dab of powder at top"; Sir Walter guessed the admiral's age to be 62 and was astonished to learn that the man was only 40, "and no more" (19–20). Also a "distress" to Sir Walter is the "rapid increase of the crow's foot about [his neighbor] Lady Russell's temples" (20). Lady Russell, for her part, is described by the narrator as "of steady age and character" and is probably Sir Walter's contemporary (5). When Sir Walter learns of the existence of Anne's friend in Bath, the widow Mrs. Smith, he disparages the friend as not only low company for Anne but also as an "old lady" that Anne could put off until tomorrow. He remarks, "She is not so near her end, I presume, but that she may hope to see another day. What is her age? Forty?" Anne replies, "No, Sir, she is not one and thirty" (157). Sir Walter's obsession with the signs of aging demonstrate his shallow character.

Persuasion has been said to use age and aging as its central theme, in no small part because of its older heroine, Anne Elliot. In chapter 1, we learn that "a few years before, Anne Elliot had been a very pretty girl, but her bloom had vanished early" (9). The narrator emphasizes this again three chapters later, when Anne is said to have suffered "the early loss of bloom and spirits" (27). Anne, at age 27, is shown to have grown old before her time. The events of the novel help her to recapture her bloom; it is envisioned as a "second spring of youth and beauty" (9) or as "every beauty excepting bloom" (77). Anne may have lost her bloom, but her older sister Elizabeth is "still the same handsome Miss Elliot that she had begun to be thirteen years ago" (10). When we are reintroduced to the novel's hero, Captain Frederick Wentworth, it is with the revelation that he appears no older than he did seven years before. He reportedly believes that Anne is "altered beyond his knowledge!" (141). But she notes that "he was not altered, or not for the worse . . . the years which had destroyed her youth and bloom had only given him a more glowing, manly, open look, in no respect lessening his personal advantages. She had seen the same Frederick Wentworth" (142). It may be inferred from the use of the word *bloom* throughout *Persuasion* that even among the more sympathetic characters and the narrator, youth and age are not measured by numbers alone.

Persuasion is sometimes called Austen's autumnal novel, because written near the end of her life. It famously concentrates on issues of time, alongside those of aging. As Janice Sokoloff argues, Austen "creates . . . an atmosphere which continuously returns the reader to issues of time and its passage: the vivid depictions of autumn; the elegiac tone so many critics have commented upon; and the recurrent and varied articulation of the experience of time."[16] Sokoloff concludes that these "features combine to create a haunting aura of chronology and mutability in nearly every character in the novel" (17). Building on the work of Sokoloff, Lamont, and others, more ought to be said on the subject of age and aging in *Persuasion*, especially its depiction of the slippery category "middle age." Though middle age is of great importance to the study of Austen and aging, it is to *Emma* instead that I turn in the remainder of this chapter, for its focus on the related category of old maid, whether in middle or old age.

Emma is an important text for studying the old in Austen, as it presents her most conspicuous old man in valetudinarian Mr. Woodhouse. We are never told his precise age, but the narrator remarks on the "disparity" of age between him and his 21-year-old daughter, Emma. The narrator explains that

Mr. Woodhouse "had not married early" and that he "was a much older man in ways than in years."[17] On the female side, *Emma* features what is arguably Austen's oldest character, the "harmless old lady" Mrs. Bates, who is an "excellent mother" to the garrulous Miss Bates (21). Mrs. Bates is called "a very old lady, almost past every thing but tea and quadrille." Her signal contributions to the action of the novel are that she breaks her spectacles and falls asleep at times convenient to young lovers (236, 240). If Mrs. Bates seems most important in the novel as an audience (receptive or not), her daughter, Miss Bates, serves as Emma's direct foil in regard to her future imagined marital status. Indeed, the novel begins with a seeming endorsement of old maidism. Before turning to a reading of the novel, however, it is worthwhile to consider cultural constructions of the old maid in Austen's era.

The Old Maid in the Long Eighteenth Century

The age at which one might be said to reach old maidenhood—whether in Austen's fiction or in the late eighteenth or early nineteenth centuries in Britain—is notoriously difficult to pin down. In Austen's *Lady Susan*, the eponymous heroine is 35. She is described as "excessively pretty" for "a Lady no longer young" (*Minor Works* 251). Women and men of "five and twenty" are regularly called young, but at 29, *Persuasion*'s hateful Elizabeth Elliot is said to have "felt her approach to the years of danger" with "apprehensions" and "regrets," though she "was fully satisfied of being still quite as handsome as ever" (7). The narrator tells us that 29 can be "a time of life at which scarcely any charm is lost," if there has been neither "ill health nor anxiety" (6). Still, the "years of danger" would seem to imply a chronological age, as well as a physical condition. Most sources point to the age of 30 or 40 as a numerical designation for old maidism in the period.

Some scholars suggest that social anxiety over old maids emerged in the Victorian era, from Charles Dickens's vengeful Miss Havisham in *Great Expectations* (1860–61), to George Gissing's somewhat more sympathetic portraits in his novel *The Odd Women* (1893), to W. R. Greg's astonishingly insulting essay, "Why Are Women Redundant?" (1862).[18] In the latter work, Greg proposes sending so-called surplus old maids to the colonies to marry them off to men who cannot afford to be too choosy.[19] It could be argued, however, that the figure of the old maid came to cultural fruition in the Restoration or the eighteenth century.[20] The *Oxford English Dictionary* locates the term "old maid" from the 1530s. It dates the first use of the word *spinster*, with the meaning old maid, to 1719. Prior to that, *spinster* was used to denote merely the common in-home activity of spinning or any woman who was not married.[21] Curiously, though the eighteenth century produced a great deal of discourse about old maids, their proportion decreased across the period. Single women went from approximately 15 percent of the population in the late seventeenth century to half that number in the late eighteenth.[22]

Old maids, declining as a portion of the population, were solidifying as a class in the cultural imagination, and stereotypes about them, too, were forming. The old maid was a stock figure who appeared in all genres of literature. Arthur Murphy's play *The Old Maid* (1761) features the 43-year-old Miss Harlow, who believes that she, not her younger married sister-in-law, is the love object of an attractive young man. Miss Harlow's brother, with whom she lives, ultimately concludes, "an old maid in the house is a devil."[23] By the end, Miss Harlow realizes her undesirability, professes herself disgraced, and says she will "hide [herself] from the world forever" (255).

Other depictions were just as punishing but far more virulent. The 1713 *Satyr upon Old Maids* calls the group "Amazonian Cannibals" (qtd. in Lanser 302). Daniel Defoe's follow up, "Satire on Censorious Old Maids" (1723), suggests that "if an Old-Maid should bite any body, it would certainly be as Mortal, as the Bite of a Mad-Dog." A 1749 poem describes old maids in hell and dubs them "gloomy," envious, and full of rage—a "lean, nauseaous, antiquated race."[24] Oliver Goldsmith's fictional dialogue in *The Citizen of the World* (1764) has two men disagreeing over whether old maids in London deserve to be treated with sympathy because they would be married if they could, or if they deserve no sympathy because they are full of "pride, avarice, coquetry, or affectation."[25] Stories illustrating the latter position take up the greater portion of his Letter 28. The once-familiar saying that "old maids lead apes in hell" also gives a vivid sense of the contempt with which this group was viewed.[26] A dictionary from 1834 notes that the saying "is still in use in the jocular sense" (qtd. in Whiting 345). As a young American woman put it about old maidism in 1762, "the appellation of Old made [sic] has always appeard to me very Formidable, and I don't believe one of our Sex wou'd Voluntarily Bare that Title if by a proper opportunity they could avoid it."[27]

Most descriptions demonstrated that old maids were held in very low esteem. In his *Father's Legacy to His Daughters* (1775), Dr. John Gregory encourages young women to marry, because old maids' tempers are infected with "chagrin and peevishness."[28] He believes such women cannot make a dignified transition from youth to "the calm, silent, unnoticed retreat of de-

clining years" (106). Old maids, it seems, are destined to make dreadful old
women and to take on many of the negative stereotypes of the female elderly
(querulousness, garrulousness) in middle age. *A Poetical Address to the Ladies
of Suffolk* (1785) also describes "antiquated virgins" as "peevish" but adds
the further description that such women are changed to a "lump of malice"
who rail alternately at both sexes, are deceitful, and enjoy cheating "simple
fools."[29] The *British Apollo* characterizes old maids as liars.[30] Later, it also offers some quasi-sympathetic reasons for the negative characteristics it sees in
old maids. In responding to a fictional correspondent who complains that as an
old maid she is "slighted and despised by all" and that people say her "looks
and qualities differ from the rest of womankind," the Apollo responds that it
is "no wonder if crosses, vexations, teasings, and disappointments shou'd alter
the looks and qualities of [such] a person" (3: 10).

Negative and farcical representations competed with more sympathetic
ones. Frances Brooke's periodical *The Old Maid* ran for thirty-seven issues
in 1755–56, under the pseudonym Mary Singleton, Spinster, the magazine's
admirable 50-year-old persona.[31] Those who study the eighteenth-century old
maid have also pointed to the work of Mary Astell (1666–1731), Jane Barker
(bap. 1652–1732), Sarah Fielding (1710–68), Elizabeth Inchbald (1753–1821),
and Sarah Scott (1720–95) as providing more positive models of eighteenth-
century spinsters. Anna Letitia Barbauld (1743–1825) early in her life wrote a
poem, published posthumously, titled "Bouts Rimés, in Praise of Old Maids."
In that short verse, Barbauld—though she belittles the life experiences of
old maids by underestimating their emotional and practical hardships—also
describes their personal strengths:

> Hail, all ye ancient maidens fair or—brown,
> Whose careless minutes dance away on—down,
> No household cares your free enjoyments—saddle,
> In life's wide sea your lonely skiff you—paddle;
> What though no lover seeks your heart to—steal,
> Nor bells salute you with a noisy—peal,
> Yet shall you never mourn your husband—fickle
> Nor children cropt by death's untimely—sickle,
> No hoyden romps shall your prim head-dress—blouze,
> No noisy sot your peaceful slumbers—rouse,
> No nurse attend with caudle and with—cake
> Too dearly bought when liberty's at—stake;

Slander against your fame shall find no—handle,
While stead of squalling brats, dear pug you—dandle.
In pleasure's free career you meet no—stop,
Greatly alone, you stand without a—prop.[32]

Through most of the poem, Barbauld imagines the life of an old maid as an uncomplicated, comfortable one, in which dogs play a major role and pleasure is probable. The last line qualifies the previous ones, with its use of "*greatly* alone," as the poem makes the old maid's life course seem courageous, albeit lonely: she (unlike those who are wives or mothers) supports *herself* to stand.

During Austen's era, full-length works of fiction appeared centering on old maids. Although purporting to be sympathetic, these novels may be viewed as overwhelmingly not so.[33] For instance, Ann Emelinda Skinn's feisty epistolary novel, *The Old Maid; or, History of Miss Ravensworth* (1771), features 40-year-old Aunt Patty, an envious, spiteful woman who has been praying for a husband "these twenty years; and all to so little purpose" (1: 27). In the end, Aunt Patty turns out not to be a virgin, discovered naked in bed with the family butler (3: 102). The heroine of the novel is Aunt Patty's spirited nemesis and niece, Emily Ravensworth, who, like Emma Woodhouse, initially determines not to marry. Emily finds the choice between matrimony and "antiquated virginity" to be a "hard" one but determines to become an old maid out of "pure spite," if her alternative is to marry a wretch (64). By the end of the novel, Emily becomes Mrs. Blanche, and her hatred of old maids in general and Aunt Patty specifically seems to be one of the reasons she ultimately agrees to "dwindle into a wife" (16).

In a fascinating essay on Skinn's notorious life and her remarkable novel, Susan Staves notes that the old maid of the title might refer either to Aunt Patty or to her niece Emily, as both are Miss Ravensworth through much of the action.[34] Staves concludes that Skinn has split "the figure of the woman alone in two, allowing Emily to fulfill her wishes and leaving the self-hatred to be projected out into Aunt Patty" (176). Skinn, Staves discovers, was herself involved in three highly publicized trials for divorce from her husband William Skinn, all of which she lost (180). The couple had separated after sixteen months of marriage in 1768. Skinn "went on to marry an army officer, who eventually abandoned her in poverty," according to Cheryl Turner, and she combined teaching, writing, and sewing to support herself.[35] Though her novel's narrator is skeptical of the goodness of actual men, Skinn is (as Staves argues) also seemingly skeptical of the degree to which one should sympathize with old maids. Skinn was in her early twenties when she wrote the book, apparently her only publication (177).

Though *The Old Maid* is in many ways sui generis, it was not the only work of fiction during the period to make an unmarried woman its titular center. Mrs. Ross's *The Balance of Comfort; or, The Old Maid and the Married Woman* (1817) features a heroine who values the single life and socializes with spinsters, though she herself also marries at novel's end.[36] A decade after Austen's death, an anonymously published novel, *The Confessions of an Old Maid* (1828), claimed to offer the narrative from young adulthood to the present of the love life of 54-year-old single woman, Clorinda Mirabelle. As a first-person narrator, Clorinda laments that any romance described from the mouth of an old maid "is ever looked upon, by a most disrespectful world, as a burlesque!"[37] But her narrative is presented as a cautionary tale, encouraging women to understand marriage as a "calculation" (3: 279) and chastising "men (many at least of them) [who] are pleased to contemplate the title of 'Old Maid' with contempt and ridicule" (287). Clorinda even offers an alternative term to old maid—"Unwedded Independent," mistress of herself (282–83). Despite all of its reassurance of good will toward the so-called sisterhood of old maids, Clorinda acknowledges that her story presents "somewhat of a caricature" (268). She encourages pride and dignity in her class and says it is a happy one, but she also acknowledges that she has fallen into the stereotypical errors of old maidism, such as not perceiving that "her day is past" where romance is concerned. The novel is said to serve at once as consolation to old maids, as well as inspiration and instruction to maids young and old (290–91).

When *Confessions of an Old Maid* was reviewed by the periodical *La Belle Assemblée*, the reviewer did not doubt that the work was "the veritable production of one of the sisterhood."[38] Others were more skeptical. The *Literary Gazette*'s brief notice calls the novel's "sketch of old-maidism . . . a caricature of the common-place character—the ancient vestal of comedy, farce, and the novel, for the witlings of long years" and suspects (rightly) that the work was written by a male.[39] (The novel has been attributed to Edmund Frederick John Carrington.)[40] Few aging single women, it would seem, were willing to publish works of fiction or nonfiction about their own "kind." Such topics were more likely to be tackled by married women or by men, whether married or not.[41] (This, too, might serve as indirect evidence of the kind of reception that an unmarried woman writer over 30 might expect, if she wrote about and became closely identified with old maids.)

Although the theory of male authorship of the *Confessions* novel was then mere speculation, it was well known that the most influential late eighteenth-century work defending old maids had been written by a man. Once-renowned poet William Hayley (1745–1820) anonymously published *A Philosophical, Historical, and Moral Essay on Old Maids* (1785), signed "a Friend to the Sisterhood." The work was almost immediately attributed to him in the periodical press, and his fascinating, troubling, and now rarely discussed three-volume defense enjoyed three editions, the latest of which incorporated significant additions and corrections (1793).[42] The *Essay* was translated into French and German and excerpted widely in periodicals of the day. From the first, the book was roundly criticized, though both fictional and nonfiction works of the period recommended it or featured characters who were reading it, and it apparently sold well. The *Dictionary of National Biography* (1891) refers to it as "one of [Hayley's] few still readable works"—a damning commentary on the poet about whom Robert Southey is alleged to have said, "Everything about that man was good, except his poetry."[43]

For contemporary readers of Hayley's *Essay*, the most puzzling question seems to have been deciphering its intentions. Many found the book a humorous lark. Others took it at face value—as a serious, valuable defense of a downtrodden group. An obituary of Hayley in the *London Magazine* (1824) sums up his accomplishment in the *Essay* as "an agreeable combination of learning, sprightliness, and arch humour."[44] Hayley, the reviewer notes, "now and then approaches to irreverence on sacred subjects, but, as I am persuaded, without any ill intention" (504). The poet Anna Seward (1742–1809), a friend and admirer of Hayley's, writes in a private letter that she reported "with freedom" to him that she believed his "wicked wit seduced him into the ungenerous conduct of betraying the cause of which he stood forth as the champion; and of increasing, by his sarcasms, the unjust contempt in which the unprotected part of our oppressed sex are held in their declining days."[45] These responses suggest readers found it to be a serious work, a satirical work, and occasionally both. Reading the *Essay* today remains a challenge.

Difficulties in construing the *Essay*'s tone arise from its first pages. Hayley dedicates his *Essay on Old Maids* to the learned Elizabeth Carter (1717–1806), a well-known classical scholar. Hayley writes, "Permit me to pay my devotions to you, as the ancients did to their threefold Diana; and to reverence you in three distinct characters; as a Poet, as a Philosopher, and as an Old Maid. . . . Your virtues and your talents induce me to consider you as the President of the chaste Community, whose interest I have endeavoured to promote in the following performance."[46] He continues by noting that the term "old maid," although it may be held inferior in "vulgar estimation" to poet and philosopher, is the one that Carter holds with "dignity" (a word later echoed in the *Confessions* novel, as we saw). That quality has made Hayley wish Carter to appear as the "Protectress" of his little volumes (v–vi). Because the dedication uses a simultaneously weighty and cheeky tone, it is hard to know whether its author meant any of it to be taken seriously. Carter was well connected and well respected and was not a common or even a likely target for ridicule.

Carter was apparently not impressed with Hayley's singling her out. In reporting her response to the dedication to her, Carter's nephew, biographer, and editor Montagu Pennington notes that Hayley anonymously sent Carter a copy of the work in an elegant binding shortly after it had been published. (One wonders what light this ought to shed on what Hayley thought he was doing in the dedication?) Pennington writes that Carter "was neither pleased, however, nor flattered by the compliment. Had that Gentleman known her personally, he would have been assured that all the wit, learning, and genius, displayed so abundantly in that performance, could never compensate, in her opinion, for the improprieties contained in it; and that no compliment to herself could induce her to excuse the ridicule thrown upon others."[47] Pennington suggests that Carter took seriously the work's dedication to her but deplored its harmful effects, if not its "learned" message—whatever she may have construed that to be.

In the first chapter of the *Essay*, Hayley seems to defuse readers' doubts that his writing this book was anything but a solemn endeavor. He urges his reader to take his project seriously and not to suspect him of questionable motives. After all, he argues, he could have written about disgraced commanders or discarded statesmen and profited from the work with a reward. He avers that "in the present case, I can have no such prospect to stimulate my pen; for, though the persons for whom I wrote cannot be said to possess the favour of the public, yet I solemnly protest, I have no expectation that any one of them will be admitted into the cabinet of any potentate or prime minister in all the kingdoms of Europe, or obtain any influence in the United States of America" (1: xviii). By the third volume of his *Essay*, Hayley reverses course on his proclamation that he will not profit from the work and concocts an ingenious way to do so. He suggests that old maids form local societies, "little convocations of their order," appoint presidents and maiden secretaries, and collect dues—an "honourable tax" (3: 252). He says he will live off of the interest, "Expecting the sum to be very great" (253), and when he dies "which

. . . can hardly be very distant," he will give the sum to reduce the national debt. Sadly for Hayley's pocketbook and for the national debt, such a scheme never took hold.[48] Though this section of the essay certainly sounds satirical, and perhaps even humorous, some readers took it quite seriously. As we will see, Hayley's work had a profound impact on discussions of old maids and on how they were represented, if not on how they actually lived.

It is unclear if Jane Austen read Hayley's *Essay on Old Maids.* She certainly knew his other writings, as she owned six volumes of his *Poems and Plays*, which she inscribed in 1791.[49] Deirdre Le Faye has also found a possible link between Austen and Hayley, suggesting that *The Loiterer* essay, which Austen may have authored, by "Sophia Sentiment," took its pseudonym from one of Hayley's productions.[50] Recent scholars have begun to link—however elliptically —Austen's novels to Hayley's *Essay.*[51] His treatise was rightly dubbed by one reviewer "singular," as the book's first volume describes the supposed character flaws and positive traits of old maids, followed by a second volume that traces the history of old maids from the classical era.[52] A third volume is filled with sermons, medical speculations, and a bizarre fantasy in which Hayley dreams he has arisen from the dead in a room filled with worshipful old maids. But the question that Hayley entertains first in his labyrinthine work is, What is an old maid? "I was on the point of defining an Old Maid to be, an unmarried woman, who has compleated her fortieth year," but then he hit unexpected difficulties (2): "This perplexity arose from my desire to fix, in the most unexceptionable manner, the aera of Old-Maidism; a phrase which I use, indeed, without authority: but as I write on a new branch of philosophy, let me vindicate the philosophical privilege of coining such new words as my original work may require" (2–3).

He decides that, in order to define old maidism, he must consult women themselves. This does not clear up his dilemma, as he learns the following: "The misses of twenty considered all their unmarried friends, who had passed their thirtieth year, as absolute Old Maids; those of thirty supposed the aera to commence at about forty-five; and some ladies of fifty convinced me how differently they thought upon the subject, by calling others, about three or four years younger than themselves, by the infantine appellation of girls; from whence I presumed they would advance the aera I speak of to the age of sixty at least" (3). Hayley, unsatisfied, consults a man who had just married a woman of 43 and had a son with her. This man rejects the label "old maid" altogether, believing that all virgins are in a perpetual state of childhood and never deserve the label "old." Hayley dismisses the position of the new father and concludes that "the world in general . . . never fail to give the unwelcome title of Old Maid to unmarried ladies of forty" (5), so he will follow suit. Hayley defines the onset of old maidism somewhat later than his culture (and than Austen) generally did, which may seem a kind of sympathetic response. But if Austen and Hayley differ over the numerical age at which old maids come into being, the two authors seem to agree almost to the letter on the personal qualities generally assigned to them.

Silly, Satisfied, Smiling, Prosing, Undistinguishing, and Unfastidious: *Emma* and Old Maidism

The Austen novel that most deserves investigation alongside Hayley's treatise—and which has not received much attention from that angle—is *Emma*.[55] Hayley's *Essay* has direct relevance to *Emma* from the first chapters of both. Austen's novel begins with conversation about a just-married woman who may be considered a former old maid. In a situation similar to that of Hayley's new father, described above, Austen's couple is expecting a child by the story's end. The woman is, of course, Mrs. Weston, heroine Emma Wood-house's former governess. We first learn about her through her long-time employer, Mr. Woodhouse. He insists on referring to Emma's ex-governess as "poor Miss Taylor" (1: 8), rather than by her married name. Mr. Woodhouse thinks it "a pity . . . that Mr. Weston ever thought of her" and later laments that "young people would be in such a hurry to marry" (52). Mr. Woodhouse in effect takes Hayley's essay, which offers advice for how old maids should and should not comport themselves, a step further, implying that the world would be a better place if there were *more* old maids. That he calls them "young" also shows his unusual relationship to this group.

Mr. Woodhouse is a ridiculous figure, fond of gruel and afraid of everyone catching cold—not a character in whom readers are to put much faith. His daughter Emma, however, offers extended commentary on old maids. Early in the novel, she lectures her young protégée Harriet Smith in ways that resonate with Hayley's treatise. Harriet warns Emma that if she does not marry, she will become an old maid like their family friend Miss Bates. Emma scoffs at the comparison: "and if I thought I should ever be like Miss Bates! so silly—so satisfied—so smiling—so prosing—so undistinguishing and un-fastidious—and so apt to tell every thing relative to every body about me, I would marry to-morrow. But between us, I am convinced there never can be any likeness, except in being unmarried" (1: 180). Emma's description of Miss

Bates catalogues the faults that Hayley describes old maids as possessing. He suggests that they suffer from four principal failings: curiosity, credulity, affectation, and envy, or ill nature. Emma's characterization of Miss Bates falls neatly in line with this list, with the exception of "envy and ill nature." Hayley links curiosity to garrulousness and nosiness, what Emma calls prosing, or telling everything relative to everybody, in Miss Bates. Hayley's quality of credulity is linked to Emma's "undistinguishing," and his citing affectation may call up Miss Bates's silly and smiling qualities. In Miss Bates, Austen has presented the stereotypical old maid, as Hayley defines her, almost to the letter.

There is more to the conversation between Harriet and Emma. Emma next refuses the category of old maid for herself, even when imagining herself aged and unmarried. She excludes herself from the category—and certainly from its reputed loathsome characteristics—on economic grounds, determining that she will not be "a poor old maid; and it is poverty only which makes celibacy contemptible to a generous public! A single woman, with a very narrow income, must be a ridiculous, disagreeable old maid!" (1: 179–80). Emma argues that a "very narrow income has a tendency to contract the mind, and sour the temper. Those who can barely live, and who live perforce in a very small, and generally very inferior, society, may well be illiberal and cross" (180).

Upon further reflection, Emma retracts some of her insults: "This does not apply, however, to Miss Bates; she is only too good natured and too silly to suit me; but, in general, she is very much to the taste of every body, though single and though poor. Poverty certainly has not contracted her mind: I really believe, if she had only a shilling in the world, she would be very likely to give away sixpence of it; and nobody is afraid of her: that is a great charm" (1: 180). Here, Hayley's good qualities of old maids come into play. He determines these to be ingenuity, patience, and charity. Emma allows Miss Bates to have patience and charity in abundance, though she appears short on ingenuity, at least in its sense of genius, talent, cleverness, or quickness of wit. It is possible to see Miss Bates's ingenuity as the talent that makes her appeal to the "taste of every body" but Emma, as a secondary eighteenth-century meaning of the word was honesty and straightforwardness. Miss Bates's ingenuity in that second sense—what we would now call a kind of ingenuousness—is something Emma, with her quick-witted ingenuity, capitalizes on in the famous, painful scene at Box Hill. There Emma unthinkingly teases Miss Bates about her inability to say no more than three very dull things at once.

After she has delivered her joking insult to Miss Bates at that climactic picnic, Emma defends her remark to Mr. Knightley by arguing that "what is good and what is ridiculous are most unfortunately blended in" Miss Bates. Mr. Knightley counters with the very economic arguments about old maids that Emma herself had voiced earlier. He lectures Emma, saying, "Were [Miss Bates] a woman of fortune, I would leave every harmless absurdity to take its chance, I would not quarrel with you for any liberties of manner. Were she your equal in situation—but, Emma, consider how far this is from being the case. She is poor; she has sunk from the comforts she was born to; and, if she live to old age, must probably sink more. Her situation should secure your compassion. It was badly done, indeed!" (3: 131). Emma had previously refused to imagine herself part of a figurative sisterhood with other unmarried women, even though she wished to remain one herself. At the end of the novel, we might say, the heroine matures at the expense of an old maid's feelings.

The little existing scholarship on Austen, *Emma*, and old maids defends Austen's characterizations as sympathetic. In her essay on eighteenth-century old maids in British women's writings, Jean B. Kern argues that Austen was "understandably gentle toward her spinster characters" and that "Miss Bates is an excellently conceived character who illustrates the faults of a spinster too anxious to please her social superiors" (210). Kern believes that Austen, throughout her fiction, "treats old maids sensitively and delicately" and dubs Austen "the best of the spinster novelists," who developed "the old maid beyond mere caricature" (212). I argue, on the contrary (through Hayley), that Austen's *Emma* was very much in thrall to the caricatures of the old maid in her time. Kern concludes that Austen "uses Emma's thoughtless discourtesy to the old maid to discipline the intelligent but self-centered heroine," which "shows how sensitive Austen is to the plight of the unmarried woman [Miss Bates]" (210). Although I agree with Kern that Miss Bates illustrates the "faults" of a spinster, I argue that Austen's treatment of this "excellently conceived character" is not particularly sensitive. The novel's climactic scene at Box Hill shows Austen's sensitivity to the plight of the intelligent but self-centered *heroine*, Emma, as well as how partial she is to her paternalistic hero, rather than to the spinster Miss Bates. For both Emma and Mr. Knightley—and for Emma in particular—Miss Bates functions throughout the novel as little more than an object—whether of pity, charity, or derision.

In her short essay on Austen, *Emma*, and Hayley, Katharine Kittredge concludes, "Austen's depiction of Miss Bates defies the most brutal aspects of the stereotype" ("Bates" 27). Kittredge directly links Miss Bates and her unmarried female author, seeing in *Emma* a critique of the fictional depictions of unmarried

women. Kittredge contrasts Austen's old maid to the decidedly more acidic portraits of the type found in the novels of Henry Fielding, Tobias Smollett, and
Frances Burney (26). But Austen's fiction did not delve into the kinds of broad
humor found in these texts, whether dealing with old maids or any other
socially marginalized group. Like Kittredge, Isobel Grundy briefly considers Austen's *Emma*, Miss Bates, and Hayley's treatise, concluding that "Miss
Bates's happiness is designed partly in support of the anti–William Hayley,
pro–old maid side of the argument."[54] I do not find such arguments wholly
persuasive. Even if we accept that Austen did not repeat the most vituperative
fictional characterizations of old maids—that they were "primping hags . . .
unaware of their physical repellence"—it does not mean that she has either
redeemed or implicitly criticized the dominant stereotype.[55]

Many critics have discussed the ways in which Emma is brought to maturity in the novel by Mr. Knightley's rebuke. What we have not remarked is
that Emma comes to this point through the efforts of a male champion of old
maids. Mr. Knightley and Hayley are similarly positioned in relation to their
texts and their subjects. Both set themselves up—unasked—as defenders of
old maids and purveyors of truth about them. They perceive that their contemporaries come up short in both areas, warranting a lecture on the subject.[56]
Where Hayley advertises his desire to be a savior to old maids in his *Essay*, the
fictional Mr. Knightley is more modestly messianic. He seeks no notoriety for
his good deeds. Still, both Hayley and Austen's hero purport to be friends to old
maids, acting on the sisterhood's behalf. Why would Austen re-enact Hayley's
characteristics of old maids in her novel and then take the further step of
making their principal defender a male?

Because Mr. Knightley chastises Emma for her narrowness, it is tempting to read Miss Bates (and Emma on Miss Bates) as Austen's response to
her culture's cruel depictions of old maids. It is further tempting to construe
Emma's actions as a warning to readers to treat old maids with greater kindness. The connections with Hayley's treatise would then be said to show that
Austen was willing to replicate her culture's stereotyping of old maids in the
name of overturning them. But are these stereotypes actually overturned in
Austen's novel? The last we hear of Miss Bates, she is spreading gossip across
the neighborhood of another impending marriage, that of Frank Churchill
to her niece Jane Fairfax (468). Miss Bates has by no means left aside her
prime failing, curiosity. She does not experience the growth and development
that Emma does. Furthermore, though Miss Bates is a good-natured fixture
in the Highbury world, she entirely drops out of the final two chapters. She

is in no way central to the portion of the narrative in which Emma and Mr. Knightley's happy marriage is concluded. In short, even if we see Emma as redeemed insofar as her poor treatment of old maids is concerned, Austen leaves Miss Bates hanging out to dry at novel's end.

From this evidence, I conclude that Austen's *Emma* does not offer a challenge (subtle or otherwise) to prevailing attitudes on old maids. What Hayley's treatise and Austen's novel have in common is a desire to speak for a population that they tacitly accept as blending the ridiculous and the good. Neither author seeks to widen the scope of old maids' characterization, instead repeating stereotypes with a vengeance, albeit from a liberal and seemingly well-meaning vantage point. Both, in other words, blend pity, contempt, and humor in their approach to old maids. Though many of us would like to get away from the pattern of defining Austen herself in the limiting framework of the morally upright spinster-author, we are still in thrall to it unless we acknowledge the possibility that, like Emma, Austen mildly disdains and even distances herself from spinsters, the group of women with whom she has been most often identified. In terms of the history of the novel, Austen's repetition in *Emma* of the common cant about spinsters should not astonish us. After all, "the novels of the century provided virtually no models for happiness in the single state."[57] Austen's fiction was, in this manner at least, not in the vanguard for women. For most of her characters, "things that are old are boring, irrelevant, or restrictive," as Claire Lamont writes (669). Though Lamont does not specifically discuss old maids, they, too, might be considered in these terms as "old things."

Dear Aunt Jane; or, This Old Maid

The reading I am offering of old maidism in *Emma* may seem surprising in light of Austen's life. We might expect a member of the supposed sisterhood to present in her fiction a more supportive picture of the class to which by the 1810s she would have been assigned. Austen "was an old maid herself," as one source puts it, so she must have "thought about her situation with a keenly analytic mind."[58] But does her identity necessarily translate into *sympathetic* fictional treatment? The question of whether or not Austen enjoyed being an old maid—whether it was an identity she felt comfortable in or embittered by—has been and continues to be debated by her biographers. In *Jane Austen among Women*, Deborah Kaplan finds Austen at home in the role. Kaplan theorizes that Austen deliberately assumed "the guise of spinsterhood" in order to spend more time with female friends.[59] Citing biographical anecdotes about Cassandra and Jane taking on the sartorial trappings of middle age earlier than was customary, Kaplan argues, "Austen was apparently exploiting contemporary stereotypes about spinsters to her advantage" (122). Through these means, Kaplan suggests, Austen was also able to recede from women's domestic social duties in favor of writing. Arguing against biographers like John Halperin, who emphasize Austen's not marrying as a source of bitter personal disappointment, Kaplan suggests that spinsterhood may have become Austen's deliberate, positive choice.

Kaplan uses as evidence a letter that Austen wrote to Cassandra in December 1808, just shy of her 33rd birthday, describing a ball she had attended. "Our Ball was rather more amusing than I expected. . . . The room was tolerably full, & there were perhaps thirty couple of Dancers;—the melancholy part was, to see so many dozen young Women standing by without partners, & each of them with two ugly naked shoulders!—It was the same room in which we danced fifteen years ago!—I thought it all over—& inspite [sic] of the shame of being so much older, felt with thankfulness that I was quite as happy now as then."[60] Five years later, in 1813, she wrote again to Cassandra, "By the bye, as I must leave off being young, I find many Douceurs in being a sort of Chaperon for I am put on the Sofa near the Fire & can drink as much wine as I like" (251). In the same letter, she refers to a conversation with a Miss Lee whom Austen determines "is at an age of reason, ten years older than myself at least." Austen may well have been growing into a happy, single middle age, rather than a stereotypically embittered, obnoxious, or self-negating spinsterhood.

It is an unfortunate fact of literary history that Austen's critics have been limited in vision when it comes to making sense of her life and career, especially in regard to her remaining unmarried. Such caricatured versions circulated during her lifetime as well. Austen's contemporary Mary Russell Mitford reported a friend saying that Austen had "stiffened into the most perpendicular, precise, taciturn piece of 'single blessedness' that every existed." As Kathleen Freeman notes, in a mid-twentieth-century biography of Austen, Mitford's "portrait is a mere cliché of a spinster" (153).[61] The "picture built up" in the nineteenth century of Austen as "a rather prim spinsterish figure who hardly knew the facts of life" (161).

The critical effects of this sense of her life are not difficult to trace. Most obvious are readings of Austen's fiction such as E. Margaret Moore's essay on

Miss Bates, which purports to be sympathetic to the character and the author. Moore takes a biographical and psychoanalytic approach to explaining the greatness of *Emma*. She suggests that Miss Bates being mistreated moves us because "Emma perceives Miss Bates to some extent as a mother-figure" and because Emma's "flirtation with Frank Churchill is a tacit reminder of Miss Bates's sexual inadequacy."[62] These interpretations are then linked to Austen's negative relationship with her mother and with Austen's "envy of the maternal role," which Moore says is "to be expected in a childless woman" (584). Out of a painful childhood (and adulthood), Moore implies, comes lonely old maidenhood and great art. This account and others like it present profoundly limiting versions of Austen's novel and of her literary career.

It is quite possible that Austen judged her own life through one set of beliefs and expectations and created the characters in *Emma* through another. Even if she herself was a happy, unconventional, and against-type unmarried older woman, her representations of old maids need not be looked to for necessary sympathy. What my reading of old maids in *Emma* demonstrates is that even if we see Austen as a feminist (as I do), we need not understand her as presenting all of her female characters through a progressive lens. Austen's heroines may range beyond dominant ideologies for women, but her old maids appear to have conformed to them.[63] Perhaps we would be asking too much of Austen in wanting her to create minor characters that break the gendered mold. But it seems that Austen did not seek to challenge representational trends where old maids were concerned. What my argument suggests is that even if she cannot be charged with cruelty and satire akin to Hayley's, and even if she did not draw on the most damaging sexual stereotypes of old maids, like Skinn's, Austen accepted limiting representations of old maids in her era. In her characterization of Miss Bates—her fiction's most prominent old maid—Austen may even be called condescending, directly echoing the least offensive material found in Hayley's *Essay*, while sidestepping the question of whether "any form of mature female sexuality that is not employed to placate a husband must be corrupt."[64]

Determining that Austen was no more a true friend to the sisterhood than was Hayley need not give any credence to the view that Austen herself was therefore a stereotypically censorious old maid. To return to that model of dismissing her and her writings—as practiced by Lawrence, Mudrick, Halperin, and others—gets us no further in understanding the nuances of her single life *or* her knotty portrayals of aging single women.[65] Her representations of old maids, like Hayley's, are complicated enough to allow for multiple readings, and we ought to continue to credit Austen's fiction with many innovations, formal and ideological. Though she may have seen beyond some of the restrictive patterns then dominant in fiction in her approaches to gendered norms, we must entertain the possibility that Austen was not so perspicacious—or perhaps simply not so motivated—when it came to fictional old maids.

Hester Lynch Piozzi, Antiquity of Bath

At my Death the Battle about my Merits & no Merits, will be renewed over my Memory. Friends wishing to save it—Foes contending for the Pleasure of throwing it to the Dogs like the Body of Petroclus in Homer.

—*Hester Lynch Piozzi, entry in her copy of* Goldsmith's Almanack, *July 1820*

Too old, by Heaven!

—*Epigraph (from* Twelfth Night*) to* Love Letters of Mrs. Piozzi, Written When She Was Eighty to William Augustus Conway *(1843)*

Though Hester Lynch Piozzi's life and writings have received significant scholarly attention, her later years have not been given their due. As we have seen in previous chapters, this is not a condition peculiar to Piozzi (1741–1821). Like many of her long-lived female contemporaries, Piozzi remained an active writer up until her last days, although in prominent biographies her old age gets short shrift.[1] Perhaps this is in part because it is received wisdom that Piozzi's most interesting years were those in which she was "Mrs. Thrale." If what is considered most compelling about Piozzi is her connection to Samuel Johnson, then her later years may fail to fascinate. But Piozzi—as those who have studied her know well—interests in her own right. Her later years, too, are intriguing and even moving, as can be gleaned from her work for publication, from her recently published letters, and from her still unpublished life writings.

In discussions of Piozzi's later years, two matters have repeatedly emerged. Both have the potential to overshadow any attempts to reassess her late literary reputation. The first is her so-called 80th birthday party in 1820. Six months before turning 79, Piozzi decided to throw herself a party and dispatched invitations to "all parts of the world" (Clifford, *HLP* 450). Approximately six hundred friends gathered at the Lower Assembly Rooms in Bath for a concert, ball, and supper. At her lavish party, for which she ran up debts, she allegedly danced with "astonishing elasticity."[2] This event is among the most chronicled of her later life, whether for good or ill, and is used as a focal point either to memorialize her or to ridicule her as an aged literary celebrity.[3]

The second matter that comes to the fore in discussions of Piozzi's late life is her friendship with the young actor William Augustus Conway (1789–1828), an episode that was sensationalized in the decades after her death. It was rumored in her lifetime and then claimed in a series of allegedly doctored letters published posthumously that she had conceived a romantic passion for Conway, a passion painted as both absurd and unrequited, proving Piozzi to be preposterously vain. Her intentions toward Conway remain subject to debate, and the matter has threatened to overshadow—and perhaps even to forestall—more nuanced discussions of her final years. This is unfortunate, because both the birthday party and the Conway episode might rightly serve as evidence of the vibrancy of her later life. I argue that these episodes, their reception notwithstanding, demonstrate the unusual ways in which Piozzi tried to take control of her position as an author in late life, after having been thwarted by the literary marketplace.

In this chapter, I look to Piozzi's writings in old age to see the ways in which she modified her understandings of herself as a writer while coming to terms with the disappearance of a mass readership. I look at her published letters, her unpublished diaries and almanacs, and her late writings themselves in order to show that her old age—though perhaps not free of folly—was neither contemptible nor pitiful. In the latter part of the chapter, I give particular attention to Piozzi's relationship with Conway, making sense of how it has wrongly come to characterize her as an irrational old woman. Revisiting this story affords us the opportunity to see her choices afresh. I argue that we ought to understand them as characteristic of an indefatigable and forward-thinking author, as well as an impassioned friend/mother/mentor figure. It is not simply to champion Piozzi's old age that I make this argument. She herself does not present that period in her life as a model or an ideal. Rather, this chapter ought to encourage us to revise our neglect of and partial conclusions about her late life. Piozzi's old age deserves to be freed from calumny, from apotheosis, *and* from run-of-the-mill neglect.

Because the age of 60 generally marked the onset of old age in the late eighteenth century, Piozzi may have been considered an old woman from the turn of the century. She was an active writer during this period, both for private and public consumption. Personally, this was not an easy time, in that she confronted outliving many of her contemporaries, both of her husbands, and most of her offspring.[4] In July 1820, she made a list of fourteen friends who had died since she left Bath. At the same time, she made a list of the "profess'd enemies outlived by H : L : P in 1820." Obviously, this list-making was not just a melancholy experience, as she reveled in having been predeceased by the likes of Sir John Hawkins (1719–89), Giuseppe Baretti (1719–89), James Boswell (1740–95), George Colman (bap. 1732–94), and Peter Pindar (John Wolcot) (bap. 1738–1819).[5] Piozzi jokingly referred to herself as "one of the Antiquities" of Bath, the city she called home for most of the last years of her life. But even if (as she suspected) she was treated as an antique curiosity by strangers and acquaintances, Piozzi was no relic in her day-to-day activities. Any account of her during this time should center on the fact that she was actively engaged in writing in—and writing about—her old age.

Attention has centered on her colorful old age, as several biographers and critics have given sustained attention to the period. As one scholar puts it, interpretations of Piozzi in old age "differ: she either enjoyed her new acquaintances at Bath and retained a reputation for impressive powers of conversation, or she spent a miserable decade, not writing anything worthwhile, increasingly isolated, disappointed in both her children and the uncertainty of social applause."[6] Critics Catherine Rodriguez (1999) and Patricia Meyer Spacks (1970) echo this difference when considering the writings of Piozzi's old age. Rodriguez's essay considers Piozzi's 24-page autobiography, written while she was in her seventies for Sir James Fellowes, a retired naval doctor and one of her literary executors. Rodriguez argues that this text presents an account of her life that shows Piozzi's fears that it has been misunderstood. Rodriguez demonstrates that "the writings from the last ten years of Piozzi's life have remained relatively obscure," offering the hope that "rereading Piozzi's late writings for their contribution to the understanding of identity issues for an aging woman in late eighteenth-century England may prove a fruitful endeavor."[7] She finds evidence of resilience in Piozzi's last writings.

Spacks, in her work on Piozzi's old age, is less sanguine. Spacks discusses Piozzi's five-volume "scrap book," or journals, written between 1810 and 1814.

The volumes were written for John Salusbury Piozzi Salusbury, Piozzi's second husband's nephew, who was also her adopted son, coexecutor, and heir.[8] Spacks offers a portrait of Piozzi as an aging female writer, looking back on her life and career, but considers Piozzi's late journals as an "extended piece of self-justification" (221), demonstrating an "unhappy" old woman relying "on the triumphs of her youth for emotional sustenance" (224, 225). Piozzi is viewed as an interesting case study of an educated eighteenth-century woman coping with a sexist culture, but her ideas in old age are considered random, puerile, and tedious (235) and her psychology pathetic (242).

In the years since Spacks's essay was published, it has become clear that Piozzi had more going for her in her old age than bitter self-defense and pathetic self-pity, though that interpretation may yet hold some weight as a portrait of the years 1810–14. During that time, Piozzi was grieving over the death of her second husband and trying to rebuild (once again) a life as a widow. A full picture of Piozzi's late life, however, would also see her as a lively and interested thinker and writer, filled with intellectual curiosity. As she put it in a letter several months prior to her death, "I must go on adding to my Stock of Ideas while Life is lent me—for who knows at 81—how soon that Power may be taken away?"[9] Piozzi seems to have lived by this dictum, as the written materials that survive from this period are voluminous.

Piozzi's writing for publication in her old age was sustained and self-conscious, and it exhibits an acute sense of how her advancing age might affect readers' responses. In her late works, Piozzi many times referred to herself as "old." The anonymous political pamphlet, *Three Warnings to John Bull before He Dies* (1798), published when she was nearly 60, is signed "an Old Acquaintance of the Public," although ultimately, it is the "public" she likens to being "in its dotage" in that work (qtd. in Clifford 396). After the appearance of her last published book, a world history titled *Retrospection* (1801), Piozzi published an anonymous short work, the anti-Napoleonic broadside, "Old England to Her Daughters" (1803). There, England—imagined as elderly—calls on her daughters not to faint or fall into fits in the face of invading French enemies but to remain strong and calm. Piozzi writes of females (whom she divides into ladies, women, and laboring women) as responsible for displaying strength, rather than succumbing to weakness. Signing the piece "Poor Old England," she argues that women alone will be able to increase glory, to add a laurel to the national wreath, or at the least to keep it from "fading upon the brows."[10]

Retrospection, too, highlights the aging process—even in the conceit of its title. Piozzi's introduction highlights her imagined readership. She offers her book as a proper object for the young of the day, who have no time to read "better books" and who are "called out to act before they *know*."[11] Her book is also pitched to the old: "Perhaps too, those who long ago have read, and long ago desisted from reading histories well-known, may like to please their fancies with the *Retrospect* of what they feel connected in their minds with youthful study, and that sweet remembrance of early-dawning knowledge on the soul" (1: vii–viii). As a writer she "recommends, and endeavours to facilitate, *Retrospection*" (17). Piozzi repeats her title like a mantra throughout the two-volume work, up to her last chapter, on 1796–1800. Then she declares, "Being arrived at the interesting moment when *Retrospection* ceases and observation is begun, our book must with this chapter end itself, and be submitted to the reader's *Retrospect*" (2: 521). In the book's subsequent twenty pages, she nevertheless invokes the term *retrospection* three more times. The word's frequent repetition, though grating, demonstrates how looking back is not only central to historiography and reading history but, for Piozzi, central to her work as an aged author. Extensive experience at having second thoughts, in memory and through the process of writing, is something she, as an aged woman, could offer the public.[12]

Old age was brought forward even more directly in Piozzi's last full-length work designed for publication. It furthered her interest in the etymology of first names and was titled, "Lyford Redivivus; or, A Granddame's Garrulity." As I argued in the introduction, Piozzi's referring to her work as stereotypically garrulous might be seen as a protest against ageist practices. It might also, however, be a capitulation to or internalization of them. Given the intricacies of Piozzi's late life self-concept, it may well be both. With "Lyford," Piozzi signed herself not with her own name, as she had done in the past, but as "An Old Woman."[13] In the preface, she includes an "Address to my Readers," characteristic of her published work in style and tone in that it is anecdotal and alternately serious and tongue-in-cheek. Piozzi maintains that the title page of the book (which quotes an epigram in two languages) is proof of her garrulity but asks that readers remember that her "little work" is "meant for the mere Amusement of a vacant hour" and is "just good enough to keep worse Books out of their hands" (Hyde Case 9 [16]). She does not claim originality but maintains that her work is "more extensive" and "may easily be more amusing, than a small Pocket Volume composed near 200 Years ago, & now scarce known in the world" (i.e., Lyford's). She gives a history of names and naming, but then maintains that she is not using "Tricks" to "give momentary Importance to our Trifle, either by a long or learned Introduction."

In these elements of apology and defense, the work resembles her previous writings but employs the stereotypes of women and aging in doing so.

In "Lyford," Piozzi highlights her own old age and the wished-for long life of her book. She ends her preface by predicting the book's future, denigrating it as frivolous, and expressing her desire that it will survive because frivolity is fashionable: "On the wide Sea of Time we find many a richly laden Vessel foundering in Gales that toss the light skiff into immediate notice, and in the busy Moments when this Book was planned, frivolous Publications had best Chance to live" (Hyde Case 9 [16]). Anticipating her critics, she then tries to disarm them with her modesty and low expectations:

> This tiny book will be easily broken down by your criticism, if not blown up by the more fortunate Breath of Caprice: and if its own nothingness does even at length condemn it as many Modern Travels are condemn'd, to travel the Remainder of their Days inside a Trunk—
>
> Or doom'd with Tarts to try the Oven's heat
> Or round Salt Butter seize my Slippery Seat;
> With rebel Will I'll ne'er oppose
> The Current of my Destiny,
> But pliant as the Torrent flows,
> Receive my Course implicitly
> —having still the honour to be
> Gentlemen & Ladies
> Your most humble Servt.
> An Old Woman—.

The destiny of the book (traveling the remainder of its days in a trunk) and the destiny of the "old woman" writer seem intertwined, with the use of the first person ("my destiny," "my Course") applying equally well to book or author. Piozzi ultimately suggests that she will not fight for or turn angry at the book's reception. But the fact of her age was given the last word, whether as apology or justification.

When she wrote this address, Piozzi presumably still had hope that the manuscript would see print. She showed it to her friend the writer and critic Edward Mangin in 1815. In his memoir of Piozzi, published in 1833, Mangin reports being impressed with "Lyford Redivivus" as "learned." As we saw in the introduction, he believed it to have "much information, ably compressed," promising an "excellent popular volume," though his subsequent praise is damningly faint. He writes that Piozzi "was . . . seventy-five; and I naturally complimented her, not only on the work in question, but [on] the amazing beauty and variety of her handwriting." Though he presented extracts from the manuscript to a London publisher, they "could not come to an arrangement" (14). Despite—or perhaps because of—her inability to find a publisher, Piozzi never forgot "Lyford Redivivus." Several months before her death, she refers to it in a letter to Fellowes, asking him, "Do you remember the *Name Book*? It ended with Zenobia" and tells him a story about a local woman with that name (*Letters* 6: 477).

Anticipating and even poking fun at the supposed garrulity of old women, Piozzi's "Lyford" attempts to hold together the categories old woman and writer at a time when this was no easy task. It seems clear simply from the titles of her anonymous published and unpublished late works that Piozzi's self-concept as an aging woman affected how she approached her authorship and how she expected others to perceive it. Her embracing a stereotype about talkative old women may be seen as an act of self-pitying capitulation, but it is also possible to read it as an act of resistance or, barring that, sassiness. In "Lyford," Piozzi was not just replaying the achievements of her youth. She was trying to add to them, perhaps realizing that she faced an uphill battle because, as an author, she had already been packed away in the proverbial trunk in the minds of many.

Imagining Piozzi Past Her Prime

It was not a personal foible that led Piozzi to mention her age in tandem with her authorship. Reviewers of her last signed publication, too, had commented on her age. *Retrospection* was dubbed by the *Critical Review* "a series of dreams by an old lady."[14] The *London Review* suggests that *Retrospection* failed because Piozzi grew old. It begins by describing the portrait of Piozzi included as the book's frontispiece: "The portrait is not what was once the gay, the sprightly, the admired Mrs. Thrale, nor yet the maturer features of Signora Piozzi. . . . Yet, after every allowance for the depredations of time, we cannot discover in the plate before us the likeness of anything, but of a *cunning* looking woman, with enormous large eyes and nose, wrapt up in a *non descript* dress. The work itself is subject to the same animadversion."[15] We might see in this comment what Jill Campbell has identified as "men's gleefully horrified rejection of the figure of the aging woman" in eighteenth-century culture.[16] Piozzi's reviewers made it clear that they thought she failed as an author because she was no longer "herself"; she was past her prime, in body as on the page.

Despite such responses, Piozzi did not step down, whether as an author or as a member of the literati. She remained in the public eye enough to become fodder for periodical gossip, particularly when she forged a friendship with a 27-year-old struggling actor, in her capacity as an octogenarian theater aficionado. In 1819, while living in Bath, Piozzi met William Augustus Conway, and the two became fast friends. Over the next two years, Piozzi wrote him devoted letters; befriended his mother; helped him navigate the Bath theater scene; unsuccessfully tried to forward his engagement to a young woman of her acquaintance; and, depending on which account you believe, developed feelings for him of an ambiguous and potentially romantic nature.

During her lifetime, rumors circulated about their relationship, some intimating that she was going to be married to the actor.[17] But it was not until 1843 that the Piozzi-Conway episode was widely publicized in print. Since then, it has featured prominently in any discussion, however brief, of her late life. In the *American Cyclopedia* (1875), a two-paragraph entry tells readers that Piozzi "survived her second husband, and in the latter part of her life became attached to the actor William A. Conway."[18] In this description, Conway is given the virtual status of a third husband. As anyone who knows Piozzi's life history must recognize, the Conway episode was hardly the first time Piozzi's love life was scrutinized and seen as beyond the pale. She was subject to such imputations when she married Piozzi. But the idea of her so-called love letters, written at nearly 80 years old, became fixed in the nineteenth-century public imagination long after it was capable of being shocked by her middle-aged second marriage to a Catholic musician.

It appears there was some knowledge of Piozzi's letters to Conway in the decades following her death, perhaps in the form of manuscript circulation. In an 1838 letter to her brother, the novelist Jane Porter acknowledges that Piozzi's old age has been a recent topic of their epistolary conversation: "You tell me a sad humbling tale of female absurdity in the narrative of poor superannuated Mrs. Piozzi, and her preposterous correspondence. Alas, for the weaknesses of human nature and particularly of old age, when once the reins [sic] is yielded to any Fancy of the Heart unbefitting the term of life!"[19] Speculating that Piozzi was driven by an evil spirit or had gone insane, Porter concludes, "In this view I regard poor old Mrs. Piozzi's calamitous Fancy for Conway" (KU MS 197). Porter, who does not seem to have seen the letters herself, believes

Hester Lynch Piozzi

Portrait of Hester Lynch Piozzi, included as the frontispiece in
Retrospection (1801)

that they should have been destroyed, both for Piozzi's sake and for the sake of old women: "For the honour of our sex and the respectability of Venerable age, I regret that such letters have been preserved. If they were in Conway's possession after her death, in Gratitude to a memory, which, (even in folly) had bestowed so much to him, he ought to have destroyed them.—And, if accident had thrown them subsequently into any other hands, reverence for the one who had once been the friend of our great moralist Dr. Johnson, and pity for the infirmities of Human age, should have withheld them from being shown to other eyes; should have determined the possessor to make an end of them." The letters, however, were not destroyed. Somehow, they came into the possession of an American woman, and apparently, without her permission, some of them were shoddily published. The story of their provenance has not been fully discovered.

The pamphlet *Love Letters of Mrs. Piozzi, Written When She Was Eighty to William Augustus Conway* (1843) was published by an anonymous editor whose identity remains unknown.[20] Called "a literary fraud" and an unsolved mystery, the pamphlet included seven letters from Piozzi to Conway.[21] Surprisingly, given the Piozzi-Conway relationship's later notoriety, the pamphlet at first appears to have received little notice. One especially negative review appeared in the *Athenaeum*, which asserts, "If we lay aside all consideration of the relative ages of the parties, the letters may fairly enough be called 'Love Letters.' We doubt, however, whether Mrs. Piozzi was ever in love— she had not the heart enough—she was a weak, vain, foolish woman."[22] The reviewer concludes that it was Piozzi who was "a far cleverer actor" and that "she played her part to admiration" (259). Why she would want purely to *act* such a lover's part is unclear.

The "love letters" came forcefully into the public eye with the appearance of Abraham Hayward's *Autobiography, Letters, and Literary Remains of Mrs. Piozzi (Thrale)* (1861).[23] Hayward repeated the hearsay about Piozzi and Conway, wavering from one edition to the next as to whether she was innocently maternal or scandalously randy. The 1843 pamphlet came to the attention of the then-owner of the letters, Mrs. E. F. Ellet. Ellet published a short piece in the *Athenaeum*, alleging that the pamphlet included "altered passages" and had "garbled and distorted" the letters.[24] She reported that she had in her possession 100 letters from Piozzi to Conway, which she offered for publication. Just a handful of them, however, were printed thereafter.

Ellet's essay and reviews of the Hayward volume set the stage for decades of debate about Piozzi's late life. Of the many things in Hayward's collection that could have caught reviewers' notice, most focused unrelentingly on the matter of Conway. The *Knickerbocker*'s reviewer proclaims the Conway episode an example of Piozzi's character "we never heard before."[25] The *Edinburgh Review* called Piozzi's feelings for Conway "a last *belle passion*."[26] The *Blackwood's Edinburgh Magazine* reviewer concluded that in her old age Piozzi had become "sufficiently fantastic now and then almost to warrant the silly imputation of renewed love-making, with the handsome young actor Conway."[27] But not all Victorian reviewers and essayists believed the claims of the 1843 pamphleteer. The *National Review* thought the letters harmless and concluded that "it was not that there was any thing to blame in Mrs. Piozzi" but twice noted that she "made herself ridiculous" in "extreme old age."[28] A review from the *Examiner* agrees with Hayward that "a relation of warm friendship . . . is of every day occurrence between youth and age that is not crabbed."[29] That reviewer normalizes the friendship by noting that "with reversal of the ages and the sexes the same thing occurred also in the strong friendship of [Piozzi's] girlhood for her preceptor, Dr. Collier" ("Hayward's Mrs. Piozzi" 121).

Perhaps because of its ability to titillate readers, commentary on Piozzi and Conway persisted. Dutton Cook's article in the *Gentleman's Magazine* (1881) gave it extended treatment, concluding that "those can best decide [whether Piozzi wrote love letters to him] who know how octogenarian ladies of vivid fancy write when they are in love, or when addicted . . . to the expression of their admiration and friendship in exaggerated terms."[30] Percival Merritt's *The True Story of the So-Called Love Letters of Mrs. Piozzi* (1927) put together all of the pieces then available about the Piozzi-Conway episode to argue his position "in defense of an elderly lady." He concludes that his efforts on Piozzi's behalf are "probably too late" because "the poison has been thoroughly disseminated."[31] The publication of the sixth and last volume of the *Piozzi Letters* (1817–21) makes available a greater portion of the Piozzi-Conway period's correspondence and offers the potential, at least, to weaken the poison. Although Charles Ryskamp indicated in 1981 that some two dozen Piozzi-Conway letters "seem to be known," the editors of *The Piozzi Letters* include 19 from Piozzi to Conway in their edition.[32] Eight brief letters from Conway to Piozzi and two from Conway to Piozzi's adopted son are held at the John Rylands Library (*H-T-P*, reel 19, MS 596). The 100 Piozzi-Conway letters that Ellet advertised as having in her possession apparently do not survive. Still, the materials that are now known offer opportunities for renewed scholarly scrutiny of Piozzi's late life, whether in its notorious or its banal aspects.

In her introduction to the *Piozzi Letters*, Gay Brack calls Piozzi's relationship with Conway "a passionate friendship so controversial that its nature is still being debated" (6: 13). She further describes it as "a close relationship on the nature of which her commentators have disagreed for more than a hundred and fifty years" (21). Brack gathers her information about the relationship from John Tearle's biography of Conway, but she promises to give full treatment to the episode in her biography-in-progress of Piozzi. Brack's introduction notes that the Piozzi-Conway episode is open to multiple interpretations. She lists three possibilities—(1) genuine passion, (2) a wish to influence the development of a young protégé, and (3) maternal or grandmotherly protection (24)—and concludes, "The truth of Mrs. Piozzi's final deep attachment, perhaps, contains elements of all these versions."

For his part, William McCarthy has characterized Piozzi's letters to Conway as expressing "intense, doting, needy enthusiasm" and their posthumous publication as having "sparked a flurry of leering innuendoes and a controversy that still occasionally flares back to life."[33] McCarthy sees Piozzi's relationship with Conway as another example of her propensity to "mothering," a role he views her as taking up in her interactions with Samuel Johnson, second husband Gabriel Piozzi, and adopted son Salusbury (*HTP* 102). McCarthy focuses on Piozzi's admission to Conway that she had been accused by her second husband of spoiling her children and was now "trying to Spoil dear Mr Conway." But as McCarthy later suggests, "Conway, for all he figures to her as her newest child, figures also as the man whose admiration her intellect requires, the father-uncle-tutor to whom, once again, her performances are delightful" (261). This is an interesting contention, but we might do just as well to see Piozzi not as seeking a father in Conway but as enacting a feminine version of the "father-uncle-tutor" role herself.

Piozzi's Innovations as Mentor-Author

Piozzi's letters to Conway apparently date from 15 June 1819 (some six months after they first made each other's acquaintance) to 6 February 1821 (a little less than three months before her death). They demonstrate a devoted attachment, in which Piozzi most often figures herself as a surrogate mother to the actor, but they also show how important literature and her attempts to fashion him as her literary progeny were to their interactions. In the close relationships she formed with men during her last ten years of life—from Fellowes to Mangin to Conway—her main objective seems to have been finding figures who would make sure that her words would live on after her. Her renewed close friendship with Penelope Pennington (1752?–1827) is more complicated, as both seemed in league in promoting Conway's career and happiness; after Piozzi's death mutual friend Helen Maria Williams (1761–1827) suggested that Pennington become Piozzi's biographer.[34] In short, Piozzi was cultivating not just an executor (she had already named two—Fellowes and Salusbury) but a number of posthumous literary agents. Naturally, she wanted all of them to get along. In a letter to Fellowes, she calls Conway a "Man of high Polish, general Knowledge, and best natural Abilities," and she warns that if he doesn't like Conway, it will vex her (*Letters* 6: 251).

Piozzi may have valued Conway precisely because he was appreciative of her as a *literary* figure, an intellectual, and an educator. Indeed, her relationship with Conway has distinctly Johnsonian overtones. She might be seen as replicating, from the other side of the partnership, some aspects of her interactions with Samuel Johnson in his later years. It may seem a stretch to compare the young Hester Thrale to the young William Conway. He was a struggling actor of uncertain birth who never married; she was a child of privilege, made "half a prodigy" by her doting parents, married to a man who apparently did not appreciate her passion for poetry. Both Conway and the young Piozzi, however, were ambitious artists. Each had distinct advantages and impediments. Conway's theatrical advantage, his beauty, was somewhat offset by an impediment, his great height. (The diminutive Edmund Kean allegedly refused to share the stage with Conway for fear of turning tragedy into farce [Tearle 131].) Piozzi's advantages—her access to social circles and her ability to foster them—were also impediments, in that she became known as a "hostess," rather than a literary figure in her own right. Her children and stepson did not follow her into a life of arts and letters. It is possible that Piozzi sought to further Conway's artistic ambitions at a time when she lacked another proper object, just after her own attempts at new publication with "Lyford Redivivus" had been stymied. In her arena of greatest influence, the arts, Conway would benefit from her patronage. In one of his surviving letters, Conway himself refers to her as his "revered Patroness" (*H-T-P*, reel 19, MS 596). If Piozzi styled herself Conway's Johnson, it was as his chief booster and cheerleader.

Conway was never a caretaker for Piozzi. If anything, she once again desired to be one for him. But he did appear to enjoy the company of this much older woman. Perhaps it was because of her access to elite cultural circles, her connections to literary and theatrical luminaries of a bygone era, or her willingness to take him seriously. Piozzi appreciates Conway's youth, his beauty (she calls him "the handsomest Man in England" [*Letters* 6: 324]), and—most of all—his promise as an actor. He seemed to put her in mind of her own bloom and offered her the opportunity to exercise her powers as a mentor. She wanted something out of Conway—not the least of which appears to have been his devotion. But her letters also suggest that she was trying his willingness to carry on her literary name. She refers to herself as his "old woman" "companion," for when he prefers "chat to reading" (337). She writes of him as if he were a divine gift: "You were sent at 27 years old to calm your headlong Monitress and Manager at Thrice your age," she tells him (335). But Piozzi frequently tries to give him something, too—the wherewithal to succeed on the stage and to believe in his own dramatic powers. She writes, "My whole Desire is to do you *good* in *Some* Way; *any* Way; May it but be in my Power! either to assist or amuse You" (308).

In a letter written over the course of a week in June 1819, Piozzi jokes that she has created "a sort of pamphlet" rather than an epistle (*Letters* 6: 282) from his "oldest and newest Friend" (280). Later, she describes this letter as "my long Letter sewed in blue Paper 13 Pages long" (289). She begins by praising Conway for his model letter to her, which she has just received. She frequently tells him that she longs to see him or to hear from him. When she contemplates the months until their next meeting, she concludes " 'tis 20 years till *then*" (279). Her maid, she says, warns her, "Why, Madam! You will not live to see Mr. Conway again, if you go on *so.*" She writes effusively of her love for him, writing of her wish that "*all* may be constrained to *admire* You as I do; altho' to love You so, is quite Impossible; as no one knows your Worth—and your Inestimable Value as it is known by Your truly and tenderly attached / H : L: Piozzi" (281). Her subsequent letters complain of his not having written, and she wonders, "shall We meet again? where when, and how? Oh I am grown so weary, it seems as if I was quite dead indeed" (330). These examples are typical of the tone of separation and loss in the letters and of her wonderment at his fine qualities.

Piozzi also writes that she considers herself "in the Light of his injured Mother" and assures him "no Parent could feel more than I have done, and still continue to do on your Account" (*Letters* 6: 281). Later, when Piozzi befriends Conway's mother, Mrs. [Susanna] Rudd, news of Conway comes through her. In less than a year, Piozzi calls him her "Youngest adopted Child" (358). And in what may be her last letter to him, she writes, "And so God bless my true and honourable Friend—who will I hope live long and happily; and die 60 Years hence in the Arms of his *own* H: L: P—The Daughter I shall perhaps one Day embrace" (493). An acquaintance of Conway's wrote, many years after his death, that Piozzi's "letters touching affairs of the heart . . . must have been deemed [by the actor] the offspring of dotage."[35] Although the letters show that Piozzi's romantic and maternal feelings are jumbled, they do not suggest senility. Nevertheless, to quote the passages above and to rehearse the anecdotes surrounding them compounds the errors of the 1843 pamphlet. It takes Piozzi's high-flown rhetoric out of context and minimizes the complexities of the relationship that are revealed in other parts of her correspondence.

In the few sustained studies to date on the Piozzi-Conway correspondence, critics have downplayed the wide variety of ideas and lessons that she covers in her letters. Nothing is too small for her notice. In one letter, she writes to him, "I hope you eat honey for Breakfast" (*Letters* 6: 308) and directs him to avoid "all strong Liquors." After he has been ill, she advises him, "live quiet, and drink Asses Milk" (333). For his part, Conway seems to have taken her advice, on occasion at least. He writes of his throat ailment not worsening "owing chiefly to the frequent application of the Gargle [Piozzi] was good enough to prescribe" (*H-T-P*, reel 19, MS 596). But most of the information she passes on to him consists of weightier fare. She reports in a letter from October 1819, "Dearest Mr. Conway has sometimes in his partial Way asked me how I came to know this and that?" (*Letters* 6: 331). In her letter of February 1820, she tells him "that you keep your Mind engaged by public and political Events delights my Heart" and follows up with remarks on Parry's expedition to the Arctic (368). She seems to relish communicating anecdotes and conversing with him about current events.

Of course, there is much exchange about the theater generally and about his own career specifically—which part he has played, which parts other actors have played, her assessments of performances and actors of earlier years and of the present day. These stories are told with an eye to encouraging him, comparing him positively to all rivals. She tells him, "You have been a luckless Wight my admirable Friend, but Amends will one Day be made for you, even in this World I know; I feel it will" (*Letters* 6: 280). She then recounts a story about her second husband's difficulties in being cruelly treated by friends and relations, likening their plights (80). In another letter, she assures him that "Accomplishment is at hand" and that he will soon enjoy great success on the stage (289). Piozzi several times refers to Conway in the same breath as her previous favorites, once coupling an assessment of "worthy Sam: Johnson and Augustus Conway" (308).

She also sprinkles quotations throughout her letters to Conway, using authors ranging from Dryden and Homer to Shakespeare and, frequently, Johnson. Last, but not least, she often refers to her own writings. In the "pamphlet" letter alone, she makes specific reference to *British Synonymy*, to an annotation she has made in a copy she has given him of Wraxall's *Memoirs*, and to a reference she cannot find in *Retrospection*, because the book does not have an index. As she laments to him, *Retrospection* is "completely useless for want of an Index. If [it ever goes] through another Edition after my Death, somebody will put an Index to them" (*Letters* 6: 282). Though this may read as a kind of hint to Conway, as well as a hope that her death will occasion a revival of her writings, no one has yet taken Piozzi up on the index or even on another edition of *Retrospection*.

Piozzi continually gives Conway direct and indirect reading assignments. She again quotes from *Retrospection* in a letter from November 1819 and points him to a specific chapter (*Letters* 6: 349). In January 1821, she advises Conway to see the biographical sketch she has written for him and "see Thraliana too" (482), which she tells him she has with her. Some evidence remains to suggest he took these reading assignments seriously. In one letter, he speaks of his desire to reperuse her *Anecdotes* of "the immortal Johnson" and "ventures to solicit the *loan* of them, for a few days" (*H-T-P*, reel 19, MS 596). Another letter refers to his return of her volume of Dryden, thanking her for its loan. He also discourses with her on their respective opinions of Sir Walter Scott, concluding that he "perfectly agrees . . . with Mrs. Piozzi, respecting the *temperate* heat of the Northern Critic." An additional piece of evidence that Conway took Piozzi's reading assignments seriously is that he kept copies of her single-authored works and her annotated works by others until his death. (He apparently committed suicide by jumping off a ship near Charleston, South Carolina, in 1828. An acquaintance described him as having suffered from a "melancholy" "nervous temperament," with a "fixed reserve" that was "beyond the reach of medical skill" [Francis 248–49].) Several of Piozzi's works and her literary gifts to him, along with her letters, were in his possession when he died and were sold at auction.

During her late life, Piozzi was perfectly clear about her project to make Conway know her as an author. She ends the pamphlet letter with the worry that "Mr. Conway will have had enough of Mrs. Piozzi and her Writings— Print and Manuscript. I will not plague You again God knows when" (*Letters* 6: 284). Untrue to her word, however, Piozzi starts another letter to him just one day later, writing "And did I actually know my Heart so ill, as to protest that I would write no more for Weeks or Months to come?" (288). She responds to a letter from him, in which he apparently encourages her to continue her education of him, or, at the least, to continue her literary bequests. She writes, "And so you want more Books, more Manuscript Stuff too" (289). In October 1819, she writes, "Live long and happily, and love my Letters; I wonder when You will Be sick of them: but I shall release you soon" (333).

She did not send him only books and letters. In August of 1819, she gave him a gold repeating watch, designed as her "last Present," along with a verse about time and tender emotion. But books seem to be her most common gift to Conway, whether volumes she has just finished reading or those valuable and unique. She writes in January 1820 of sending him Leslie's *Truth of Christianity Demonstrated* and Spence's *Anecdotes* (1820), offering to "bind them for You beautifully if you will read them" (*Letters* 6: 360). In June 1820, she writes that she has not had a letter from him since April and complains that he "will not employ Three Fingers for five Minutes to give me unspeakable Pleasure"; she tells of her intention to give him "a French Rasselas given to Doctor Johnson by the Translator—and bestowed on me by the Immortal S. J. half a Century ago" (393). Regretting that she does not have means to serve Conway further, she writes, "I *can* give you *that*" and tells him that she will leave the book for him with his mother. When she did send the *Rasselas*, she also gave to him her copy of *The Percy Anecdotes* (1820). Making reference to *Rasselas*, she says it made her think of her own verses, which she also sent to him—a poem about time, death, and eternity (398). Time figures prominently in her interactions with the actor, whether past, present, or future.

Piozzi linked the past to the present through Conway in imaginative ways. In addition to professing her own love for him, she assured him that Johnson would have loved him. She writes: "Dr. Johnson said You know, that Admiration is a short-lived Passion, I have not found it so; but then We never knew a Mortal who could heap Fewel on the *Flame as You* have done—*he* would have loved my Conway—not as I do, because no one but Mrs. Rudd *can* do *so;* but he would have praised and petted, and made every one else—*appear* as if sensible to Your Merits" (*Letters* 6: 408). In a triangle of Piozzi's design, Johnson oversees their relationship. But rather than imagining Conway as her Johnson replacement, Piozzi understood herself as the mediating mentor and Conway as the would-be protégé.

We know that Piozzi inscribed an autobiography, which she titled "The Abridgement," in Conway's copy of her *Observations and Reflections Made in the Course of a Journey through France, Italy, and Germany* (1789). It is not the only time she completed a brief autobiography, but it is, perhaps, the latest one she produced. She inscribed that copy of *Observations* with the following note: "These Books do not in any wise belong to me; they are the property of William Augustus Conway . . . who left them to my care, for purpose of putting notes, when he quitted Bath, May 14, 1819 . . . Hester Lynch Piozzi writes this for fear lest her death happening before his return, these books might be confounded among others in her study."[36] Piozzi seems to have considered writing out her life for Conway as a last act performed for him. As Terri Premo has argued, "Autobiographies in old age often tell us more about the writer's unique old-age perspective than about specific events in life," and Piozzi's bears this out.[37] She makes direct references to Conway in the account, addressing him as a reader in multiple passages. She even pokes fun of her enterprise, writing, "poor H. L. P. turns egoist at eighty, and tells her own adventures" ("Original" 616). She ends the autobiography with a tribute to Conway: "Your talents roused, your offered friendship opened my heart to enjoyment. Oh! never say hereafter that the obligations are on your side. Without you, dullness, darkness, stagnation of every faculty would have enveloped and extinguished all the powers of hapless H. L. P." (622).

Later, when Piozzi moved from Bath to Penzance to cut down on her expenses, she wrote to ask Conway to visit her. She positively discouraged her adopted son from coming, writing a friend that she should be "sorry" if Salusbury comes but would "rejoyce" if the "same fancy" would take Conway "by the brain pan" (*Letters* 6: 426). She put pressure directly on Conway: "And I wonder if you recollect a certain Friend of mine, named Augustus; who said in Camden Place A.D. *1818;* I could be happy in a Prison, with dear Mrs. Piozzi and her Anecdotes. . . . Come here in the Winter and *Try* 1821—Imprisonment with H: L: P. and *Her Castle* by the Seaside" (416). Though Conway never came, Piozzi saw him several months later when she returned to Clifton. She died there, in what was probably one of Conway's mother's apartments.

Conway, in a moving letter to Piozzi's adopted son, indicates as much. On 30 April 1821, Conway writes to Salusbury that Hester Piozzi is "so much reduced as to afford, I fear, no reasonable hope of her *recovery.*" He tells Sir John not to lose an instant in coming, "if you hope to see poor Mrs. Piozzi alive." Mrs. Piozzi, Conway says, "has at present taken apartments at my Mother's, with whom I at present reside," at 10 Sion Row in Clifton. Conway asks that this information not be attributed to him, however: "I rely upon your honour, Sir John, never to name me as the source of your authority for setting out. My motive for addressing you is good to some, and harm to none, and I therefore stand acquitted to myself for my conduct" (*H-T-P,* reel 19, MS 596; *Letters* 6: 32). Piozzi died on 2 May 1821. Despite Conway's warning, Salusbury did not arrive until three days after her death.

Few of Conway's letters to Piozzi appear to have survived, and one wonders if that means there were only a few. The Conway letters at the John Rylands Library in Manchester—many quite short and cryptically dated—do not allow much insight into his sense of their relationship. The letters are extremely polite, often apologetic, and unusually grateful, suggesting that, even if he is not as attached to her as she is to him, he placed a high value on knowing her. As he puts it in one letter from early in their friendship (26 Mar. 1819), "Mr. Conway is really at a loss to express in adequate terms his sense of Mrs. Piozzi's very kind and flattering attentions to him, but though he cannot *express,* he *feels* them most strongly, and begs to offer her his sincere and heartfelt acknowledgements for the same" (*H-T-P,* reel 19, MS 596). Two years later, in a letter to Salusbury from 23 July 1821 (some months after Piozzi's death), Conway thanked him for sending the books Piozzi apparently meant for him to have. He writes that they "are indeed invaluable." Whatever the relationship was to her or to him, from what we can gather, it was one that revolved around flattering attentions on both sides and around conversations about books. Conway appears to have indulged, and perhaps even enjoyed, the attention.

Throughout her late life (indeed, throughout her life) Piozzi made eccentric choices. Like Macaulay before her, she seems not to have anticipated or to have cared about how her unconventional personal life would be judged. At the same time, like Macaulay, Piozzi appeared to care deeply about what would become of her reputation as an author. Instead of working to overturn the ill effects of negative reviews, Piozzi tried to establish her own miniature "reading public," demonstrating a kind of creative ingenuity. When Fellowes could not find a publisher for "Lyford," when she was stymied in her attempts to reach a mass audience, she continued her now-famous private writing, in the form of letters and journals, virtually to her last breath. It was through these vehicles—looming large among them the letters to Conway—that Piozzi served as her own literary agent, one reader at a time. She may have assumed that these readers were well placed enough to influence others after her death.

More proof of this assumption is a large Bible, inscribed to Conway's mother, now housed at the British Library, which features Piozzi's characteristic marginalia throughout.[38] She opens the text with this comment: "It was an imperfect Copy bought cheap for Love of the *Prints;* in 1819 & intrusted to my Care; who restored the Text & wrote Notes to it, for Love of the possessor and her Heirs: *not* those of H : L : P."[39] Piozzi makes predictions for the Second Coming, reference to historical and religious works, and reference to her own published and unpublished writings. That she thought the book valuable because of her marginalia is evident. The Bible itself was an "imperfect Copy" "bought cheap." Still, Piozzi believed it worth protecting, indicating that it ought not to be passed down through her own heirs.

As Piozzi desired, the Bible became the property of the Rudd-Conways. The 1830 will of Mrs. Rudd stipulated that it be given to her grandson, Frederick Bartlett Conway (ca. 1819–74), illegitimate son and heir of her late (also illegitimate) son, William Augustus Conway.[40] Whether Piozzi knew of her darling Conway's progeny is unclear; there is no mention of his birth in her letters or papers. That she assumed, through evidence in this Bible and elsewhere, that the Rudd-Conways would carry on her good name to posterity, however, seems obvious. As one critic put it, though Piozzi's marginalia show her "pursuing her own train of thought she is also mindful of her audience, the reader who will be reading this Bible with her even after she is gone" (Jackson, *Readers* 182). Perhaps Piozzi hoped that these readers would "restore" her, when her reputation was "intrusted" to their care. Her choices were not entirely misplaced. Frederick Conway, too, became an actor, and his children enjoyed modest success on the stage and in the theater. But Piozzi's connection to the Conways kept her in the public eye in ways more damaging than salubrious.

To some, the fact of Piozzi's old age itself should have protected her from venomous posthumous response. An 1862 reviewer wrongly concluded that her status as a granddame would "at once [disarm] criticism, and [leave] few contemporaries able to criticize" ("Lives" 423). On the contrary, Piozzi became either a touchstone for or a laughingstock in conversations about old women dancing or about May–December romances. Chivalrous catering to her old age did not carry the day, and commentary on Piozzi was profoundly mixed. The *Christian Examiner* (1861) concluded, "Piozzi can hardly be treated worse by posterity than she was during her life."[41] The *St. James' Magazine* (1861) argued that Piozzi "has been too hastily lynched by posterity."[42] But for every Piozzi defender, there was a detractor. An 1861 essay in the *Atlantic Monthly* held that "the last forty years of her life were not as charming as the first," describing her as sprightly and good natured, though sad, feeble, undignified, filled with pretense, and lacking freshness ("Original" 615, 622). But perhaps the worst treatment she faced was from those who thought her life and writings were forgettable. One such reviewer concluded that "Mrs. Piozzi is not a woman . . . who merits much posthumous blame or praise. . . . She is, in short, one of those persons of whom we like to read, but whom we do not care to remember" ("Memoirs" 392).

Piozzi has been remembered, and rightly so, but how she is remembered is just as crucial as that she is remembered as an old woman. We ought not, wittingly or unwittingly, repeat the nineteenth-century tradition of caricaturing her last years as those of a shallow, happy-go-lucky woman (the "birthday party" Piozzi) or as a would-be seducer in her dotage (the Conway episode). The shallow, happy-go-lucky distortion is typified by an 1861 reviewer for the *New Monthly Magazine,* who offered a dissenting though apologetic opinion: "Though [Piozzi] *dared to give a ball at eighty,*" the reviewer opined, "her old age was beautiful."[43] Throughout this chapter I have taken issue with commentary on Piozzi casting her as an aged seductress. In addition to potentially undoing these caricatures, then, renewed attention to Piozzi's old age allows us the potential to understand her writing career more fully, whether or not she was reaching a mass audience.

Piozzi may have used her interactions with Conway to extend her literary powers to the next generation, during a period when she was unable to find receptive readers through former channels. Needless to say, if this was one of her aims, the plan backfired—at least in part. Long after both had died, Conway indeed kept Piozzi's name before the public, but in none of the ways she might have hoped. Throughout the nineteenth century and into the twentieth, the Piozzi-Conway episode served to characterize Piozzi as an irrational and self-involved old woman and to imagine Conway as her victim. What this chapter proposes is that we might see Piozzi's befriending Conway as an innovative and resourceful choice, rather than as a desperate act. Viewed in this way, the friendship's contours mirror many of the other late-life activities in which Piozzi engaged. Piozzi, according to James Clifford, would "talk, talk, talk away the last years of her long and active life."[44] We might rather say that she wrote, wrote, wrote, with an eye to ensuring that her writings would be remembered.

CHAPTER FIVE

"One generation passeth away, and another cometh"

Anna Letitia Barbauld's Late Literary Work

> The part of monitress I dare not play,
> Nor scarce accept the def'rence thou wouldst pay,
> But know a kind illusion gives it rise,
> And blush thy simpleness should count me wise.
>
> —*Lady Louisa Stuart,* "Upon Growing Old" *(1757–1851)*

Poet, critic, and essayist Anna Letitia Barbauld (1743–1825) remained on the fringes of literary history during the Victorian era, when many eighteenth- and early nineteenth-century women writers vanished. That may mean little for the woman whose fame was once described as "second to none among the female writers of her country."[1] One critic predicted that after her death Barbauld would be remembered for her well-circulated works for children, but before her late twentieth-century rehabilitation, Barbauld was remembered primarily as the attractive old woman who wrote a harmless poem about old age.[2] This poem, titled "Life," was supposedly learned by heart by William Wordsworth (1770–1850), who is said to have wished he had written it himself, and recited at bedtime by Frances Burney (1752–1840), as we have seen.[3] For a time after her death, Barbauld was known best—what little was known of her—as a model elderly woman writer.

Barbauld's "Life," first published in her posthumous works (1825), is a 30-line poem, written circa 1812. Only its last stanza was cited at the centenary of her death, as William McCarthy and Elizabeth Kraft note (318):

> Life! we have been long together,
> Through pleasant and through cloudy weather;

'Tis hard to part when friends are dear;
Perhaps 'twill cost a sigh, a tear;—
Then steal away, give little warning,
Choose thine own time;
Say not Good-night, but in some brighter clime
Bid me Good-morning!

As clever as it may be, this verse is unrepresentative of the variety and depth of Barbauld's poetic, not to say literary, contributions. The stanza is not even representative of the poem "Life," which displays greater complexity and questions the relationship of life, identity, and the afterlife. The poem takes as its epigraph the beginning of Roman emperor Hadrian's alleged deathbed verse, "Animula, vagula, blandula" (sweet little soul, fickle, yet cuddlesome)—itself no simple comment on the end of earthly existence. Barbauld's poem begins, "Life! I know not what thou art, / But I know that thou and I must part," and goes on to mention the "valueless clod" that will hold the speaker's corpse, once she is dead, and to wonder "in this strange divorce" (from life), "where I must seek, this compound I?" (166). The second stanza imagines what might make up Life's essence, wondering if Life's existence ever changes, asking "Yet canst thou without thought or feeling be? / O say what art thou, when no more thou'rt thee?" The poem's last stanza is far more optimistic and unquestioning than its first two.

It has been said that the last stanza of "Life" should have been inscribed on [Barbauld's] tomb 'by way of Epitaph'" (qtd. in McCarthy and Kraft 318). "Figuratively, it has been," as McCarthy and Kraft conclude, offering evidence of the ways in which "the eight lines seem to have entered popular culture" as "a set piece for mortuary consolation."[4] Barbauld was remembered as an ideal elderly woman, successfully performing happy old age, a type of memorializing unusual among women writers of the period. For Barbauld's best-known contemporaries, it was more customary to endure tributes to their early works and criticism or ignorance of their later ones. Barbauld came to be appreciated as a young person's old person. American Unitarian minister William Ellery Channing (1780–1842) declared that he had never seen a person of Barbauld's age "who had preserved so much of youth; on whom time had laid so gentle a hand. Her countenance had nothing of the rigidity and hard lines of advanced life, but responded to the mind like a young woman's."[5] Those who wrote about celebrated women writers' looks in old age seem either to remark on their premature haggardness or to celebrate loudly their uncanny youthfulness. The latter, too, has its costs; although Barbauld was able to sustain posthumous renown for having inhabited a "grandmotherly" role in late life, that persona necessitated that she be viewed as harmless and noncontroversial—a condition dependent upon the neglect of the most noteworthy long poem published in her late life.

The extent to which Barbauld experienced the happy old age that "Life" presents is difficult to conclude.[6] In posthumously published letters, Barbauld makes several disparaging comments about the prospect of old age, but her December 1813 letter to Susanna Estlin is perhaps the most profoundly negative: "If you ask what I am doing,—nothing. Pope, I think, somewhere says, 'The last years of life, like tickets left in the wheel, rise in value.' The thought is beautiful, but false; they are of very little value,—they are generally past either in struggling with pains and infirmities, or in a dreamy kind of existence: no new veins of thought are opened; no young affections springing up; the ship has taken in its lading, whatever it may be, whether precious stones or lumber, and lies idly flapping its sails, and waiting for the wind that must drive it upon the wide ocean" (*Works* 1: 308). This statement alone is enough to suggest that "Life" serves us ill as a summary of Barbauld's late literary career, but her letter to Estlin may be no more representative of her experiences than the poem. Contrary to what she states in this letter, Barbauld's late work as an author shows that she had opened—and would continue to open—new veins of thought in her old age.

Today, Barbauld is studied for her work in a range of genres, not simply for brief, allegedly cheerful verses. Critical commentary on Barbauld has never been more robust. A good deal of this work has centered on her poetry, especially her shorter poems, perhaps because they are easily anthologized and pleasurable to teach.[7] When critics have looked to Barbauld's writings in other genres, it has been primarily to her works for the young. It is only recently that much interest has been taken in Barbauld's other literary contributions. For instance, Claudia Johnson, Catherine Moore, and Katharine Rogers have written about Barbauld's groundbreaking editorial work for the fifty-volume series *British Novelists* (1810).[8] As Johnson has noted, Barbauld's "work as an editor of fiction receives relatively little attention" (166). We might add that editorial, biographical, and literary critical work constitutes a significant portion of Barbauld's authorial contributions, particularly in late life and that it has been little attended to.

In the first half of this chapter, I address this lack by examining Barbauld's editorial and literary critical projects from the 1790s to the 1810s, in order to

argue for that labor as an important feature of her later years, showing its consequence as an authorial choice. Rather than seeing it as work she undertook
because she could not pursue more challenging writing (as her nineteenth-
century biographers surmised), we ought to consider her critical work as an
attempt to make a different kind of contribution to literary history. Barbauld's
own comments show that she thought it important to bring before the public
authors of the previous generation whose works deserved another hearing,
positioning her work as a kind of literary public service. Barbauld may have
been doing for the rising generation what she hoped would be done for her
in the next—reviving under-read or almost forgotten texts for a public that
needed reminding of their quality.

A look at Barbauld as editor and critic sets up the latter part of the chapter,
in which I consider her last published work and its effect on her reputation in
old age, as well as her posthumous reputation. Barbauld's *Eighteen Hundred
and Eleven* (1812) imagines a future with London in ruins and in which global
power has shifted to the Americas. The poem was excoriated by prominent
British reviewers and received one particularly damning review. A great deal
of commentary on the poem has appeared in the past decade, much of it seeking the reasons why *Eighteen Hundred and Eleven* proved a critical failure.[9]
There is at least one angle that few critics have investigated—the possibility
that negative stereotypes about old women played a role. My chapter deepens
the work of previous scholars by returning the fact of—and the factor of—
Barbauld's old age to our speculations about the reception of this important
poem. Reconstructing Barbauld's authorial activities in her old age serves to
refocus our conversations on the extent of the literary contributions she made.
It demonstrates the ways in which the poem "Life" has long skewed our sense
not only of Barbauld's career as a whole but of the variety and vicissitudes of
her written work in old age.

"A Work of the First Excellence Cannot Perish": Barbauld as Editor

When "the effervescence caused by the French revolution had subsided,"
Barbauld "could seldom excite herself to the labor of composition, except on
the spur of occasion," according to her niece, biographer, and editor Lucy Aikin (1781–1864) (Barbauld, *Works* xxxvii). Aikin belittles Barbauld's efforts,
explaining that in the 1790s Barbauld "gave nothing more to the public for
a considerable number of years, with the exception of two critical essays,"

on Akenside and Collins. It was not long afterward that Barbauld's selections from the *Spectator, Tatler, Guardian,* and *Freeholder* and her biography and correspondence of novelist Samuel Richardson appeared—both in 1804. Neither of these works ought to be characterized as slight, and they could not have been produced on the "spur of occasion." The former arose, according to Aikin, from "a warm attachment to the authors of what has been called the Augustan age of English literature," resulting in Barbauld's "most successful" effort in literary criticism (xxxix, xl). Despite this praise, Aikin repeatedly downplays Barbauld's motivations for and agency in undertaking editorial and critical work.

Barbauld's reasons for pursuing this work are presented by Aikin as a reaction to negative circumstances. As we saw above, she first asserts that Barbauld had no political impetus to write. When describing her aunt's editing and critical efforts in the early 1800s, however, Aikin alleges that that work was undertaken "chiefly as a solace under the pressure and anxieties" of her husband's unnamed (but by then well-known) ailment: mental illness (Barbauld, *Works* xliii). After his death in 1808, Barbauld is said to have sought "relief from dejection" in editing and literary criticism because she was "incapable as yet of any stronger effort" (xlix). In other words, Aikin would have it that Barbauld chose this kind of work first because she was living in a politically unexciting time, then because she was looking for something to relieve anxiety, and finally, because it was effortless work in which she might drown her grief. It seems peculiar to explain away many years of dedicated labor as either accidental or easy. At other points, Aikin presents Barbauld as having been drawn into editorial and critical work not by circumstances but through pressure from others. According to Aikin, Barbauld "was *prevailed upon* to undertake the task" of editing Richardson's letters (xliii; emphasis added). Barbauld "*consented to* employ herself in these *humbler offices* of literature." In each case, Aikin's message is clear: Barbauld incidentally—or perhaps even as a result of coercion—set aside her literary talents. To serve as an editor and a critic, Aikin implies, is an act of little consequence for a successful author.

This version of events has seemed to stick in subsequent accounts of Barbauld's career. The anthology *Women Critics 1660–1820* (1995) mistakenly claims that "Barbauld's career as a critic began when she edited the letters of Samuel Richardson."[10] But it was almost a decade earlier that Barbauld had written a substantial introductory essay for Mark Akenside's *Pleasures of the Imagination* (1795) and the works of William Collins (1797). She followed up these projects with the Richardson correspondence and her selections from the *Spectator* and *Tatler* (1804), then with the fifty-volume *British Novelists* (1810), as well as with a further collection titled *The Female Speaker* (1811). For several decades, the lion's share of Barbauld's publications consisted of editorial projects or substantive literary critical introductions on eighteenth-century writers. It was arguably the most significant published work of her early old age. In no sense, in terms of labor or length, was this minor work. As one critic points out, Barbauld's life of Richardson is "the longest work she ever did," at approximately two hundred pages.[11] Kraft and McCarthy conclude, "The critical neglect of Barbauld's poetry is baffling" (xxi). We might add that the critical neglect of Barbauld as an editor and literary critic is baffling as well.

Perhaps the best place to examine Barbauld's critical and editorial work is through a study of "the longest work she ever did," her prefatory essay to Richardson's correspondence and the editorial work that followed it. Barbauld undertook this ambitious six-volume project when few of the eighteenth-century novelist's letters had been previously published. She also wrote the first full-length biography of Richardson. Still, there has been little twentieth-century appreciation of Barbauld's contributions. References to her in Richardson criticism have followed A. D. McKillop, who chastises Barbauld's "ruthless hand" as editor and refers to "the slashing strokes of her editorial pen."[12] Editor John Carroll also characterizes Barbauld's editing with such words as "unaccountable," "erroneous," and "altered."[13] Where she has been mentioned, it is generally in a footnote of little substance or complaint. It is also true that Barbauld may get short shrift in scholarship on Richardson because there is so little attention to his correspondence per se, as Peter Sabor points out.[14]

If there is little mention of Barbauld in studies about Richardson, however, there is even less of Richardson in studies of Barbauld.[15] This seems surprising, because editing and introducing the *Correspondence of Samuel Richardson* (1804) was an important event in her publishing career, particularly if the reception of the work is any indication. Discussing Barbauld as editor, critic, and biographer affords us the opportunity to examine the ways in which she framed her work and to consider the import of the glowing critical responses the project met with. In this section, I examine Barbauld's contemporaries' views of her critical and editorial work on Richardson, seeing them alongside more recent concerns about her editorial choices and practice. In the process, I draw conclusions about what the work may have meant for Barbauld's later life and reputation, as well as her career in full.

Barbauld's editorial practices vis-à-vis Richardson's letters have already been expertly evaluated by William McCarthy. In an essay published in *Studies in Bibliography* (2001), McCarthy compares surviving Richardson letters with texts printed in Barbauld's edition, arguing that her edited letters "may not be first-class citizens of the Richardson canon" "but they are not aliens to it."[16] He offers four conclusions: (1) Barbauld abridged letters by an average of 30 percent; (2) all of the letters "depart from their originals in occasional details of wording" (SiB 207); (3) very few (just 5%–6%) bear directions to conflate; and (4) based on his findings, approximately 90 percent of the 280 letters known only from the Barbauld *Correspondence* "can be trusted to represent with accuracy the originals" (208). McCarthy stresses that Barbauld should not be held solely responsible for departures from the manuscripts. Richardson, too, left editorial markings. As McCarthy reminds us, "Richardson's editing, like Barbauld's later, was not based on the ethic modern editors work by" (205). McCarthy's work overturns previous conclusions about Barbauld's hand in Richardson's correspondence. Twentieth-century criticisms of Barbauld as a shoddy editor ought as a result to strike us as anachronistic.

Further information deepens these claims—first, by contextualizing how important editorial and critical work was to Barbauld's late career and, second, by examining the responses to her edition of Richardson. Barbauld was not a green editor, by any means, when she tackled the Richardson project. She was a seasoned, experienced, and well-respected critic—and an author who valued editing. In the preface to the Richardson edition, Barbauld writes, "It was the favourite employment of [Richardson's] declining years to select and arrange [his letters], and he always looked forward to their publication at some distant period."[17] What critics have overlooked is the way in which Barbauld's description of Richardson's employment mirrors her labor on his behalf. She appears to have found selecting, arranging, introducing, and remarking on the works of other authors a favorite employment of her *own* declining years.

Barbauld's "Life of Samuel Richardson With Remarks on His Writings" begins not with his life or writings but with a twenty-page discourse on novels and romances. (She would later draw from this piece in her introductory essay to the *British Novelists* collection.) Barbauld's biography of Richardson follows, with twenty-five pages summarizing his life. She then provides approximately thirty pages of summary and commentary each on *Pamela* and *Clarissa. Sir Charles Grandison* is given nearly twenty pages of coverage, and *Familiar Letters* receives two pages' worth. From there, Barbauld considers literary matters such as Richardson's style, his relationships with female correspondents, and the effects of the piracy of Dublin booksellers. Next, Barbauld spends thirty-five pages describing Richardson's moral character, covering his love life, his beliefs about and relationships to women, his religion, his faults (according to Barbauld, Richardson was vain), his physical description, and his daughters. She proceeds to a ten-page account of Richardson that she has received from a woman acquainted with him in her youth. Finally, Barbauld presents in twenty pages short sketches of Richardson's main correspondents, from Aaron Hill to Lady Bradshaigh.

In her introduction, Barbauld argues that the value of an author's correspondence is that it functions as a kind of time travel or as a way to commune with spirits beyond the grave. She writes, "Nothing tends so strongly to place us in the midst of the generations that are past, as a perusal of their correspondence. To have their very letters, their very handwriting before our eyes, gives a more intimate feeling of their existence, than any other memorial of them" (*Correspondence* ccx). As Barbauld describes it, reading correspondence is a retrospective activity, particularly suited to the aged or to those inclined to look backward. As I discussed in the introduction, such manifestations of having-done-this-ness are common in aged women's writings. For Barbauld, the sensation is linked to reading the words—especially the very handwriting—of others. Her sense of the *Correspondence*'s function and audience paved the way for its reception. The *Critical Review* thought that the volumes would be attractive to two kinds of readers—first, "modern ladies" who want to see the objects that entertained their mothers and grandmothers, and second, the old themselves: "those who lived nearer the period" who "will feel their former pleasures revived, by the renewal of the impressions with which they were once so much delighted."[18]

Barbauld's Richardson edition was reviewed widely, and, as Peter Sabor notes, reviews were "mixed"—a mix worthy of scrutiny.[19] Of the six major reviews that appeared, only one (the *Anti-Jacobin*) approached its task as starting and stopping with a volume-by-volume description of the contents of the *Correspondence*, and one provided extracts from the letters themselves (*Imperial Review*). The others concentrated almost exclusively on Barbauld's essay. In these reviews, nearly as much attention was paid to the achievements of Barbauld as to those of Richardson. Some reviewers questioned whether Richardson was too out of fashion to be brought back into the public eye, as the *Monthly Review* wonders that, "after so long a repose, we should now conjure up [Richardson's] ghost."[20] The *Critical Review* claims, "of the rising generation few have heard of Pamela" (162). In the strangest proof that

Richardson was seen as old literary news, one well-meaning critic calls him "the greatest literary luminary of the seventeenth century" (*Monthly Review* 31). Each reviewer argued that one or more of Richardson's literary achievements would endure, making his biography and correspondence of abiding interest.

Notable in these reviews is not just the estimation of Richardson's importance but the lavish encomiums on Barbauld. The *Imperial Review* praises publisher Phillips for his "judgment in submitting these valuable documents to the critical inspection of Mrs. Barbauld. The good sense and the delicacy of feeling by which the writings of that lady are distinguished, afforded an ample pledge that she would discharge the office of editor with taste and fidelity." The reviewer is not disappointed with the results: "Upon inspection of the contents of these volumes, we confidently declare our conviction that this pledge she has not forfeited."[21] The *Eclectic Review* describes "the judicious selection, and the elegant composition of Mrs. Barbauld, which will naturally be cherished. . . . She has at once done justice to *his* fame and to her own; she praises with discrimination, censures with candour."[22] The *Literary Magazine*, too, thinks Barbauld's choice of subject and her work itself could not have been better executed: "a more congenial subject could not possibly have been afforded to [Barbauld's] pen. Richardson has experienced a good fortune, which rarely falls to the lot of deceased merit. His will appears to have been literally executed at the time he himself prescribed, and by a hand more worthy of his genius than any other which England could at present furnish."[23] The reviewer believes that Richardson himself, were he living, would have chosen Barbauld for the editorial and critical task: "the only pen in England which Richardson's sublime and disembodied intelligence would have selected, is, most probably, that of Letitia Barbauld" (533). Making Barbauld Richardson's editor was seen as a perfect pairing because she was considered as talented a writer as he.

If reviewers were enthusiastic about Barbauld as editor and critic, they were less pleased with the letters themselves, which were most often described as trifling. The *Critical Review* finds them "seldom containing any particular subject of inquiry or discussion," with "little that is particularly interesting" on literary information of the era (284, 285). After its warm praise, the *Eclectic Review*, too, turns sour: "But after every exertion of candour, we must avow, that in reading these letters, we have betrayed symptoms of weariness, and even of disgust" (123). Because of the repetition of subject and the frequent idolizing of Richardson in the letters, the reviewer proclaims, "we cannot wholly suppress emotions of mingled pity and contempt." Many of the reviews spent little space on volumes 2 through 6—the letters themselves. As the *Eclectic Review* puts it, "Having dwelt thus long on two-thirds of the first volume, our readers will not wish us to enlarge on the correspondence which occupies the rest of this publication." The chief complaint was that the letters did not contain instruction and advice, whether moral or literary. Instead, they were found wearisome in "ringing incessant changes on Pamela, Clarissa, Grandison" (*Eclectic Review* 123). For Francis Jeffrey's *Edinburgh Review*, the novels of Richardson "will always be read with admiration," but "certainly can never appear to greater advantage than when contrasted with the melancholy farrago which is here entitled his Correspondence."[24]

Still, the reviewers generally praised rather than blamed Barbauld when addressing this "problem." They were grateful for, as she put it, her "necessary office of selection" from the "very numerous" letters in the papers purchased by publisher Phillips (1: vi). But six volumes were more than the reviewers thought appropriate. As one critic jokes, "Mrs. B. has formerly written [a poem] '*The Groans of the Tankard*,' and if correspondence of this kind be often published, we recommend it to her to write the *Groans of the Press*" (*Monthly Review* 38). Francis Jeffrey's *Edinburgh Review* assessment was less jocose; after remarking that Barbauld "has suppressed about twice as many letters as are now presented to our consideration," Jeffrey concludes: "Favourably as we are disposed to think of all for which she is directly responsible, the perusal of the whole six volumes has fully convinced us that we are even more indebted to her forbearance than to her bounty" (23). The *Eclectic Review* wishes the correspondence "had been comprised in two or three volumes" but considers itself "obliged to Mrs. Barbauld, that we are let off with the perusal of six" (123). Some blamed Barbauld for the length of the project: The *Monthly Review* wishes that "the fair editor" had "discreetly suppressed with a bolder hand" (31). Barbauld showed, as she says, "mercy on the public" by not printing the complete letters, but, the *Monthly* adds, "this mercy should have been farther extended." Only the *Anti-Jacobin Review* finds "the whole correspondence is interesting"; it determines that "the selection of [the letters] confers high honour on the judgment of the editor."[25]

Whether the letters seemed too many or just right in number, Barbauld was credited with editorial and critical excellence. She was thanked by almost all of her reviewers for keeping back some of Richardson's letters. Since the early twentieth century, critics have complained about Barbauld's liberties in (to invoke McKillop's aforementioned phrase) "slashing" Richardson's correspondence. But for her earliest critics, Barbauld did not cut out enough. Not one contemporary source complained that Barbauld brought out too little material. This suggests that, rather than the radical editor most twentieth-century criticism would make her out to be, Barbauld was, for her time, quite conservative, putting into print much more of Richardson's correspondence than her contemporaries wanted to see. It is unclear what directions she had as to length from her publisher, but it is possible that we owe a debt to Barbauld herself for preserving for posterity *so much* of Richardson's correspondence.[26]

As a biographer of Richardson, Barbauld received almost universal high praise. The *Critical Review*'s assessment is typical: "We have scarcely even seen a biographic sketch more elegant, better discriminated, and more appropriate" (156). As a critic, Barbauld also received compliments from reviewers, though with some minor complaints about her interpretations.[27] What the reviewers do not agree on is Barbauld's style. Some criticize its "freedom and boldness" (*Eclectic Review* 123), while others found the writing too old fashioned. The *Monthly Review* concludes that "Mrs. Barbauld's Memoir is, in general, written with purity and elegance: but occasionally we meet with expressions which modern correctness and taste do not tolerate" (48). Examples of her outdated diction follow. Whether or not the six volumes of Richardson correspondence were being read cover to cover, contemporary readers' comments suggest that Barbauld's introductory essay was being read closely in the years after its publication. Although it is difficult to establish both critical and popular acclaim, it would seem Barbauld's Richardson edition enjoyed both.

The elaborate praise that Barbauld received from reviewers may seem excessive. Traditional scholarly wisdom would have it that Richardson is more worthy of our interest than Barbauld, but it is clear from the critical response to the *Correspondence* that at the turn of the nineteenth century, Richardson and Barbauld were held in equally high esteem. According to one reviewer, "The world is indebted to . . . the discernment which selected an editor so peculiarly fitted for doing justice to the writings and character of Richardson. Mrs. Barbauld has genius, taste, and sentiment more congenial to those which have been displayed in Pamela, Grandison, and Clarissa, than probably any other writer of the times, even including those of a similar direction, if perhaps we should except the author of Evelina and Cecilia" (*Anti-Jacobin Review* 177). The reviewer prefers Burney, presumably because she knows more about novel writing, although Barbauld arguably knew more about editing and literary criticism, and what she produced was almost universally applauded. Her reviewers did not consider editorial, critical, and biographical work beneath Barbauld's notice, as she was perceived as at the height of her powers in all three areas—a fortuitous combination for literary history.

What did Barbauld think of her editorial, critical, and biographical work? Was turning editor and critic of Richardson, as Aikin suggested, Barbauld's reaction to political boredom, a search for solace, or a response to dejection? Reviewer Jeffrey senses that Barbauld does not approve of Richardson's letters because, according to him, she "does not venture to say much in favour of the collection" (34). That may be so. But it appears more likely that she found the letters absorbing. In a private letter to a former pupil, Barbauld refers to her work on Richardson, suggesting that the job is proving fascinating, if challenging: "I am very busy; being . . . deeply engaged in the job I have perhaps rashly undertaken. Indeed I have at present a splendid opportunity, which I think I might as well use, of getting clear with my correspondents, at little expence of my own invention. For cannot I send them some brilliant paragraphs from Richardson, from Sheridan, from Mrs. Carter, from Dr. Young all whose letters lie before me at my mercy?"[28] Here Barbauld imagines herself channeling the voices of literary predecessors, as she envisions using their words—indeed, their paragraphs—as her own. Barbauld seems entranced by the power of editing and criticism. In a letter from January 1805, she writes to Maria Edgeworth asking her and her father for specific criticisms on the Richardson essay: "I shall be much obliged to Mr. Edgeworth or you for any criticisms of the *life*, because Phillips talks of publishing it separately."[29] Phillips appears never to have done so, but it seems unlikely that Barbauld would have sought criticism on a piece of published work that she did not much value.

Why did Barbauld invest so much of her energy in late life to editorial and literary critical work? Though the Richardson edition offers some indication of what was at stake for Barbauld, her other editorial efforts provide further information. In the prefatory essay to *Selections from the "Spectator," "Tatler," "Guardian," and "Freeholder,"* Barbauld again begins—as she did with Richardson—by invoking a retrospective trope: "It is equally true of books as of their authors," she writes, "that one generation passeth away and another cometh."[30] She asserts that "new authors are continually taking possession of the public mind, and old ones falling into disuse" (1: v). The task of the editor, she implies, is to forestall this "falling into disuse" by bringing old authors before the public. When she notes that "the fame of writers is exposed to continual fluctuation," not just for ephemeral productions but also for "books that have been the favorites of the public," she could just as easily be speaking of the work of Richardson, of many of the volumes she later selected for inclusion in *The British Novelists*, or indeed, of her own work. Her hopeful belief is that classics have a special status and cannot die, though they must age.[31] As she puts it, a classic is withdrawn from everyday public view to be laid on an honorable shelf: "It is true, indeed, that a work of the first excellence cannot perish. It will continue to be respected as a classic: but it will no longer be the book which every one who reads is expected to be acquainted with, to which allusions are often made, and readily understood in conversation; it loses the precious privilege of occupying the minds of youth; in short, it is withdrawn from the parlour-window, and laid upon the shelf in honourable respose. It ceases to be current coin, but is preserved like a medal in the cabinets of the curious" (vi).

This statement may stand in support of all of Barbauld's editorial and critical work. To preserve like a medal the work of previous years is a gift that an old critic-author can give to "the minds of youth." Imagining herself intergenerationally from both sides—among those who came before and after her—seems to have led to a desire to turn editor. For Barbauld, this appears as a selfless response to retrospective thinking. Editing or reintroducing important literary works plays a role in making them classics, available to young and old readers alike. Barbauld is ostensibly discussing the early eighteenth-century periodical essay, and especially the work of Joseph Addison, which she holds in high regard.[32] It is also possible to read her statement as the philosophical reflection—at one remove, no doubt—of an aging author herself.

Barbauld in the 1800s and 1810s must have understood firsthand the vagaries of literary fame, as well as the potential power of books. Not one to despair for the future of great books (at this point in her old age, at least), she demonstrates confidence in the ability of future generations to recognize a classic. She discusses situations that might lead to an early forgetting of a work, but she reaches the conclusion that "in reality, nearly all [books] are preserved to us that are most worth preservation . . . what has perished is chiefly made up of the residuum of science, and the caput mortuum of literature" (*Selections* x). In particular, she notes, literary works that describe manners "rise in value as their contents become more obsolete." She writes, "To an antiquary the Spectators are already a great source of information, and five hundred years hence will be invaluable; though it must be observed, some discernment is necessary to separate the playful exaggerations of humour from the real facts on which they are grounded." Did Barbauld consider her own literary efforts as ones that would "rise in value"? Was she doing unto authors of the past what she hoped, or even trusted, would be done unto her, whether later in life or posthumously?

Her own writings may not have been foremost in her mind when she made such statements, but it is difficult not to see them lurking in the background of her discussions of the fate of past literary compositions. In her preface to *The Female Speaker* (1811), Barbauld refers to the importance of reading in youth and in age. As she puts it, "a familiarity with the most striking passages of our best authors" has an "advantage" "in future life" that is "not small."[33] These striking passages from the best authors are "equally relished in age as in youth. Whoever has been conversant with them in early youth, has laid up in her mind treasures, which, in sickness and in sorrow, in the sleepless night and the solitary day, will sooth the mind with ideas dear to it's [sic] recollection; will come upon it like the remembrance of an early friend, revive the vivid feelings of youth, feed the mind with hope, compose it to resignation, and perhaps dismiss the parting breath with those hallelujahs on the tongue, which awoke the first feelings of love and admiration in the childish bosom" (vi). Good literature may guide us successfully from cradle to grave, she argues. Reading such works is especially important as a youthful investment in creating the conditions for a contented late life.

Although Aikin would have it that her aunt's labors in editing and literary criticism arose almost by default, whether in response to world or life circumstances, it is possible that Barbauld's critical work was chosen as an aging woman's literary gift to posterity. She presented to the public the old letters of, original critical essays on, and new editions of the authors of her youth—the ones that presumably served as her solace in old age—so that their words would not be lost. In the years following her death, Aikin and others would attempt to do the same for Barbauld. That Aikin (herself a long-lived author of no small reputation) undertook this labor at all, given her apparent low regard for editorial and critical work, is something for which we ought to be grateful.[34] Today, it seems a shame that she and her successors did not bring more of Barbauld's manuscripts into print or did not say more about them. It is especially unfortunate because a large number of papers were destroyed in an attack on London during the Second World War (McCarthy and Kraft xxxv).[35] Barbauld's faith in posterity's ability to recognize the "best authors," if she herself may be admitted among those ranks, was not misplaced, but she could not have anticipated that such recognition would come half a century too late to do as much for her as she had done for others.

Barbauld Sallies Forth

When she was engaged in her most influential works of criticism, Barbauld was just over 60 years old—in her green old age. After nearly ten more years of publishing principally editorial and literary critical work, she published new poetry. Her long, prophetic *Eighteen Hundred and Eleven* (1812), and the negative press it generated, is alleged to have ended her career. Such stories appear all too frequently in our literary histories. The publishing careers of Hester Lynch Piozzi, Frances Burney, and Barbauld were all said to have been halted by negative press.[56] In Barbauld's case, the stories are literally untrue, as she continued to publish and to contemplate publication after 1812. In the cases of Burney and Barbauld, it was the same anonymous reviewer who eventually stood accused: the acerbic conservative writer and politician John Wilson Croker (1780–1857) of the *Quarterly Review*. In this section, I look afresh at *Eighteen Hundred and Eleven* and its reception, with an eye to gender and old age, in order to further our sense of what effects this poem's initial critical failure may have had on Barbauld's late career and, ultimately, on her posthumous reputation.

A prophetic poem, *Eighteen Hundred and Eleven* envisioned Great Britain's fall as a world power. Recent critics have been almost of one voice in praising it as a poetic achievement, though assessments of what caused its failure have been enormously varied, with gender, religion, and political climate foremost among the reasons explored. For critic Lucy Newlyn, it was the "generic unclassifiability" of the poem—its "juxtaposition of the familiar and the unfamiliar through prospect and retrospect, its conflation of the elegiac and the satirical, the political and the sentimental" that prevented it from being fully appreciated. Barbauld's "sheer ambitiousness" and "the authority to which she lays claim" are what "offended her contemporary readers."[57] Nicholas Birns argues that it was the impending War of 1812, considered alongside Barbauld's prophetic poem about the costs of globalization, that made her critics so uncomfortable.[58] William Keach finds in the poem a "decisive break" from Barbauld's "meliorist historical perspective," which he suspects was off-putting to her readers, even those who shared her progressive Dissenting ideology (577). It seems likely in this case, as in so many others, that a number of factors contributed to *Eighteen Hundred and Eleven*'s poor reception. One factor among the many that has not yet been given a hearing is old age and ageism.

In Barbauld's own day, most reviewers cited political reasons for their condemnations of the poem. Conservative periodical writers were incensed at Barbauld's message of national doom and her trenchant antiwar criticism, but the poem also made some liberal commentators uncomfortable. They responded "nervously at best" to her becoming a Cassandra of the state (McCarthy and Kraft 310). Although it predicts the future, the poem begins solidly in the present, describing Napoleon's conquests, other nations' capitulations, starving British peasants, dead soldiers, and bereaved mothers, widows, and friends anxiously seeking locations of battles that ended their loved ones' lives. Barbauld's poem moves into the realm of prophecy with the declaration that Britain's "Midas dream is o'er" (154). She makes clear that her country is by her "beloved, revered, / By every tie that binds the soul endeared." It seems obvious that she did not enjoy the poetic vision that she drew—one of London in ruins. That scene was one in which she imagined that foreign travelers would look on the city with "mingled feelings" as its "faded glories rise to view" (157). Great Britain would be honored for its literature and philosophy, but as a national power it would have been decimated, in Barbauld's poetic vision.

Though there is no date named at which the ruin Barbauld imagined would be accomplished, she implies that it has already begun:

> But fairest flowers expand but to decay;
> Thy worm is in thy core, thy glories pass away;
> Arts, arms and wealth destroy the fruits they bring;
> Commerce, like beauty, knows no second spring.
> (McCarthy and Kraft 160–61)

These lines, near the poem's end, describe the reasons for her prognostications. She sees a national fall as inevitable once the country has taken a destructive course. These lines also depict the aging process, linking seasonal and bodily aging to national aging. Barbauld describes it as inevitable that as seasons pass (and flowers decay), as humans age (and beauty fades), so the glories of countries—especially those without a love for liberty—pass away. She predicts that "Genius" will fly from "Europe's desolated shores" to the place where she sees freedom blossoming—the Americas (161).

One need not be an aged writer to use the trope of a body's (or a season's) decline in order to imagine a nation's decline and fall. In Barbauld's hands, though, such a comparison had special resonance. It was universally known that *Eighteen Hundred and Eleven* was the work of a venerable female author. Barbauld's first publication, a critically acclaimed collection of poems, had appeared some forty years earlier. Reviewers emphasized her advanced age in their assessment of the late poem's effectiveness. Many used the fact of her long career in framing their remarks. Most placed their reactions to Barbauld's work in the context of a long line of prior responses they had had to her productions, comparing the present poem unfavorably to her previous works, finding in it the peevishness and joylessness supposedly typical of female old age. The implication seems to have been that reading *Eighteen Hundred and Eleven* was like being disappointed by an old friend, an old teacher—or simply by an old woman writer. At least one reviewer expressed this sentiment directly.

Most reviews merely hinted at Barbauld's old age. The *Monthly Review*'s Christopher Moody focused on a wish that Barbauld had given the poem a later date for its title and expressed the desire that the writings of Barbauld and others would act to "defer the period" of the end of Britain's greatness. Moody also noted that the poem disappoints "as a picture of the present era," implying that Barbauld was not at her best perceiving or writing about the current age, even if it accepted her as a prophet for future ones.[39] The *Anti-Jacobin Review*, which reviewed not only the poem but also the *Monthly Review*'s positive review (no surprise, given Barbauld's association with it), focuses on Barbauld's having been "bred and educated a Dissenter" and argues that she would not have received the *Monthly*'s approbation otherwise.[40] The two reviews did share some elements, however, as the *Anti-Jacobin*, too, marks Barbauld out as old-fashioned.[41] The reviewer writes, "Poets may predict, but the age of *prophecy* has long passed" (204). Barbauld's poem, it would seem, was evidence of her being out of touch with the age in which she lived. The *Eclectic Review* acknowledges the poem's style to be vigorous and "not very common in the productions of a female pen."[42] The reviewer focuses on the poem's departure from Barbauld's previous productions, remarking, "Disposed as we are to receive every performance of Mrs. Barbauld with peculiar cordiality, yet her choice of a subject in this instance . . . is so unfortunate, that we scarcely ever read a poem of equal merit with so little pleasure" (475). That was then, the reviewer implies, but this is now.

In private letters, too, readers wondered about how their responses to *Eighteen Hundred and Eleven* ought to be squared with Barbauld's advanced age. Sir Walter Scott is "sorry the Quarterly Revw. has been savage on Mrs. Barbauld for whose talents I have had long and sincere respect," even though he could not condemn the principle of their criticism.[43] The poet Elizabeth Cobbold (apparently personally unacquainted with Barbauld) writes to her friend Sir

James Edward Smith on 26 March 1812 that she has read the just published poem and cannot approve of it: "It is in a high strain of poetry, and possesses a fire of genius and force of language which I should not have expected from her advanced age and what I had seen of her earlier productions; but if I were offered the powers of genius, together with the feelings manifested in that poem, I would reject the combination as a dangerous and deadly gift."[44] Smith disagreed heartily in his reply of 30 March 1812, telling Cobbold that "I did not doubt your admiring Mrs. Barbauld's *poetry;* indeed, I think this poem (without any allowance for her age) may take its stand amongst the most lofty productions of any poet, male or female" (2: 178). He then quotes from one of her hymns, first published in the 1770s, and says that it is the most sublime and poetical of its kind ever written, without making any allowance for her *youth* or her sex. In each case, Barbauld's age becomes important to the reader's evaluation of her poetry.

Several reviews also linked Barbauld's aging to the poem's political message in terms similar to those she herself had used. The *Eclectic Review* understands the poem as "almost . . . unfilial" (475). In a reversal of the way we might expect a long admired female author to be discussed, the review imagines the poet as a faithless daughter and Great Britain as her aged mother:

> Such is her [Barbauld's] eagerness to read a lecture on morbid anatomy, and display her knowledge of the appearances *post mortem*, that she actually begins to demonstrate on the body of her venerable parent [Great Britain], while she is yet in very tolerable health; and in doing this preserves all the while such perfect composure, as to us is absolutely astonishing. The old lady herself will not relish this treatment, we are sure. She will undoubtedly observe, that she considers herself a very good life at present, and has so little doubt of surviving all her existing progeny, that instead of punishing her graceless daughter [Barbauld] by cutting her off with a shilling, she will frown on her through life, and finally take ample vengeance by inscribing an epitaph on her tomb. (474–75)

On a first reading, it is unclear which "old lady" the reviewer might be referring to. Is it Barbauld or her country? But it becomes evident that "old lady" Great Britain will have the last laugh over "old lady" Barbauld—herself made to seem youthful in comparison—by writing her epitaph.

The notorious review—the one that led Maria Edgeworth to write to Barbauld about her "indignation" and "disgust" and that nearly provoked her to snatch up a pen and respond—was the *Quarterly*'s, now attributed to Croker.[45] He begins his diatribe on the author and the poem by invoking the age of the former: "Our old acquaintance Mrs. Barbauld turned satirist! The last thing we should have expected, and, now that we have seen her satire, the last thing that we could have desired" (309). Croker then emphasizes his own comparative lack of age—at the risk of impugning his own wisdom—to highlight Barbauld's advance in life: "May we (without derogating too much from that reputation of age and gravity of which critics should be so chary) confess that we are yet young enough to have had early obligations to Mrs. Barbauld; and that it really is with no disposition to retaliate on the fair peda-gogue of our former life, that on the present occasion, we have called her up to correct her exercise?" (309). Croker imagines Barbauld, the aged teacher of his far-away youth, changing places with him and playing ignorant pupil to face his supposedly reluctant corrections. This infantilizing rhetoric is con-tinued when Croker implies that Barbauld may be losing her literary facul-ties, describing her as having "wandered from the course in which she was respectable and useful" (309). He writes of her composing from a misguided sense of "irresistible impulse of public duty" that compelled her to "dash down her shagreen spectacles and her knitting needles" and to "sally forth" as the author of the poem under review.[46]

In his description of Barbauld sallying forth—giving up the usual garb of an old woman or spinster for the costume of political pamphleteer—Croker paints a picture of an aged female Quixote, foolishly leaving hearth and home to save the world.[47] Though he doesn't know where Barbauld lives, Croker says it is not on Parnassus and must be in some "equally unfrequented" re-gion (310). Unbeknownst to her, Barbauld has become humorously isolated, beyond her prime, and working outside of her own abilities, Croker implies. He ends his review with a serious message—that Barbauld's "former works have been of some utility" and, though not displaying much taste or talent, "are yet something better than harmless" (313). He warns her that she should "desist from satire," it being "satire on herself alone" (313). He couches this reproach in generational terms, claiming to speak to age for all youth, ear-nestly begging "she will not, for the sake of this ungrateful generation, put herself to the trouble of writing any more party pamphlets in verse" (313).

The tradition has been to report that Barbauld was "deeply wounded by the insults and personal remarks which this poem . . . received from the preju-dice and malignancy of a critic" (Ellis 278–79). There seems no reason to doubt that she was upset, but the myth that Croker's review ended Barbauld's publishing career seems to have originated with her first biographer. Aikin writes in her 1825 memoir, "This was the last of Mrs. Barbauld's separate publications. Who indeed, that knew and loved her, could have wished her to expose again that honoured head to the scorns of the unmanly, the malignant, and the base?" (Barbauld, *Works* lii). Aikin especially laments this "unmanly" review because Barbauld would have welcomed, been cheered by, and had her energy revived by the respectful greetings "which it was once the generous and graceful practice of contemporary criticism to welcome the re-appearance of a well-deserving veteran in the field of letters."[48] Barbauld was treated in a manner neither befitting her sex nor her age, Aikin claims. The result was said to have been devastating to Barbauld in her remaining years, though she put her faith in posterity: "She even laid aside the intention which she had entertained of preparing a new edition of her Poems, long out of print and often inquired for in vain;—well knowing that a day must come when the sting of Envy would be blunted, and her *memory* would have its fame" (liii). The *Quarterly's* review, Aikin alleges, prompted Barbauld to leave her writings in the hands of future editors, rather than to arrange them herself, for fear of inciting further criticism. If Aikin is correct, Croker's review was highly persuasive. It convinced Barbauld to avoid putting her work before the ungrateful generation that Croker claimed to represent until after her death.

There is good reason to question Aikin's version of events about the effect of the review on Barbauld's publishing career. *Eighteen Hundred and Eleven* was not the last time she published new work. Her poem, "A Thought on Death," first mysteriously published in the United States, appeared in the *Monthly Repository* in 1822, advertised as Barbauld's and "written in her *Eightieth Year*"; this publication was followed a month later by a signed note from her, offering a corrected version of the poem, both of which the *Monthly Repository* printed.[49] She wrote a memoir attached to a publication by her friend Dr. J. P. Estlin and continued to publish short poems (signed, unsigned, and pseudonymous) in the *Annual Register, Monthly Magazine, Monthly Repository,* and *Ladies Monthly Museum.*[50] She continued her extensive anonymous reviewing in the *Monthly Review.*[51] The accuracy of Aikin's statement may rest with how we understand "separate publication." If it means a single-authored book, Aikin is accurate, but her words have circulated as something more wide ranging. It is customary to claim that the negative review led Barbauld *never again* to seek print.[52] This is simply not the case. She continued to write and sought publication for poems and prose.

Aikin also claims that the *Quarterly's* review stopped Barbauld's plans to edit a volume of her poems, but it is unclear whether or when Barbauld gave up her plan to prepare a new edition. In a letter to Joanna Baillie from 2 February 1822, Barbauld expresses reluctance to provide her with verses requested for a proposed collection to be published for charity: "With regard to your request I cannot say it is particularly agreeable to me to part with one of my poems for a collection, because I have not entirely relinquished the intention of publishing them myself, & I have so very few that I hardly know how to spare one" (Rodgers 242). She accedes to the request because she cannot refuse Baillie or the good cause, offering a poem that has been previously published, one apparently suggested by Baillie. A 20 March 1822 letter asks Baillie please to publish both the "trifle" and the "other" poem which she had thought of before.[53] Then Barbauld changes her tone, suggesting that the publication of her verses by Baillie "would not hinder me, I presume, from printing either of them should I think of collecting my scatter'd pieces, as I sometimes do, but many are the things I think of & never accomplish. If at the close of life some may be tolerably acquitted of having done the things they ought to have done, very few of us indeed are not sensible of having left undone those things we ought to have done." Barbauld's intention to prepare an edition of her poems for publication seems more equivocal in these letters than the decided refusal that Aikin's posthumous memoir pronounces. It is possible that Barbauld's letter itself deserves our skepticism, as her note to Baillie may have been written as a kind of press release to a fellow author. The March 1822 letter, in particular, seems to seek encouragement for completing the task, and it is conceivable that Barbauld hoped Baillie would take a role in seeking an editor. In the end, Barbauld (unlike Baillie) apparently had no hand in preparing for publication her own "complete works."[54]

Barbauld's *not* editing her own writings in late life cleared the way for Aikin's account of the effect that *Eighteen Hundred and Eleven* had on Barbauld's career. It was the principal one that circulated after Barbauld's death, though it also competed with less sympathetic interpretations—following Croker—about the soundness of Barbauld's mind. Jerom Murch, in his study of Barbauld, suggests that the widely held belief at the time her last long poem was published was that Barbauld was losing her faculties, as a result of the death of her husband in 1808. Murch writes, "It has been stated with reference to her last important poem that her mind had not regained its usual healthy tone. There is no doubt that she long suffered severely, but the poem should be judged on its own merits, and few persons would admit that it deserved the bitter criticism with which it was assailed."[55] After thus giving some credence to the likes of Croker, Murch returns to the line of reasoning offered by

Aikin: "Mrs. Barbauld lived fourteen years after the publication of this poem. Her powers were still vigorous; her fancy retained all its brightness, but the harp was hung upon the willows. She felt so deeply the misconstruction of angry critics that she wrote nothing more of much importance, though her kindness and gentleness were more conspicuous than ever" (86). As if these myths were not damaging enough to Barbauld's reputation as an author in old age, an American biographer of women, Sarah Hale, further perverted the distortions of Aikin and Croker. Hale claimed that Barbauld's "husband died in 1808, and Mrs. Barbauld has recorded her feelings on this melancholy event in a poetical dirge to his memory, and also in her poem 'Eighteen Hundred and Eleven.' "[56] Barbauld's controversial and moving political poem is misrepresented as an elegy on her late husband.

Traditional versions of her late life—Barbauld the happy-go-lucky old lady, Barbauld the silenced prophetic poet, or Barbauld the accidental editor/critic—do not hold much water. Ageist responses of the literary public during her lifetime and well-meaning misconstructions by her own niece and others thereafter continue to warp our perceptions of Barbauld's important, sustained late work. Barbauld's namesake and great-niece Anna Letitia Le Breton left an account of Barbauld's final years that may provide a helpful springboard for revisionary work. The elderly writer's steadfast independence during her last years is illustrated by her response to a robbery in her home:

> [The burglars] entered a small parlour on the ground floor, and completely sacked it, as well as the dining room adjoining it, actually taking up and carrying off a large carpet among other things. My aunt [Barbauld] slept in a room above adjoining the drawing-room; not only alone, but two stories below the [two female] servants, whose room was reached by a separate staircase. We were dreadfully alarmed for her when the news came to us in town; . . . she was perfectly cool and calm, however; only remarking how lucky it was they had not come up stairs, as she had a good deal of money in her desk; and she would not be persuaded to alter her arrangements, or have a maid near her. (Le Breton, *Memories* 42)

Barbauld appears to have been equally unflappable in her late travels and correspondence. Her last journey was to Bristol, where she paid a visit to her "old friends," Dr. and Mrs. Estlin (49). From there, she went to see her "very old friend" and fellow writer Hannah More (1745–1833), with whom she stayed for several days. In a letter to her brother John Aikin, Barbauld describes her visit to More and her sisters, who were "all good old maids."[57] Barbauld reports that she and More "exchanged riddles, like the wise men of old," an amusing redeployment of the common linkage of old age and masculine wisdom (50).

At least one nineteenth-century literary critic seems to have more accurately captured the outlines of Barbauld's late life. In *Looking toward Sunset* (1865), an extremely popular collection of writings on old age designed as "words of consolation and cheer" to the old, American writer Lydia Maria Child predictably included the last stanza of Barbauld's poem "Life." Child introduces the poem, noting that Barbauld "lived to be nearly eighty-two years old. She employed the latter part of her life in editing a series of the best English novels and essays, accompanied with biographical sketches of the authors; and compositions in prose and verse continued to be her favorite occupation to the last."[58] This short paragraph on Barbauld's old age encapsulates its professional contours, albeit in sentimental, romanticized terms. Nonetheless, it is an important example of an older woman author grasping the varied writing life of another. As studies of Barbauld deepen and evolve, the full impact of her long life and late career—both on their own terms and in terms of literary history—deserve more nuanced retellings. This chapter provides a springboard for future work, by returning Barbauld's late life critical and editorial contributions to the record, speculating on what motivated this work in her old age and demonstrating the ways in which the harsh reviews she faced were centrally buttressed by ageism, even if driven by political, sex-based, and religious prejudice.

CHAPTER SIX

Jane Porter and the Old Woman Writer's Quest for Financial Independence

My sunshine of youth is no more!
My mornings of pleasure are fled!
'Tis painful my fate to endure—
A pension supplies me with bread!
Dependant at length on the man
Whose fortunes I struggled to raise!
I conquer my pride as I can—
His charity merits my praise!
>   —*John Cunningham, "Verses by Mr. Cunningham,*
>   *Written about Three Weeks before His Death" (ca. 1773)*

Jane Porter (bap. 1776–1850) did not enter into her twilight years unthinkingly. As an author who lived much of her adult life with her beloved sister (author Anna Maria Porter [1780–1832]) and their widowed mother, Porter knew that old age brought financial challenges for the unmarried woman writer.[1] Though the sisters enjoyed early fame and considerable acclaim, by the time they reached middle age, supporting themselves by writing had become a burden. Jane Porter had a vision of a female author's ideal old age. She longed for the steady income not common to writers, just as she hoped to revive her literary reputation. She began very deliberately to try to build toward this vision in late middle age. Repeatedly, however, her plans were derailed, whether by a death in the family, a bank's failure, an unrealized sum from a promised bequest, or a rejected request for monetary assistance. Although each part of her story deserves a more complete telling, it is Porter's quest for a pension—and the ways in which that episode has played a heretofore unknown role in her career as an author in late middle and old age—to which I turn in this chapter.

Porter published no new full-length works in old age. She did not pursue a late life novel or memoir, as Frances Burney and Maria Edgeworth did, and she does not appear to have completed book-length nonfiction works designed for publication, as Hester Lynch Piozzi did. Porter did not pen poems about history or old age or edit and introduce the works of previous generations, as did Anna Letitia Barbauld. But like Catharine Macaulay before her, Porter appears to have felt acutely the waning of her laurels, and she lived long enough to fight for her reputation, in private and public, under her own name and anonymously. Some of this struggle is evident in the voluminous prefaces and postscripts she added to her most popular novels when they were republished in new editions during the last decades of her life. The bulk of the information about her struggles, however, lies in her unpublished manuscripts and letters.

Porter's labors in late life were not tied up with working toward new success in the literary marketplace, but she did engage in efforts to make it possible to retire comfortably. Perhaps she knew, as historian L. A. Botelho writes that "the foundations of how one's old age would be experienced (both materially and emotionally) were often laid in youth and middle age."[2] Porter's is a story worth telling, as it provides a picture of a different kind of resourcefulness in old age from those we have seen in previous chapters. Porter did not want run-of-the-mill charity, assistance she viewed as insulting her respectability and assaulting her dignity, but she was not above making pleas for state monies as she sought remuneration coupled with recognition. In her own day, from among the limited means that were available to women writers, Porter aspired to a royal or governmental pension to honor her literary service. Though she never received the pension she so doggedly sought, her petitions resulted in compensation that contributed to her ability to maintain, however precariously, a middle-class standard of living. Porter's case demonstrates that it was possible for a celebrated aged woman author in reduced circumstances to live off of her former fame.

Jane Porter and the Royal Assignment

In the early 1820s, Jane Porter took on a project that a fellow female author had refused. Late in her life, Porter wrote of having accepted an assignment from a royal emissary, who asked her, on behalf of the king, to write a historical novel based on his royal forebears. If this story sounds familiar, it is because Jane Austen was encouraged to do the same—and famously declined. In her 1816 letter to Royal Librarian James Stanier Clarke, Austen writes:

> You are very, very kind in your hint as to the sort of Composition which might recommend me at present, & I am fully sensible that an Historical Romance, founded on the house of Saxe Cobourg might be much more to the purpose of Profit or Popularity, than such pictures of domestic life in Country Villages as I deal in—but I could no more write a Romance than an Epic Poem.—I could not sit seriously down to write a serious Romance under any other motive than to save my Life, & if it were indispensable for me to keep it up & never relax into laughing at myself or other people, I am sure I should be hung before I had finished the first Chapter.—No—I must keep to my own style & go on in my own Way; And though I may never succeed again in that, I am convinced that I should totally fail in any other.[3]

Instead of writing Clarke's desired royal historical romance, Austen worked on *Persuasion* (1818). The exchange between Austen and Clarke now looms large in accounts of her life. The episode is read by some as displaying her steadfast irony and by others as revealing her straightforward self-deprecation. In either case, the interaction with Clarke is generally presented as a momentous one in Austen's career as an author.

In a story earlier told but now much less circulated, Jane Porter, too, was said to have received such an invitation from Clarke. We know the details from Porter's own pen, as she described it in the "Recollective Preface" (1840) attached to the newly revised edition of her popular novel *The Scottish Chiefs* (1810). According to that account, Porter's invitation from Clarke came— unbeknownst to her—several years after Austen's. Though Porter's narrative is less well known, her interaction with Clarke was, if anything, more significant. Twenty years after the fact, Porter describes for the public the circumstances of Clarke's proposal: "Dr. Clarke . . . librarian to our then Sovereign George the Fourth . . . told me that his Majesty . . . took my early published volumes from the royal shelf, and was so satisfied with the historical fidelity of the heroes they portrayed that Dr. Clarke was commanded to communicate to me his Majesty's gracious request that my next subject should be 'The Life of his great and virtuous progenitor, Duke Christian of Luneburg.' "[4] Porter attributes her invitation to chance (the king happening to take her book off of the shelf) and to a virtual royal decree (a "gracious request" that was also a "command"). Her fictional account of the royal family's ancestors appeared as *Duke*

Christian of Luneburg; or, Tradition from the Hartz (1824). As Porter put it in
1840, "I could but obey so distinguishing a command, and the royal goodness soon
furnished me with many original documents for the building up of my story. . . .
When it was published, I was honoured by an assurance from my gracious
Sovereign that 'it had been completed to his fullest wishes'" (1: 39–40).

Why would Porter have been tempted to complete a novel to the "fullest
wishes" of her sovereign? Unlike Austen, Porter published her major works
under her own name and achieved great fame in her lifetime. Her most successful novels went through many editions, regularly republished into her old
age. *Thaddeus of Warsaw* (1803) was her novel of a fictional Polish military
hero in the 1790s. *The Scottish Chiefs* (1810) told the story of William Wal-
lace and Scotland in the thirteenth century. Her third best-known novel, *The
Pastor's Fire-Side* (1817), featured the imaginary English son of the Spanish
duke of Ripperda in the 1720s. Each of these novels went through multiple
editions. Could not Porter, like Austen, afford to reject a bid for profit and
popularity—the terms through which Austen saw Clarke's invitation? Porter's
letters show that the circumstances that led to the writing of *Duke Christian*
differed from those she would later claim in print. Choosing to write a historical romance based on the royal family's ancestors was driven by concerns for her
financial well being in late life. Bringing an account of the episode out of the
archives deepens our sense of the relationship of Porter's aging to the literary
careers of Austen and Sir Walter Scott, as well as to other writers who sought
(successfully or not) to turn their early fame into a regular late-life income.

The overlapping circumstances and opposite choices of the two Janes have
always reflected more poorly on Porter and more admirably on Austen. Austen
is said to have stood her ground and maintained her authorial dignity, choosing to "go her own way," rather than to capitulate to His Majesty or mam-
mon. Austen's refusal is called "polite," while Porter's acceptance produced a
work whose hero was so perfect that it "not surprisingly" "met with full royal
approval."[5] One twentieth-century critic comments slyly on Porter's choice, as
if it is risible—and a joke that Austen herself would have been in on: "One
can imagine how Jane Austen, had she lived, would have smiled" (Jones 136).
A recent short biography of Porter labels her "more cooperative" than Austen
where the royal invitation was concerned.[6]

Characterizations of a fawning, malleable, or greedy Porter and an upright,
self-determining Austen are not of recent vintage. Early twentieth-century
literary critic Mona Wilson, contrasting the two writers, cites the demurring
letter of the "greater Jane" and notes that Porter, "on the other hand, duti-

fully wrote" for Clarke and the king.[7] Before Wilson, Sarah Tytler thought it strange that "two such women as Jane Austen and Jane Porter—equal in moral worth, though standing on very different intellectual heights—should have eagerly availed themselves of the permission to dedicate books to George IV."[8] Tytler writes, "what is if possible stranger, is that the Prince Regent should have been, even professedly, an admiring, assiduous reader of the novels —altogether apart in literary merit, but alike in good tone and taste—of these two upright and blameless women" (29). Defending Porter as a woman but selling short her literary skill, Tytler admits that the "so-called historical novels were in Miss Porter's way and not in Miss Austen's" (30).

These stories have given us one view of Porter's late life—that of an unsuccessful, fawning sycophant. Because she accepted Clarke's invitation, Porter has long been viewed in contrast to Austen as having degraded herself, prostituting her talents in order to advance her success at court. This is an incomplete if not inaccurate version of Porter's old age. As her unpublished correspondence shows, Porter's desires for advantage from *Duke Christian* were directed, on the one hand, toward her brother, the travel writer, military man, and artist Robert Ker Porter (1777–1842). She was anxious to secure Robert's future as a diplomat and wistfully envisioned herself sitting at his feet, happily serving as his private secretary.[9] Jane hoped that favor from the king might advance Robert's career as a diplomat, relieving her of the need to publish, as well as freeing her brother from having to scramble to provide financial support for his mother and sisters.[10] The personal economic benefit that Porter most hoped to receive after writing *Duke Christian*, though, was a royal pension to support herself and sister Anna Maria in their old age.

The story of *Duke Christian*—Porter's last single-authored novel—is one undergirded by the fear of an impoverished old age. In 1821, when Porter first contemplated writing *Duke Christian*, she was in her late forties, unmarried (as she would remain), and in need of money. Her most recent novel, *The Pastor's Fire-Side*, had taken years to write and, though respectably successful, was not as profitable as her previous efforts had been. *The Scottish Chiefs* "was one of the most widely read and influential texts produced during the Romantic period," Gary Kelly notes.[11] But it had been ten years since its publication, and Porter's writing career was in a slump. The Porters perpetually struggled financially to maintain their place in polite society.[12] They were in debt for hundreds of pounds to their friends, to their publishers (who regularly provided them with advances against their next novels), and to their creditors, who they feared would realize their plight and take collective action. Porter's choosing to write a novel on assignment takes on a different meaning in such a context. By the late 1810s, she felt she had been passed over for the literary accolades that were her due. Using her writing to please a potential royal patron—and perhaps to secure a pension—may have seemed a better bet than counting on renewed success with the fickle reading public.

The idea of Clarke's asking at least two women to write a historical romance is not in itself surprising. The genre was extremely fashionable. Today we associate it principally with one name: Sir Walter Scott, long seen as its originator. Many of his contemporaries, including Austen, suspected that the anonymously published *Waverley* (1814) was the product of his pen. In an 1814 letter to her niece Anna, Austen complains, "Walter Scott has no business to write novels, especially good ones.—It is not fair" (*Letters* 277). Because "He has Fame & Profit enough as a Poet," Austen quips, he "should not be taking the bread out of other people's mouths." She concludes, "I do not like him [Scott], & do not mean to like Waverley if I can help it—but fear I must." Joking or not, Austen was obviously frustrated with Scott's successful move into *her* genre, despite leading Clarke to believe two years later that she thought historical romances and fictional pictures of domestic life were very different.

Scott was neither the first nor the only author writing historical fiction during the Regency period. Indeed, the phrase "historical novel" was used as the subtitle of several productions of the 1790s, including E. M. Foster's *The Duke of Clarence* (1795) and *Jaquelina of Hainault* (1798); and *Charles Dacres; or, The Voluntary Exile* (1797), which proposes to *"shew men as they are."*[13] But the phrase long predates that period, found as a subtitle in fiction translated from French, such as *The Count de Rethel* (1779), Claudine Tencin's *The Siege of Calais* (1740), and *The Lady's Philosopher's Stone* (1725).[14] Though its significance no doubt changed across the period, the term "historical novel" was in use in the early eighteenth century.[15] Fictional works with "historical romance" or "founded on facts" in their subtitles appeared in significant numbers in English texts from the 1760s on but particularly after the late 1780s. Until Scott, however, few of these novels rivaled in popular success Porter's contributions to the genre. P. D. Garside shows that Scott, in "inventing" the historical novel, drew heavily on the fiction of female predecessors. Garside argues that "the Waverley novels first emerged at a time when male authorship was at an unusually low ebb; though from 1820 the position changes sharply, and by the later 1820s, no doubt partly because of Scott's influence, male novelists are dominant."[16] This claim is supported with statistical evidence drawn from publication histories that demonstrate how

Scott and his historical fiction, directly or indirectly, had a hand in squeezing women novelists out of the literary marketplace.

As it turns out, at least one of Porter's contemporaries also noticed the phenomenon. The anonymous reviewer of *Reginald Dalton* (1823) writes, "It is, we apprehend, chiefly to be attributed to the success of the 'Waverley novels,' that so many men of distinguished talents have within these last few years devoted their pens to works of imagination" (200).[17] This rise of the male novelist, the reviewer recognizes, is a change, "for, fifteen years since, all the popular novelists of the day, with a very few exceptions, prefixed Mrs. or Miss to their names" (200). He lists, "Miss Edgeworth, Miss Austen, Miss Benger, Miss Owenson, the two Misses Porter, Mrs. West, Mrs. Brunton, Mrs. Opie, &c. &c." The reviewer then implies that the women have been forced out because they have not produced new work:

> Since that period, however, the ladies have been almost driven from the field of fiction by the hosts of powerful writers of the masculine gender who have occupied it. The most serious incursion has been made by our neighbors the Scotch, the well-known "Unknown" [Scott] leading the way. . . . These masculine writers have at length almost entirely superseded their feminine predecessors. Even Miss Edgeworth's pen has been idle since the publication of her *Patronage*; and Miss Anna Maria Porter's romantic heroes now seldom make their appearance. Mrs. Opie's Tales have become "few and far between," and if we except the fair writer of "The Favorite of Nature," no new female writer has for some years past appeared before the public with any claims to celebrity as a novelist. (200)

Some of this reviewer's claims are preposterous. Austen could not have produced new works, as she was no longer living, but others on the list must have been enraged to see the falsehood spread that they had stopped publishing.[18] New works of fiction by Anna Maria Porter had appeared in 1817, 1818, 1821, and 1822. Indeed, the very month in which this review was printed, Jane Porter published *Duke Christian*.

Scott himself may not personally have been to blame for stealing the thunder of these women writers, though as Ina Ferris, Michael Gamer, April London, and others have shown, Scott was both aware of and trying to distance himself from the "femininity" of the novel.[19] Scott ultimately credited some women writers, such as Maria Edgeworth, for spurring his move into historical romance. In the postscript to *Waverley* (1829), Scott cites Edgeworth and two other female authors, Elizabeth Hamilton (1758–1816) and Anne MacVicar

Grant (1755–1838), whose work he says prompted his own.[20] Despite his grati-tude, he goes to great pains to distinguish his writing from that of all three women. Edgeworth, he says, he emulates in a "distant degree," as she is deal-ing with Irish subjects (5). The work of Elizabeth Hamilton, he claims, is "confined" to "rural habits," while Anne MacVicar Grant's work is "distinct from fictitious narrative." But in acknowledging these female authors as hav-ing reinspired him—after he allegedly started *Waverley* but put it away in a drawer and mislaid it for some years—he ignores authors who might more obviously be classed as his predecessors. Nowhere does he mention Jane or Anna Maria Porter, whom he apparently had known since childhood, infor-mation that would make his omission all the more striking.[21] By 1845, it could be claimed that Porter and Maria Edgeworth followed Scott into historical fiction, after he "made this way of writing at once popular and catching."[22]

Much remains to be said about the Porters' complex personal and autho-rial relationship to Scott.[23] It is enough to note here that Jane Porter felt the lack of homage from the Waverley author strongly. Indeed, she and her sister believed that the writer stole his ideas for, if not actual material from, their works. In 1819, Anna Maria writes to Jane that the Waverley author "evidently uses *our* novels as a sort of store house" from which "he draws unobserved whatever odd bit of furniture strikes his fancy for his own pompous edifice. I do not say he steals the thing itself, but the idea & fashion of it, and if he had the honesty to shew that he thought well of our writings, by a hand or two of such commendation as he liberally give to works that have no resemblance to his own, I should say the conduct was fair and allowable. But I quarrel with the self-interestedness of working the hints we give him, yet never owning that he does" (HL, POR 819). It is important to note that Scott was not the only author against whom the Porter sisters leveled charges of neglect or out-right theft. In another letter to her sister Jane in 1815, Anna Maria complains that she reads poet Robert Southey's work with a little "mist-rising" because he has "rifled" "unacknowledged" all of the "best parts" of one of her nov-els (728). A letter from Jane to Anna Maria shows that she agrees with her sister. Jane writes of Southey as having stolen from their novels in his latest poem, complaining, "It is monstrous how these poets play the vampire with our works.—I beg of you to read it.—Some time or other, I think I shall be provoked to give the public the real Genealogy of these matters" (1707).

For many years, Porter appears to have resisted being so provoked. It is pos-sible that she had a hand in one of the published reviews of *Duke Christian*, which refers to Porter as the author of a "new species . . . of literary fiction" and to Scott as "only a follower in her wake."[24] Further references to her fictional innovations would follow, eventually in a work to which she signed her own name. In her "The Author to Her Friendly Readers," a preface to the Standard Novels edition of *Thaddeus of Warsaw* (1831), she broke her silence, laying out the matter as she had long seen it. There, she claims that it was "Sir Walter Scott; who did me the honor to adopt the style or class of novel of which 'Thaddeus of Warsaw' was the first:—a class which, uniting the personages and facts of real history or biography, with a combining and illustrative machinery of the imagination, formed a new species of writing in that day."[25] She reiterates that her *Thaddeus of Warsaw* and *Scottish Chiefs* were "both published in England, and translated into various languages abroad, many years before the literary wonder of Scotland gave to the world his transcendent story of Waverley" (vi).

Porter's claims were received with skepticism. One critic published a sarcastic letter addressed to Porter, in which he mocks her with, "What is Sir Walter Scott but an imitator of Miss Jane Porter?"[26] The letter writer, who signs himself "Peter Puff," comments directly on Porter's claims of having been the first to form a new species of writing: "Believe us, Miss Porter, when we read this fine passage, we blushed as red as our morocco slippers at our disgraceful ignorance. Well acquainted with your novels as we were, and having a little more intimate acquaintance with Sir Walter Scott's, we assure you we never discovered that Sir Walter had adopted the style of your romances, until you so kindly informed us that such was the case. When the great truth at last flashed on our minds, it is impossible to describe our feelings" (553). Puff tears into Porter for her supposed lack of modesty and teases her about who precisely has copied—or even plagiarized—from whom. Porter's own statements, Puff writes, "render any criticism on your works almost superfluous" (556). He scornfully claims that the world has been unaware that "Sir Walter Scott has been enjoying the honours rightly due to Miss Porter!" (553). Scott, he writes, "has been made a baronet by George IV, while you, Immortal Madam, have languished in untitled obscurity, and your works been read only by the discerning devourers of circulating libraries!" Scott's favors from George IV in comparison to Porter's lack of them ran deeper than this writer may have known.

"I have a hope": Jane Porter's Dream of Independence

Given Porter's longstanding sense of Scott's literary debt to her, it is not surprising that Scott himself (or at least the idea of Scott) played a role in her writing of *Duke Christian*. In one of Jane Porter's long, private letters to her brother Robert, she gives an account of the genesis of her royal romance. In September 1821, Jane asks Robert to save her letter, "because hereafter, I may like to recall to memory, some exact account . . . on the principle of the work I have in meditation" (HL, POR 2045). When she had an occasion to recall to memory those circumstances to the public many years later, Porter elected to gloss over and even to alter some of the key details. Some of those suppressed particulars relate to flattering comparisons to Scott, while others relate to her hopes for the work as a vehicle for a comfortable old age.

In her old age, as we have seen, Porter led readers to believe that she had been "commanded" by George IV through Clarke to write *Duke Christian*. This is at best a partial version of events. If her 1821 letter is the more accurate account, as seems likely, the major player in forwarding the idea of a work of fiction based on the king's ancestors was not Clarke but Sir Andrew Halliday (1781–1839), physician to the duke of Clarence, later William IV. Halliday, himself an author, published treatises on lunatic asylums and on military and historical subjects, and he first met the Porter sisters on their visit to Carlton House. As Jane tells Robert,

> last May, when I went up to town, to personally thank Dr. Clarke for the really handsome manner in which he had at last obtained the Royal Permission for the Dedication of your Work [*Travels in Georgia, Persia, Armenia, Ancient Babylonia, &c. &c.: During the Years 1817, 1818, 1819, and 1820* (1821)], I was, as I before mentioned to you, then so very unwell that I could not go over Carlton House with the good Doctor, who wished to shew Maria its state-rooms & c.—I remained below in the Library, with Sir Andrew Haliday [sic], a man of Letters, and a warm-hearted Scotsman.—I had never seen him before; but he soon got on my old ground of William Wallace; and I found that book had given me a friend in him. (HL, POR 2045)

Halliday and Porter had a conversation about literary subjects, and it was he who introduced the idea of her writing a historical romance about royal ancestors. The hook that Halliday used to get Jane Porter's rapt attention was a story comparing her novels to Scott's.

Halliday is said to have confessed to Porter that, one year earlier, in the very room in which they were talking, the king and Scott had had a conversation. After "much admiration" was "expressed of the Tales of My Landlord and Waverley," Halliday told Scott, "Well Sir, who ever may be the author of those Novels; you, Sir Walter, must allow that the foundations of them all, were laid by Miss Porter in her Scottish Chiefs." (HL, POR 2045). Scott's reply was said to be, "I grant it . . . there is something in what you say." One can only imagine how gratifying a story like this must have been to Porter. This compliment alone might have been enough to predispose her toward Halliday's project. "Whether this conversation had made the king think more highly of my talents, I know not," Jane tells Robert, "but in the continuation of our discourse Sir Andrew suddenly asked me, whether I had ever turned my mind towards the interesting annals of His Majesty's Hanoverian ancestors?" Porter was ashamed to admit she had not, as she said they had never entered her head.

Halliday suggested as a subject for her next historical romance the admirable Duke Christian of Brunswick Luneburg. She reports that Halliday added, "with a peculiar emphasis, 'I can assure you, nothing would please the king so much, as your writing a romance on that hero!'" This line seems to have hit Porter like a bolt of lightning: "I was struck with Sir Andrew's manner; and with the opening that Providence appeared to be laying before me, for some future advantage, possibly, to myself and family; and in some emotion at heart, for I did not let it be seen, I replied, that nothing would delight me more, if the subject really struck my feelings; for without the sort of inspiration which enthusiasm gives, I could do nothing.—And in this, I said the fact" (HL, POR 2045). Based on her first thoughts of potential future advantage, Porter promised to go home, read the book Halliday had loaned to her treating the archives of Brunswick, and write to him about whether she believed she could manage the subject. She ended the conference with the request not to mention the matter to anyone. The exception to this dictum was, of course, Clarke and the king, to whom Halliday was to bring the matter. Porter was assured that, once an agreement had been reached, the matter would remain a secret until the novel was published.

Porter's letter to her brother is explicit about the kind of future advantage Porter imagines might result from her taking on the royal assignment: "I have a hope, that hereafter Maria's old age & mine may be rendered moderately independent by some pension from His Majesty. Indeed, I think, should my work really please him, that he may volunteer such a work in his favour"

(HL, POR 2045). In this wish, she claims also to be thinking of Robert. Jane writes, "should we get any pension from the king, then, my beloved Robert, of not another guinea would we ever again so cruelly deprive you." Her subsequent letters to her brother reinforce her private wishes, adding the additional wrinkle—apparently alluded to by Halliday—that it was the king's intention to bestow another knighthood on Sir Robert as soon as Jane would present the Royal Library with her work on the Brunswick hero (2047).[27]

A friendship with Halliday developed quickly, but the historical romance came along slowly. By January 1823, Jane tells Robert that she "shall leave no stone unturned in interest for you" but that her "own work [i.e., *Duke Christian*] has not advanced"; she then hopes to finish it by May, if she is able to make herself a hermit (HL, POR 2059). By the following November she anticipates its publication in January of 1824, and it was finally published in February. When the work was about to launch, Porter began her attempts to use it to secure herself a pension. She tells Robert, "by the time you could arrive here . . . I should have fully known whether *I* am to get anything for ourselves, from the Royal munificence. I mean to consult Lady Anne Barnard about *properly presenting* the Work, when it is ready; and *how* to put the K[ing]—in possession of the fact, that a pension would be most gratefully received.—I would *briefly* give a story of ourselves to H. M.—to Interest, but not to *lower* us in *any way*. The Sentiments of my Work, dearest Robert, are loyal to the heart, and they are Magna Charta!—I 'would not flatter Cesar for his disdain!' Hence, if I win gold, I may wear it honourably" (2067). She ends her letter feeling optimistic about the possibility of *Duke Christian* prompting a diplomatic post for Robert and reiterates, "should it yield me a pension too, how it would smooth our paths every where!"

The path did not run smooth. In Porter's dedication of *Duke Christian* to George IV, she describes him as "a father in the bosom of his family" in his "comprehensive care" over an empire.[28] But he did not immediately take the flattering hint to offer charity to her as a poor relation of the nation. When the work was published, the king was confined to bed with gout (HL, POR 2068–69). Seeing this as a stroke of bad luck, Porter bemoaned the fact that the only way the book could be presented to the king was through the librarian and that she would therefore not have the chance to deliver her plea for a pension or make her case for royal charity directly to the king. Porter heard thirdhand from Halliday that the king was pleased with her book, but she expressed doubt about whether a pension would be the reward for her efforts.

Consoling herself that a warm public reception would compensate for the lack of notice from the king, she writes that she is "perfectly satisfied all will be for the ultimate Best" and believes her "Reputation, seems so heightened by the work itself, that my profits hereafter, can hardly fail of increasing" (HL, POR 2069). It may ring a bit false, but she proclaims herself "a hundred-fold more satisfied with success from the Public, than even a large Income" from the king. Porter overestimated the public; though *Duke Christian* received several positive reviews, readers did not welcome it as warmly as they had her previous novels. In the end, Porter got neither the wished-for pension to serve her in old age nor the anticipated renewal of public acclaim.

Porter's *Duke Christian* is a novel difficult to summarize. It features a signature Porter hero—perfect in filial duty, unlucky in love, fortunate in battle, and universally admired (especially by women) for his moral uprightness. Christian is one of seven brothers, who, at their father's deathbed, draw lots to see which will carry on the family line, the rest of them to live celibate. Though the father hoped that Christian would draw the lot, it was instead his brother George to whom that honor fell. Christian had been secretly betrothed to the young orphan Adelheid, who had been taken in by Christian's family and raised as his sister. He is distraught but committed to his promise to his father, rather than to his promise to Adelheid, whom he declared to be the only woman he could ever love. Conveniently, Adelheid dies by the end of volume one, and Christian is free to be hopelessly beloved by other women for the rest of the novel.

Next, he travels to England with his brother George. There he meets the daughter of England's James I, Princess Elizabeth, who reminds him of Adelheid and whom he admires extremely. She falls in love with Christian, but when she learns that he cannot marry, she ultimately gives her hand to Frederick V. (In volume 3, she becomes the short-lived queen of Bohemia.) The England portion of the novel also features William Shakespeare as a character. Shakespeare and Duke Christian are introduced to each other (by King James's son Henry) as mutual admirers (2: 268). Christian determines Shakespeare to be "a statesman—a sage, a hero—every thing!" and like a being from another sphere (272). Later, Shakespeare serves as the brothers' escort to Dover as they return to Germany (388).

Back on the Continent, there are many battles, treacheries, and women who cross-dress to advance the battles and forestall the treacheries. At the end of the novel, Elizabeth, having given birth to a daughter, Sophia, and being reconciled to the foolishly misled Frederick, puts the hand of her husband into Christian's with a "convulsive sigh" (3: 396). Elizabeth and Christian are described as like brother and sister. Brother George fulfills his promise to re-produce and marries Eleanor of Darmstadt. Their friend Wulfenbuttel mar-ries Isabel de Vere, whom he long thought was a male page but who reveals herself a woman. Elizabeth and Frederick's daughter, Sophia, is baptized, with the hope that she will "live to take her part in binding both countries in the firmest bonds of peace" (398). As readers would have known, Sophia would grow up to become the mother of Great Britain's first Hanoverian king, George I.

If the novel is difficult to recap, however, its reception is not. Despite Porter's best hopes, it was no runaway success. Her publishers prepared a large print run of 3,000, in anticipation of brisk sales that did not material-ize, though the book enjoyed an American audience and was translated into French and German (Longman Archives, Reel 39 H11 22).[29] Still, for all this, *Duke Christian* received minimal public notice, primarily in short, mildly en-thusiastic reviews. The *New Monthly Magazine* acknowledges that Porter's "merits as a novelist" are "well known" but says that *Duke Christian* "does not . . . equal some of Miss Porter's former productions."[30] The plot, the re-viewer claims, wants unity, and the love plots are not well managed, though the martial descriptions are complimented. The period Porter has chosen is considered favorable to romance, but some elements of the book are called vapid. An 1825 letter from the Longman publishing house refers to the "non success of *Duke Christian*," for which they had negotiated more handsome terms than for Porter's past productions. As a result of the novel's modest showing, the Longmans, both long-time publishers and personal friends, in-dicate that they cannot offer so generous an advance for any of Porter's future works.[31]

For some months after *Duke Christian*'s publication, Porter hung on to the hope that she would emerge a financial winner. She admitted (and then brushed off) a concern that would turn out to be prescient. She acknowledges to her brother Robert that, "had the work sunk in the esteem of the World," she "might have been branded as a Court-flatterer, & therefore lost the repu-tation for a High Principle, which is the stronghold of my usefulness as a Writer, and of my eminent station in society" (HL, POR 2069). Porter's worst fear was realized—posthumously, if not during her lifetime. She emerged in literary history as a royal sycophant, especially when judged alongside Austen.

Porter was nearly fifty years old when *Duke Christian* was published. One wonders if she would have accepted the royal assignment had she been invited to consider it earlier in her life, when her literary fortunes were greater and her future more promising. Because her family was relatively status conscious, and because they were frequently in debt, it is possible that Porter would have agreed to write such a work even at the height of her popularity. (More interesting to speculate about, perhaps, is whether Austen, were she in Porter's late-life shoes, would have been so steadfast in her refusal.) Porter's reputation as a court toady was sealed long before it was known that she took on the project with fervent wishes for financial independence in old age. For this reason, we ought to revisit the *Duke Christian* episode to examine its context, seeing this moment in her career in the larger framework of British women writers' late-life challenges and quests for financial independence.

It was not long after *Duke Christian* was published that Jane Porter's hopes of obtaining a pension from the king began to dwindle. She writes, "from all accounts, I now think, there is 3 chances in 4, no proposal whatever of any Literary Golden Laurel, will be afforded to me"; she consoles herself that she has "ample fame from the royal House" and that the book may do Robert's own appearance some good as well (HL, POR 2069). Despite her continued machinations, she received no royal accolades in return for her literary labors. She watched as over the coming years her contemporaries, some of them female, got the pension she so coveted. Ultimately, her dashed hopes turned to anger.

Her rancor is evident in a biographical essay she appears to have written for the *Edinburgh Literary Gazette* in 1829. The draft copy, in her own hand with corrections, differs in significant ways from what was ultimately published in the journal, so that even if the memoir was not written by her, we might conclude that it had her approbation. The essay outlines her long literary career, and when describing in the third person Porter's authorship of *Duke Christian*, it includes an appended note in a more rushed hand:

> Note—We are sorry to learn that Miss Porter has never yet received even the slightest mark of approbation from our own Sovereign—Though written with the avowed purpose of making the renown of his Majesty's illustrious Ancestors more familiar to the British Public "Duke Christian" has hitherto escaped the Royal Notice—so we must suppose—and we account for it in this way. Dr. Clarke had left the Royal Library before it was published—His successor was too anxiously engaged in seeking his own advancement to care much for the views or feelings of authors and the present Librarian has neither health nor temper to become an available Patron of Literature.[32]

What this appended footnote sets out to accomplish is unclear, though it does vent frustration with George IV and his librarians. An attempt to blame the librarians would seem to open up a space for the king to right their alleged wrongs. Disappointments from *Duke Christian*—financial and otherwise—continued to affect Porter's career many years hence. As the draft memoir's angry footnote suggests, Porter (or some supporter of hers) acutely felt the failure of that project five years later. For a myriad of reasons, she did not enjoy fame or fortune from any single-authored, full-length work after *Duke Christian*.[33] Was she trying to prod the king into belatedly recognizing her efforts?

The note was not published as written in the "Memoir of Miss Jane Porter," whether because of its author's second thoughts, the editor's judgment, or some other reason. The printed version includes this more tempered statement: "We are not aware, however, that Miss Porter has ever received for [*Duke Christian*] even the slightest mark of approbation from our own gracious monarch, whose reign has not been more distinguished by the overthrow of Napoleon, than by the patronage so unweariedly extended to the arts and sciences."[34] If George IV ever read this sentence, there is no record of its having spurred him to action. The anonymous memoir of Jane Porter was published in late September of 1829; by late June 1830, George IV was dead.

For Porter, more worrying deaths were to follow. She no longer needed to struggle to secure the financial futures of her sister and her elderly mother; both died in the early 1830s. Jane Porter would live for more than twenty-five years after the publication of *Duke Christian*, earning an irregular income through miscellaneous writing. Her next best option for financial support would have been her brothers. She must have known, as her contemporaries would not have, that this avenue was not a promising one. She received modest assistance from her diplomat darling brother, Robert, by then a widower living in South America, himself in chronic financial trouble. Jane spent significant amounts of time wrangling with his debtors throughout his life and as his executor after his death in 1842, when he left debts in excess of £1,500.[35]

Ultimately, she lived with her physician and author brother, William Ogilvie Porter (1774–1850), with whom she had a conflicted relationship and whose existence she often did not acknowledge in her correspondence. In her late middle age, he frequently disappointed her through what she saw as his greed and miserliness and his shirking of filial duty. Though she had joined him in Bristol by 1844, she says he made it clear to her that his "tied-up circumstances" meant that his only assistance to her would be a roof over her head; she claims he never inquired into her circumstances or what she calls her "ways and means."[36] Unless she wanted to or could keep producing written work—something she felt the pressure of and increasingly found exhausting—Porter needed to find another route to support herself.

British Women Writers, Pensions, and the Royal Bounty

Though described by a contemporary and well-wisher as "totally destitute or nearly so," Porter was not among the truly hard-luck cases among the elderly in her own day.[37] Before and after she moved in with her brother William, she often found shelter as a houseguest, circulating for weeks and months at a time among her wealthy friends, presumably joining them at table, asking them to frank her letters, and relying on their servants. This was a kind of genteel poverty. For the less fortunate, few of these advantages were possible. Many of the impoverished English elderly received financial help through the parish Poor Law authority. Small payments of two or three shillings per week were the nineteenth-century norm, a modest amount equivalent to the average income that workers in rural areas earned.[38] An astounding "seventy percent of all women in England, married or unmarried, rich or poor, who were seventy years of age or more were receiving regular cash assistance . . . during any one week" via Poor Law assistance, along with about half the men from that group. For people in their sixties, the proportion fell to half of women and a lesser proportion of men.[39] Those not receiving Poor Law aid, as David Thomson points out, included "the wealthy, the propertied and the salaried; persons with pensions, superannuations, allowances or annuities from former service to government, military or private employers; persons who remained in employment . . . and persons sheltered at community expense in hospitals, charity housing, asylums, and workhouses" (268). Jane Porter assiduously sought to join the pensioners and just as assiduously worked to remain out of the category of laborers or the publicly maintained. Her former fame shielded her from the fate of the majority of the elderly poor, as she received more exceptional forms of financial help.

Royal charity (which one scholar dubs the "welfare monarchy") expanded during the reign of George III and exploded during Victoria's rule, although across that period Parliament worked to rein in the Crown's civil list expenditures, including pensions.[40] Civil list monies (established under George III, with the surrender to Parliament of income arising from hereditary land revenues) included the sum assigned by the government to cover both the expenses of the sovereign and his or her family and some expenditures of the state, such as pensions. The history of royal pensions is a complicated one, as, after George III and before Queen Victoria, pensions could derive from four sources: the civil list pensions of England, the civil list pensions of Ireland, the pensions charged upon the hereditary revenues of Scotland, and the pensions charged on the 4½ percent duties. In short, during the reign of George III and thereafter, certain kinds of royal preferment became increasingly more difficult to get, as the government capped the amount sovereigns could spend annually.

Under George III, the government also curtailed the practice of discharging royal debts incurred from civil list expenditures, something that had routinely been done previously, often to the extent of hundreds of thousands of pounds. During the Regency, an auditor was put in place for the civil list for the first time. By the time William IV came to the throne in 1830, English civil list pensions had been reduced from nearly £100,000 pounds to approximately £75,000.[41] At the beginning of Queen Victoria's reign, "in lieu of the pension list of £75,000, her Majesty was empowered to grant pensions annually to the extent of £1,200" (May 1: 166). The 1837 formation of the Select Committee on Pensions meant close scrutiny of how such monies were being spent, something that apparently prompted many to resign their pensions. This period of increased pension regulation roughly corresponds with Porter's lifetime, as well as with the late lives of the first generations of professional women writers. Porter gained her knowledge of pensions during what in retrospect seem to have been their boom years, but with each successive monarch, she witnessed the pension system undergo further belt tightening.

Civil list and royal pensions were the most sought after of the available options for royal charity. As Victorian historian Thomas Erskine May put it, "No branch of the public expenditure was regarded with so much jealousy as that arising out of the unrestricted power of granting pensions by the Crown" (May 1: 173). Under George III, when there was "no limit to the amount of the pensions so long as the civil list could meet the demand," pensions were awarded to several noted intellectual women. Writer Elizabeth Hamilton was awarded a royal pension in 1804, and before her, Bluestocking artist and letter writer Mary Delany (1700–1788) received a pension of £300 per annum and a house at Windsor.[42] Pension monies could be quite generous—the celebrated Corsican politician Pasquale Paoli (1725–1807) received a civil list pension estimated at £1,500 per annum—and they could be transferred to spouses or kin; for example, military man and courtier Sir Herbert Taylor (1775–1839) received a pension of £1,000, which passed after his death to his widow.[43]

In her initial quest for a pension, Porter dealt not with the generous pension-giver George III but with his dissolute son. Despite his early spendthrift ways, however, George IV had kept up some of his father's charitable impulses, as a patron of artists and a friend to widows and orphans (Porchaska 39). Some of them he knew personally. In 1825, he offered a royal pension to the playwright John O'Keeffe (1747–1833). According to reports given to the king, O'Keeffe was "stone blind," and George IV acknowledged he "knew a little of him formerly."[44] The king did not limit his support of needy authors to pensions; he gave the Literary Fund for Indigent Authors (the Royal Literary Fund) a total of £5,000 over twenty-five years (Porchaska 39). His personal spending was great, however, and "applications for royal favour bombarded the Palace from all sides" (41). Porter had good reason to hope for preferment from him after writing her royal historical novel, but her case may have come at the wrong time, or perhaps her personal circumstances or even her writings (despite Halliday's account) did not appeal to the monarch.

It was not merely the fact that she was a female author that prevented her success, as other women were more fortunate in their supplications. Anne MacVicar Grant (1755–1838) succeeded where Porter had failed. In 1825, Grant secured a royal pension from George IV, with the assistance and support of her powerful male friends among the Scottish literati. According to her son, Grant's path to the royal pension was cleared by the "joint representation of Sir William Arbuthnot, Sir Walter Scott, Lord Jeffrey, Mr. Henry Mackenzie (author of the Man of Feeling), Sir Robert Liston, and Principal Baird, who, in the memorial presented on the occasion in Mrs. Grant's behalf, which was written by Sir Walter Scott, attest their opinion that 'the character and talents of Mrs. Grant have long rendered her not only a useful and estimable member of society, but one eminent for the services she has rendered to the cause of religion, morality, knowledge, and taste.' "[45] Though her son's memoir of his mother does not acknowledge it, Anne Grant's case was also presented directly from her own pen in a petition to George IV. Grant's compellingly told life story was far more moving than anything Porter could narrate.[46] Porter's situation—that of an "old maid" novelist, with a celebrated brother and an equally well-known author-sister—pales in comparison to Grant's challenging circumstances. In addition, Porter did not or could not assemble the pantheon of male power that Grant attracted in old age.

Porter's senior by twenty years, Grant was already an old woman in the 1820s. She had turned to writing after her husband's death, enjoying great success with her *Letters from the Mountains* (1806), *Memoirs of an American*

Lady (1808), *Essays on the Superstitions of the Highlands of Scotland* (1811), and poetic works. The proceeds from this writing were said to have allowed her to raise, educate, and set up in life her eight children. As it turned out, all but two of them had died by the early 1820s, two sons in military service and several daughters from illness. (Another daughter, ill at the time of Grant's petition, would also pass away.) As a final stroke of personal tragedy, Grant had been made lame from a fall. After communicating these details in her petition to the king, she modestly declares reluctance to approach him for assistance. She writes that she "could hardly be in any circumstances reconciled to it, otherwise than by the consciousness that in circumstances of great affliction and successive calamity, she has hitherto neglected no means within her power to avert such a necessity; and that it is not until it has pleased God in so many respects to diminish her powers of exertion and to deprive her of the natural supports to whom she looked for assistance in her declining age, she now prefers her claim for such share of the Public Bounty as your Majesty's Generosity may think proper to assign" (BL Add. 38300 f. 11).[47] The result of her request was a pension of £100, which Grant collected for the remaining dozen years of her life (Grant 1: 29). Scott's correspondence demonstrates that Grant may have been less humble—and more designing—than she declares in her petition. She apparently balked at the sum she was being offered. Scott expresses surprise, as he tells a friend that securing a pension is like "hunting a pig with a soap'd tail, monstrous apt to slip through your fingers."[48]

That Scott was among those who led the charge for Grant—and that George IV would choose to reward Grant when he continued to pass over Porter—must have been a hard pill for Porter to swallow. To make matters worse, in 1837, the relatively well off Lady Morgan (Sydney Owenson) (1776?–1859) was granted a generous civil list pension of £300 per year.[49] Lord Melbourne is said to have written that he "had much pleasure in doing that which may in some degree alleviate the pressure of the infirmity under which, I very deeply lament to hear that you are suffering" (Morgan 2: 420). Lady Morgan's infirmity was her failing eyesight, though it improved enough for her to read and write, most notably her *Woman and Master* (1840), which one reviewer described as "a work without one claim to notice except the antiquity of its author."[50] It is said that even on the last day of her life, Morgan had "called for her desk and papers and begun to write a letter on business but on the entrance of her doctor reluctantly gave up her pen" (547–48). Porter—despite her greater financial need—was again passed over for a pension in favor of an acquaintance and rival.

Porter's quest, which had begun in 1821 with *Duke Christian,* continued to within a month of her death, in 1850. From the late 1830s onward, she regularly appealed to the crown and the government for financial assistance. Aware that June was the month in which new pensions were generally bestowed, her campaigns would begin some months earlier.[51] Each year she wrote a series of letters to a dizzying number of powerful people, some of her accounts more accurate than others and all highly pathetic. Typical among them is her 1844 letter to Prince Albert, with a petition to Queen Victoria, describing her "lonely and enfeebled age" and asking for "some small annual Pension, from any public Fund under your Majesty's benign control for such benevolent purposes," that would "afford a simple but respectable shelter and subsistence, to the last days, of a once honoured contributor to the literary service of her country during a period of above Fifty years!"[52] To add insult to injury, given the *Duke Christian* episode, Porter received one reply from Sir Robert Peel informing her that such pensions were awarded only to those who had given "personal Service to the Sovereign, Eminent public Service, and distinguished literary or scientific merit."[53]

We might say now that it was foolish of Porter to set her sights on a royal or civil list pension—that it was akin to hoping to win the lottery—but her hopes were not outlandish. Her celebrity was on a par with that of those selected, even if her literary stock had fallen sharply after Scott turned novelist. Also, Porter had some knowledge of the workings of the patronage system, which she may have come by as a result of her work on behalf of her diplomat brother, Robert. (Porter's mother had a widow's pension, from her husband's military service, so the family knew well the stability that regular income promised.) In the 1830s and 1840s, Porter even spearheaded successful campaigns for funds from the Royal Bounty for at least two needy women friends: Sarah Belzoni (1783–1870), widow of the famed Egyptologist Giovanni Battista Belzoni (1778–1823). (In a strange twist of fate, Mrs. Belzoni was awarded a civil list pension the year after Porter's death.)[54] Porter's correspondence mentions Mrs. Belzoni having been paid in excess of £600 pounds in one-time assistance from the Royal Bounty; this was more than Porter herself would ultimately receive.[55] The second woman Porter championed was Mrs. Dwyer, the widowed half-sister of naval war hero—and Porter's lifelong unrequited love—Sir Sidney Smith (1764–1840). Porter organized the campaign to raise funds for Dwyer, netting £400, a good portion of it donated by Queen Victoria; it was apparently used to purchase an annuity.[56] Sir Sidney Smith himself had enjoyed a £1,000 pension granted from the 4½ percent duties.[57]

Porter came to know a good deal about who had been recognized with a pension. She more than once named their names in the hopes of being placed among them. She asked Prime Minister Peel in 1842 to consider her "not undeserving of some share in the munificent provision which has at different times been dispensed to the merits, or necessities, of British authors and authoresses;—and in my own time, on Mr. Thomas Campbell, Mr. Thomas Moore, Mrs. Somerville, Lady Morgan, and several others."[58] Science writer Mary Somerville (1780–1872) had been awarded a civil list pension of £200 in 1835, increased to £300 in the face of further financial difficulties.[59]

Poet Moore (1779–1852), who struggled with late-life financial difficulties, outlived all of his children, and by his own account was "sinking into a mere vegetable" in the late 1840s, had been given a royal pension in 1835 (£300; Select 69) and a civil list pension in 1850.[60] Other names might have been added to Porter's list, as they were published in the 1838 Select Committee on Pensions report, along with their ages, pension amounts, and details about why they were considered worthy. A section of the report is devoted to describing "Pensions Connected with Literary and Scientific Eminence, and with Useful Inventions and Attainments in the Arts" (66). Named there, and unnamed by Porter, is Mary Russell Mitford (1787–1855), "authoress," age 51, receiving £100 per year (69). Most of the women included in the 1838 list are described as worthy because they are daughters or widows of eminent men, but several were authors in their own right.

Porter regularly asked the prime minister "to award to her, what ever donation of Pension, his goodness may deem proper to bestow" (BL Add. 40510 f. 76). Peel's repeated rejections inform her that he cannot recommend her for a pension, that the whole amount of the Pension Fund is spoken for during the current year, that there is no opening, and that he never makes promises for the future (40522 ff. 188). She became more bold in 1844, writing to a friend asking him to take up her case with Peel. She pleads, "I feel that you take a too sincere interest in the final result of my recently inspired Hopes towards some little Establishment, from a certain High Quarter for my future comfort in Life—Lonely, and desolated, as it has become in my old age!— not to excuse the present expression of an awakened anxiety concerning it."[61] Porter's idea is to have her friend work behind the scenes to secure for her the pension of the recently deceased poet, Campbell (1777–1844): "Yesterday, I saw in a Newspaper of the Day, a Notice of the Death of Mr. Thomas Campbell, the Well-known Poet of 'The Pleasures of Hope,' & C. at Boulogne—I believe he for many years possessed a Pension from Government, in honour of his Poetical Works:—What its amount was, I do not know.—But it has struck me, that if, with Propriety!—The Premier, at this favourable moment, of a Literary Vacancy having thus occurred in the Pension Lists, this Goodness might probably embrace the occasion to bestow it upon me."[62]

Porter's reasons for considering herself deserving are then detailed. It is unclear whether Porter knew more of Campbell's situation than she lets on here, as the two authors had been friendly. The 1838 report published his pension amount as £184 (Select 67), a sum he had been awarded long before, apparently used to support his widowed mother and sisters.[63] In giving her reasons for thinking herself worthy to replace Campbell on the pension list, Porter tells her friend that "Time, does indeed wear on me!" and calls herself "a Sojourner with Friends alone!" (neglecting to mention that her miserly brother William was still alive). She writes that she is in the decline of life as well as in a decline of health (BL Add. 40547 f. 147). She speaks of her fear that she may "perhaps die under some one of [her friends'] kind roofs (not having one of my own!)." This last was a repeatedly voiced worry in her letters.

Ultimately, Porter claimed she was no longer able to earn a living by writing. Throughout the 1820s she was doggedly pursuing authorship, but by the 1840s, she writes about being physically unable to continue what had been her livelihood. She frequently reports in her letters that she is no longer able to take up her pen. The fact that so many of her letters survive from this time may prompt us to question her veracity, but she obviously felt more able to compose short, formulaic begging letters or to work toward republishing her earlier novels than to engage in writing new, full-length imaginative works. Begging may not be the appropriate term for Porter's efforts, however, as she refused to become a public charity case. When some supporters tried to organize a subscription to raise money for her shortly after her brother's death, she recoiled. She replied that a public subscription campaign would "destroy all my future comfort in life" because it would not allow her to live by her fixed principle of "self-dependence, under God."[64] In the same letter, though, she reiterates her desire for a "humble home" (HL, POR 2171). Porter wanted charity, without being made a visible charity case.

Her epistolary requests did prove profitable, even if not in the way she had first envisioned. Countless hours netted her several one-time funds from the Royal Bounty and the Royal Literary Fund, which she appears to have accepted without scruple. The first was apparently a grant of £100 from Queen Victoria made to her in 1839.[65] In a stroke of very bad luck, Porter lost the money when the bank in which she deposited it failed.[66] In 1842, after her brother's death, she received £50 from the Royal Literary Fund.[67] In 1845, Peel awarded her a one-time grant of £150 pounds, while refusing the pension request.[68] In October 1846, new Prime Minister Lord Russell wrote that he intended to ask Queen Victoria to grant Porter another one-time amount of £200 and wrote in terms more encouraging than Peel ever had to say that this would not prevent her from being considered for a pension in the future.[69] It appears that the sum was not made available to her until May 1848, unless Russell provided her with a second such amount, which seems unlikely.[70]

During this period, Porter explored other avenues for financial independence. Letters and memos from the 1840s describe her business affairs. Early in the decade, prior to moving in with her brother William, Jane wrote letters looking for a place to live rent free. She asked Leopold I, King of the Belgians, "for a Free Cottage, at Esher, or Claremont," or for an apartment, when one becomes vacant, at Hampton Court Palace.[71] Other documents speak of her holding a life annuity on government security. It was perhaps this annuity that was purchased in the mid-1840s for £400, at a return of £40 a year, possibly with her Royal Bounty and republishing monies.[72] This may have been the first time in more than three decades that Porter was not struggling to repay family debts. The annuity purchase indicates clearly the importance Porter placed on having a regular sum paid out to her twice yearly.[73]

Other aged authors were more inventive—or more fortunate—in their quests for financial independence. Among the fortunate, we might count Elizabeth Carter (1717–1806). When she became a widow, Bluestocking writer Elizabeth Montagu (1720–1800) settled a pension on her friend, as she had on Sarah Fielding (1710–68).[74] The idea of wealthy women settling annuities on admired authors had entered the public imagination to a significant enough degree that it features in Jane Austen's *Sense and Sensibility*, when Edward Ferrars teases Marianne Dashwood that if she were to come into money, "the bulk of your fortune would be laid out in annuities on the authors or their heirs."[75] Porter seemed to have no friends willing to settle a pension on her, though they were generous in offering her places to stay with them, even long term.

More inventive approaches include William Hayley's, about whom we heard in chapter 3. Hayley, poet and author of the *Essay upon Old Maids*, worked out a deal with a publisher to sell his then-unwritten memoirs, to be published posthumously, in return for an annuity until his death. Poet Robert Southey called Hayley "perhaps the only person who ever dealt with his posthumous reputation as a post-obit, and converted it into a present income."[76] The aforementioned actor John O'Keeffe, also a playwright, sold his remaining copyrights and unpublished plays in return for an annuity from Thomas Harris, the manager of Covent Garden.[77] Notable women writers of the era apparently did not or could not broker similar deals. In any case, Porter, though she annotated her papers in late life, did not have the wherewithal to write a memoir and apparently had little unpublished work she was willing to sell.

She was more successful in adding new prefaces and postscripts to her still well-regarded novels. This effort was not without obstacles in that Porter found herself battling for the return of her copyright. After protracted legal wrangling, she settled with Richard Bentley (of the Standard Novels series), and she saw the revised texts of *Thaddeus of Warsaw*, *The Scottish Chiefs*, and *The Pastor's Fire-Side* through to new illustrated editions. Her new publisher, George Virtue, paid her £200 for a preface to *The Scottish Chiefs* and for her remaining life interest in the copyright.[78] In 1844, she even looks forward to the year 1852, when the copyright for *Duke Christian* will revert to her.[79] Some months later, she writes of selling to Virtue the whole, entire, and exclusive copyright of three novels (presumably *Thaddeus of Warsaw*, *The Scottish Chiefs*, and *The Pastor's Fire-Side*) for £300 pounds, except for rights to the works in the Standard Novels series.[80] A new market for old novels was helped by the genre's rise in status, as well as by Porter's ability to claim that she was offering to the public improved, corrected versions. The extras included her collected recollective prefaces, postscripts, and appendices.

As well as financial vehicles, Porter's paratexts served by her own admission as a substitute for writing an autobiography.[81] They also kept her books in the public eye and gave her a platform to argue for her importance to literary history, as we saw earlier in her self-comparisons to Scott. But Porter's attempts to keep her name before readers were not merely an act of personal vanity or even, as we saw in Piozzi's case, a way to ensure future readers. Porter's efforts were, if not a matter of life or death, a matter of relative comfort versus dependent genteel poverty. Fighting to regain the copyright to her novels and writing seemingly endless prefaces to her works, Porter was no doubt trying to resuscitate her once shining literary star. In monetary terms, her republication efforts seem to have been equally as successful as her quest for royal funds, each netting her several hundred pounds over the course of a decade. Some of this money, as we saw, was lost in a bank failure, and a portion of it likely went to pay off debts contracted years earlier, by herself and her brother. Neither the Royal Bounty nor the republications delivered the financial stability she sought.

Although a beneficiary of the "welfare monarchy," Porter's success was relatively modest. It was certainly because of these monies that Porter was able to continue to employ a maid, Elizabeth Bullen, to the end of her days. But when the novelist experienced a collapsed lung, she went into debt getting the medical treatment she was ordered to seek—a removal to the fresh air of Clifton.[82] More than providing a context for these personal financial travails, however, what we see in Porter's late-life attempts to support herself as an author is that producing new works in old age was not the only way for a woman writer of this era to make money. Porter poured her energies into trying to profit from her reputation. She capitalized on emerging methods and markets for doing so, demonstrating that even a literary star on the wane could turn old work into new capital. Trading on their former fame, elderly authors like Porter employed new tactics to try to make a living. Porter may well have been in the (until now, hidden) vanguard, with her indefatigable efforts to secure a pension and to revise and republish her novels. Others—more fortunate, pluckier, or more skilled—would serve as the visible exemplars.

Posthumous Porter

After her death, Porter's novels enjoyed frequent nineteenth- and early twentieth-century reprintings. *Thaddeus of Warsaw* went through at least eighty-four nineteenth-century editions and printings, and *Scottish Chiefs* went through roughly seventy-five editions and printings (Adams 264). Even *The Pastor's Fire-Side* enjoyed some thirteen editions by 1892 (Jones 136). *Duke Christian* was not revived after 1824. The work that was to have made her late life financially easy failed even to enhance her literary reputation. Still, enough of her work survived for Porter (like Macaulay before her) to join the ranks of those authors repeatedly remembered as forgotten.

In 1897, Ina M. White, publishing portions of Porter's diary, tells readers, "Few of us in the present remember the name of Jane Porter, and still fewer have ever read her works. The copies of *Thaddeus of Warsaw* and *The Scottish Chiefs*, over which our parents bestowed their tears and enthusiasms, are now relegated to shelves in the lumber-room."[83] In 1905, *Thaddeus of Warsaw* was edited by E. A. Baker, for a series titled, "Half-Forgotten Books."[84] In 1924, Mona Wilson included a chapter on Porter in *These Were Muses*, which sets out to tell the stories of "all these ladies whose renown has faded."[85] Wilson concludes, "If Miss Porter's ghost is still anxious about her fame, she must not expect a fresh outburst of enthusiasm for her works" (142). In 1931, Herbert Vaughan began his chapter on Jane, Anna Maria, and Robert Ker Porter by noting that it is "somewhat curious that the high reputation of the Porters should have collapsed so completely. The novels of Jane and Maria are absolutely unknown to the present generation, though, as a schoolboy, I can remember [Jane Porter's novels] . . . being sold and read in cheap editions by young folk."[86] In a 1940 *Notes & Queries* article, a critic writes that "Jane Porter's romance of *The Scottish Chiefs* . . . is now, perhaps, forgotten."[87] In one of the only successful attempts to date to write Porter's biography, a 1942 master's thesis, Robert Tate Irvine Jr. indicates that he has chosen to trace the comet trail of Porter's fame, "to record its fast fading light before it goes out entirely" (3). These comments, made over such a long period, offer evidence of Porter's tenuous staying power, mirroring the rhetoric of her supplicating letters and the republications of her novels in late life. It is possible that the republications themselves, implicitly admonishing readers not to lose sight of her, contributed to this perpetual "half-forgetting" over a century and a half.

Regardless, the twentieth century was not as bleak for Porter as it was for many of her female contemporaries. In 1921, the edition that would secure Porter's twentieth-century endurance was published. *The Scottish Chiefs* was issued as a Scribner's Illustrated Classic, featuring the illustrations of the renowned N. C. Wyeth.[88] In 1950, the novel was featured in the Classics Illustrated comic book series as no. 67, several times reprinted over the next twenty years.[89] Some claim that Porter's novel served as an inspiration for Mel Gibson's *Braveheart* (1995).[90] Pickering and Chatto published a series, *Varieties of the Female Gothic* (2002), edited by Gary Kelly, which includes *The Scottish Chiefs*.[91] In what might be termed Porter's breakthrough in the twenty-first century, a paperback edition of *The Scottish Chiefs* (2007) has been edited by Fiona Price and published for classroom use.[92] It seems that Porter's posthumous luck is beginning to turn. Though her vision for creating a financially comfortable, independent life in old age while resting on her literary laurels was thwarted, her corollary efforts to ensure that the celebrity she enjoyed in her youth would be revived may well be—surprisingly—realizable.

Conclusion

"Old women now-a-days are not much thought of; out of sight out of mind with them, now-a-days"

In *The Work of Writing* (1998), Clifford Siskin describes what he calls "The Great Forgetting" of women writers, enjoining us to keep in mind that "there is much remembering to be done, and admirable progress has recently been made. But . . . we also need to find out how we forgot."[1] In the wake of what we might now call our great remembering of early modern British women writers, spearheaded by feminist literary criticism, we ought to extend Siskin's admonition to ask how—and why—have we forgotten so many women writers of this era in old age? Despite the burgeoning of recent feminist work on early modern women writers, why have we continued to ignore or downplay so many subjects' achievements and trials in old age?[2]

The great forgetting of the first generations of aged British women writers (and their selective remembrance as a group in the nineteenth century) may stem from what we would now call ageism, whether malignant or benign. The chapters of this book demonstrate a commitment to the explanatory power of this theory. It seems evident that many older female authors' works were devalued because of their age and sex, though these may not have been the only obstacles to critical or popular success. Readers and critics were fixated (usually negatively) on women writers' old age when it was known—a virtual inevitability with the most famous of them. Many seemed to have an investment in conceiving of women writers in old age, even those once considered great, as past their prime or perhaps past being worth listening to. Critics today carry this misapprehension forward, as British women writers' late works from the eighteenth and nineteenth centuries are on the whole infrequently read, taught, republished, or commented on. The findings I have presented in this book suggest that, to no small degree, ageism or proto-ageism (often in concert with and inseparable from other ideologies) played a role in the neglect of many women authors in their late lives. This conclusion should function as an invitation to further research.

If limited understandings of gender, old age, and authorship have prevented our seeing the full range of a subject's life course, however, so has literary historical periodization. The ways in which literary history has been packaged has affected our ability to see all but the most visible (traditionally, male and canonical) writers across their entire careers. In particular, the first generations of elderly professional women writers, especially those who published over many decades, have become marooned in our literary histories. When we as scholars of the eighteenth century or the Romantic era stop attending to the works "our" authors published after 1800, 1832, or 1837—and when Victorian studies compatriots also consider those authors as "ours"—it is not difficult to see how partial views of long careers may take hold. As we have seen, Edgeworth becomes an eighteenth-century author (despite having published as late as 1848), Austen is admonished to worship at Burney's grave (though Burney died two decades after she did), and late careers are diminished in literary biographies as life epilogues.

Literary history would look radically different if organized by authors' death dates. This is not, of course, a serious suggestion, but it makes for a provocative thought experiment. Jane Austen (1775–1817) and Sir Walter Scott (1771–1832) would come before Maria Edgeworth (1768–1849) and Frances Burney (1752–1840); William Godwin (1756–1836) would come long after Mary Wollstonecraft (1759–97). William Blake (1757–1827), Samuel Taylor Coleridge (1772–1834), and William Wordsworth (1770–1850) would come after John Keats (1795–1821), Percy Shelley (1792–1822), and Lord Byron (1788–1824). Attending to the long lives even of the most canonical poets makes problematic traditional designations of "early" and "late" Romanticism. Although we might argue that these designations arose from what has been considered each author's most important work(s), the case of British women writers is more complicated. Most hold either very new or largely exceptional places in the literary canon, and therefore, we have only scratched the surface in the project of determining what ought to be considered their most important contributions.

Focusing on works, rather than authors, may provide some advantages. In her landmark study, *A Literary History of Women's Writing in Britain, 1660–1789* (2006), Susan Staves uses this method, emphasizing "texts rather than authors' lives" and using "dates of texts rather than biographical dates."[3]

This is a promising approach, for many reasons. As Staves notes, a focus on texts rather than lives for her chronology allows her to treat Eliza Haywood's (1693?–1756) early and later work in separate chapters, "suggesting ways in which it was representative of more general trends" (10). There is great potential in this for allowing us to comprehend the entirety of writings across an author's life (e.g., the early vs. the late Haywood) and across traditional literary periods, but this approach also has drawbacks. If we focus on works and downplay authorship, we may not be in a good position to tell whether late lives and works deserve reconsideration, and we hamper ourselves in attempting to study late works with an eye to literary, cultural, and historical issues of age qua age.

Recent moves toward claiming a long eighteenth century (1660–1830) or a Romantic century (1750–1850) offer greater possibilities for looking at some writers' old ages within reconfigured periods, and such shifts could also open new windows for age studies. Even so, it would remain difficult to see Edgeworth and Frances Trollope (1779–1863) as near contemporaries, to use the example cited in the introduction. An additional challenge is the matter of whether we ought to focus on dates of publication or dates of composition in the study of women's writing (Staves 11). The current scholarly emphasis on first editions as the preferred standard texts also means that we may have additional work to do to consider authors' revising and editorial practices in late life. What might we learn—about literary history, politics, gender, and or aging—if we look to the individual (and perhaps even generalizable) ways in which authors rewrote their earlier printed texts for late-life publication? We have much to do to share subjects and scholarly questions across the literary periods that have traditionally separated us; age studies provides yet another impetus for doing so.

It is also possible that our neglect of eighteenth- and nineteenth-century British women writers in late life stems from insufficient scholarship on how old age is represented in literature. In the introduction, I outlined a number of stereotypes of old age (e.g., garrulity, trifling qualities, querulousness, and virtuousness) that might have influenced perceptions of elderly women's writings. We do not yet have a substantial body of work documenting prevalent literary treatments and cultural stereotypes of old age in early modern Great Britain; this would seem a necessary foundation for determining whether and how women writers responded to conventional understandings of gender and age. Differences in the representations of old age across decades, nations, classes, and genders have been drawn only in vague terms. As we add to this work and seek to categorize those representations, we ought to be mindful not only of what seems clearly prejudicial but of what Betty Friedan calls (in a contemporary context) "compassionate ageism"—that is, well-intentioned, "sympathetic" attitudes that nevertheless have negative effects.[4] (We might say that this kind of response was at work in the posthumous treatment of Anna Letitia Barbauld's "Life.") Finally, as we seek to describe the features of old age in the lives and works of the old, we should not expect to find only sympathetic renderings of old age, as my reading of Jane Austen and old maidism serves to remind us.

Some female authors worked against rather than embracing or accepting sexist and ageist representations in their writings and their careers, while others acceded to strictures for enacting proper old womanhood, and still others combined these two approaches. A recent study of twentieth-century French literature contrasts these extremes as "age rage" versus "going gently."[5] Catharine Macaulay, witnessing her historical work criticized and labeled as old fashioned, did not go gently, using her old age to urge a better reception for her later works. Others sought channels beyond the literary marketplace to further their aims. Hester Piozzi may have forged an unusual friendship with a young actor to create her own "reading public," when unable to secure publication (and maintain or re-establish literary reputation) through former channels. Some writers left aside fictional, poetic, or dramatic pursuits and took up literary-critical ones. By commenting on the great books of the previous generation and bringing them to the attention of the rising generation, Barbauld did unto other authors as she may have hoped would eventually be done unto her. Some writers tried to live off of their early literary success in old age. The aged Jane Porter, no longer able or willing to craft new full-length works, sought to capitalize on her former productions through republication and through a quest for a pension. This book's chapters ought to lead us to conclude that unless and until we get a better grasp on the finer points of authorship and old age in the early modern period, we are bound to reproduce incomplete pictures of British literary history.

What specifically can be done to complete the picture? To begin with, more studies are needed of aged writers as a group. How often did aged female authors—and when did they or how did they—maintain professional relationships with publishers, other female writers, or men of letters of all generations? Do patterns appear in women writers' romances, marriages, maidenhood, or widowhood, and how do these relate to authorial careers?[6] How did having children—or not having children—have an impact on later years as a female author?[7] It has been estimated that up to one-third of women who lived to age 65 in seventeenth- and eighteenth-century England had no surviving children (Thane, "Social" 102). We might guess how this affected wealth, but did it have a similar impact on authorship? Did economic well-being have an impact on whether authors continued to seek or to achieve publication? When women writers were unable to care for themselves, who served as their caretakers? How did illness, health, and medical treatment relate to the ability or desire to continue writing? Did political affiliations become more conservative or more progressive? Might some of these questions be answered in the same ways for aged male as well as aged female authors, and if so, what does that mean for age studies and feminist studies?

We ought to ask, too, if there were genres in which it was more acceptable to write as an old woman. Was it a greater challenge to remain "fashionable" in a masculinized or a feminized genre? My preliminary research suggests that the late eighteenth- and early ninteenth-century novel, with its increasing emphasis on presentism and fashionability, became a more challenging nut for older women to crack. Even historical novels, with their focus on the past, proved difficult for some, particularly after Scott. Letters and conduct books appear generally to have been a more acceptable form for female authors in old age, particularly when an experienced narrator offered expert advice to a young charge. By the end of the period, private letters published posthumously were becoming almost genteel. What conclusions might we draw about writing or publishing works of drama, poetry, history, travel writing, or natural philosophy in old age? Were certain areas of the literary marketplace more open—or less open—to granddames? Or did success depend less on the genre and more on the approach to an audience—or some other factor or factors as yet unnamed?

Many stories also remain to be told and questions remain to be asked and answered at the level of the individual. In the remainder of the conclusion, I briefly recount some of these stories, which could provide chapters or book-length studies of their own. The long-lived Bluestockings offer fascinating subjects for the study of writing and old age.[8] Elizabeth Montagu (1720–1800) seems to have worked out a system for thriving in late life, involving periodic trips but much solitude and considered reading. As she writes in a 1780 letter to Elizabeth Vesey (ca. 1715–91), "a quiet life is suitable to my age, & my taste. I love society, but to be perpetually in company makes fools of ye young, & dotards of ye old; as it adds to ye natural inconsiderateness of youth, & imbecilities of age. I have enjoyd more real satisfaction in my few retired hours since I came hither, than in a month of Bath life. I wd by no means live always out of ye World, but intervals of perfect retirement in every month of ye Year, & solitary hours in every day, wd be my wish. There are books in every kind, excellent in their kind, whether ye mind is indolent or active, serious or gay, suitable to its disposition."[9] In another letter, Montagu recommends the kinds of reading that ought to be contemplated in late life: "The least agitating of all employments is reading of what is past; one calmly peruses *the tale of other times*. The ruin of Carthage, the Sack of Rome, the destruction of Babylon, do not give such emotions while one reads them, as hearing a nightingales or Robins nest has been plunderd in ones garden" (HL, MO 6413). Positing history or romance as a genre suited for the old, Montagu implies a great deal about what she thinks old women ought to write, as well as what they ought to read.

Montagu published two works during her middle age, *Dialogues of the Dead* (1760) and *An Essay on the Writing and Genius of Shakespear* (1769), but she wrote many letters throughout her life. In the years after her death, some of them were published, but editors most often selected those letters written before she was 40. Some of the letters of her late life have now seen print, though the task is by no means complete. We have much yet to learn about Montagu and other important Bluestocking women. In some cases, establishing the basic facts of their late lives provides the next step. For the aforementioned Vesey, for example, Deborah Heller has made a speculative diagnosis of Alzheimer's disease; this promises to reconfigure our understandings of Vesey's late life and those of her Bluestocking friends in their later years.[10] Another Bluestocking writer whose late life deserves more of our attention is Hester Mulso Chapone (1727–1801). Her very successful conduct book writings used a mature female narrator speaking directly to a young woman.[11]

Many other individual writers merit continued research into their later careers because of their heretofore unrecognized ingenuity. The line of inquiry I have begun on Piozzi, Barbauld, and Porter—that each tried in her own way to direct her posthumous reputation—might be extended to the poet Anna Seward (1742–1809). She left instructions to try to conduct her writing career from the grave. In her "Posthumous Letter from Anna Seward to Mr. A. Constable" (1807), she asked publisher Constable to follow the directions in her will in bringing her letters into print. She gave him the exclusive copyright to a dozen quarto volumes, writing that they contained "copies of letters, or of parts of letters, that, after I had written them, appeared to me worth the attention of the public."[12] Seward intended for Constable to bring out two volumes annually, in chronological order, as he found them transcribed. Despite these directives, he published all twelve volumes at once in 1811, even leaving out some of the letters she had selected because he saw them as unfit for public consumption.

Other writers used indirection when attempting to influence audiences in late life. Jane West (1758–1852) titled her last novel *Ringrove; or, Old Fashioned Notions* (1827), effectively defusing any criticism that it was aiming at being fashionable. The novel's end can be read not only as a character's but as an aged author's farewell. The final paragraph, in an old woman's voice, begins, " 'Yes,' she said to me, after she had given Ellen's hand to Frederic at the altar, 'my duties now seem all terminated. Yet, believe me, I retire in charity with the world; for I rise from the feast of life satisfied, and vacate my place for a younger guest, without envious regret.' "[13] In her old age, West is said to have suffered from a growing feeling of isolation, describing herself as "an old Q in a corner whom the rest of the world has forgotten."[14] She outlived her husband and sons—and her celebrity—but saved her letters and read them as "bon bons to gratify" her old age, until her eyesight began to fail (Lloyd 669). Her papers were left to a grandson, but they are as yet untraced, suggesting yet another danger of outliving one's literary fame.

West appears to have maintained her politically conservative slant throughout her career, but other writers have reputations for late life political shifts. Mary Hays (1760–1843), one-time compatriot of Mary Wollstonecraft, has sometimes been understood as leaving behind her radical politics to become a late-life monarchist, but this hardly seems a fair assessment. Hays is "interesting not only for her achievements but also for her longevity," according to Marilyn L. Brooks.[15] Hays ended her publishing career in her sixties with *Memoirs of Queens: Illustrious and Celebrated* (1821). In the preface to that work, Hays mentions herself as writing "cheerfully," though "declining in physical strength and mental activity." She also puts her authorship at one remove, speaking of compiling it at "the request of her publisher," heading off any potential criticism that she has had the audacity to seek print of her own accord.[16] She apologizes for the lack of novelty in the work and notes, "sickness retarded its progress," in effect asking for her audience's forbearance in judging her harshly, because of her old age (viii). In fact, portions of the book recycle her own earlier work; half of its seventy "memoirs" are found in some form in her earlier work, *Female Biography* (1803). Some have claimed that she used the 1821 work to make connections to her 1790s feminist ideals, but measuring in detail the continuities and differences of Hays's early and late political positions remains an unfinished project.

In late life, Hays complained "more than once that 'the world forsakes me.'"[17] In a letter from 1842, she tells a friend that should he be unable to see her in the near future, he should "seek my remains in a humble grave in the Newington *cemetery* with the simple memorial *Mary Hays* engraven on the headstone" (qtd. in Ty 160). Hays "lived through the 1830s and into the early Victorian period, but she published nothing more and dropped out of contact with literary life," according to Gary Kelly.[18] Biographer Gina Luria Walker argues that Hays had an "unspoken wish . . . that Mary Shelley, a professional writer, would memorialize Hays as well as her father [William Godwin] and mother [Mary Wollstonecraft]" at the end of her "lonely, idiosyncratic struggles over the last 50 years" to gain recognition for her own and other women's contributions to history.[19] Brooks finds Hays in old age an "embittered recluse" (x). Much more might be done to make sense of these statements and arguments and to contextualize Hays's late life.

Arguments that a woman author gave up writing and publication in old age are sometimes easily refuted. The late life of Ellis Cornelia Knight (1758–1837), best known today as the author of *Dinarbus* (1790), is a case in point. She published novels, poems, and histories from the 1790s to the 1810s, although her service to the likes of Lady Emma Hamilton, Queen Charlotte, and Princess Charlotte has proven to be of greater interest to some. After close connections with the court came to an end, Knight left England for the Continent, returning to England for short visits. It was said in the introduction to her posthumously published *Autobiography* that in her old age, "she devoted herself more to Society than to Literature" and "gave nothing to the world beyond a few fugitive pieces."[20] This is untrue, as she published a novel in 1833, *Sir Guy de Lusignan*.[21] One twentieth-century critic considered it "the most remarkable of her works."[22] Fragments of later works apparently survived her as well (Knight, *Autobiography* 1: x). There is clearly more to say about the post–court service portion of Knight's life and about her decision to publish a new work of historical fiction in her mid-seventies.

In other cases, an author's reputation for ceasing publication in old age seems based on sound evidence, though the story may be more complex than it appears at first glance. Susan Ferrier (1782–1854) is said to have made a positive decision to stop publishing in her late life, though her reasons for doing so remain debated. The author of three novels—*Marriage* (1818), *The Inheritance* (1824), and *Destiny* (1831)—Ferrier's fortune as a writer grew with age. She received £1,700 for *Destiny* and respectfully dedicated it to "Sir Walter Scott, Baronet," from "an obliged friend, though anonymous author."[23] It sold 2,400 copies in four months.[24] In 1837, she was offered £1,000 "for a *volume anything from you*" and declined, saying she had made two attempts to write something and did not please herself, so she would not publish "anything" (Latané 100). Did Ferrier choose not to seek publication because she was "aware of the inferior quality of" her last work?[25] Was this decision "wise," as one critic would have it?[26] Are there other factors at play here, such as her alleged growing blindness, which may have deterred her from further writing?[27] Did she choose to focus on family duty over (anonymous) authorship? Manuscript fragments of late work survive, and more remains to be considered.

Still other kinds of stories of authorship ought to be retold in the context of gender, authorship, and old age. The brief accounts I have offered in earlier chapters of the late life activities and attitudes of Hannah More, Sydney Owenson, Lady Morgan, and Anne MacVicar Grant deserve expansion. Dozens more stories, ranging from tantalizing to tragic, await further research. What might be learned, for instance, of the late life of Adelaide O'Keeffe (1776–1855?), author of poems for children and religious novels and caretaker daughter of John O'Keeffe, the playwright who had been financially savvy and fortunate in his late life? Another promising subject, Eliza Fenwick (1766–1840), author of the novel *Secresy* (1795) and other works, apparently did not pursue literary fame in late life. She moved abroad with two of her children, first to the West Indies and then to the United States, only to witness their deaths. She began by running boarding schools and then, in old age, a boarding house, subsequently moving from New York City, to Niagara, Toronto, and Rhode Island. In 1832, she encountered a friend of Jane Porter's, prompting her to send a letter to her fellow aged author, saying that she had often boasted of their friendship.[28] Despite having left the literary scene in England, Fenwick remained connected to it through trans-Atlantic correspondence.

Another promising subject for the study of authorship and old age is Amelia Opie (1769–1853), known best for her novel inspired by the lives of Godwin and Wollstonecraft, *Adeline Mowbray* (1804). Opie published her last work of fiction, *Madeline*, in 1822. Her career as a fiction writer ended when she joined the Society of Friends in 1825 and renounced novel writing.[29] She decided to leave unfinished a novel already under contract. Still, she continued to publish as a Quaker. Her *Lays for the Dead* (1833) consisted of retrospective poems in memory of loved ones. In late life, she engaged in charity work and antislavery activism. Much has been written about her, both in the nineteenth century and in recent years, but little interrogates the contributions she made (and did not make) as a writer in old age.

Science writer Mary Somerville (1780–1872) was one of the rare women authors who published a memoir with "old age" in its title, though it was published posthumously. There she writes proudly of retaining her faculties into her early 90s: "I am now in my 92nd year (1872), still able to drive out for several hours; I am extremely deaf and my memory of ordinary events, and especially, of the names of people, is failing, but not for mathematical and scientific subjects. I am still able to read books on the higher algebra for four or five hours in the mornings, and even to solve the problems. Sometimes I find them difficult, but my old obstinacy remains, for if I do not succeed to-day, I attack them again on the morrow. I also enjoy reading about all the new discoveries and theories in the scientific world, and on all branches of science."[30] A recent writer says of Somerville's last published scientific book, *On Molecular and Microscopic Science* (1869), that, "though its science was largely out of date, [it] was kindly received out of deference to its author, then in her eighty-ninth year."[31] What does it mean that Somerville was "kindly received"? Was her reception typical, or did it represent change in the way old women writers were treated as the nineteenth century progressed? Was it a matter of genre or an anomaly? Was it possible to publish scientific work as an old woman in this period and *not* be perceived as out of date?

In addition to the ordinary there are as well the unusual aspects of female authorship in old age. Prophetic writer Joanna Southcott (1750–1814) promised to give birth to Shiloh, the next Messiah, and showed signs of pregnancy at age 64. She died many weeks after the blessed event was to have occurred, an autopsy found no fetus, and her followers conjectured that Shiloh had "mysteriously disappeared."[32] One contemporary denounced her prophecies as "the witless efflorescences of a distracted old woman."[33] Ann Radcliffe (1764–1823), though she did not survive far into old age, had a mysterious late life, and it was rumored that she was driven crazy by her own Gothic novels. Though little is known of her last years, in which she seems to have gone silent, her fiction features scores of garrulous old servants. One, in *The Italian* (1797), complains of her lot, "old women now-a-days are not much thought of; out of sight out of mind with them, now-a-days!"[34] This comment by a minor character might itself serve as a backdrop for many of the writings, experiences, and attitudes we have seen throughout this book.

Although British women writers deserve to be studied across their careers and across the life course, what this book has sought to demonstrate is that their late lives present us with thorny issues and factual and methodological questions that persist at the level of the group and the individual. Until we take seriously the idea that studying gender and old age in the past presents its own set of concerns, we are bound to ignore or mischaracterize female authors' late lives. We risk following Victorian critic Jerom Murch by seeing women writers in old age as "calm and gentle," living out an inoffensive, graceful coda. We might carry forward other limiting frameworks, such as viewing old persons in the past as powerless to respond to cultural stereotypes or, on the contrary, as being able to set their own terms and agendas. We have, for more than a century, comprehended the late lives of early modern British women writers too rosily, too darkly, or more often, not at all. We owe it to our subjects and to our literary and cultural histories to investigate British women writers in old age through emerging frameworks, some of which are enacted in the chapters of this book. If old women remain overwhelmingly out of sight in our scholarship, there is no reason any longer for them to remain out of mind.

Abbreviations

BL   Department of Manuscripts. British Library

KU MS 197   Porter Papers. Department of Special Collections. Kenneth Spencer Research Library. University of Kansas, Lawrence

PC/NYPL   Jane Porter Papers. Pforzheimer Collection. New York Public Library

Preface

1. Murch, *Mrs. Barbauld and Her Contemporaries*, 175. Hereafter cited in text.

2. See "Modern Old Age." Hereafter cited in text.

3. The excerpt on long-lived literary women was republished as "Brainwork and Longevity."

4. Madden, *Infirmities of Genius*.

5. Rev. of *The Infirmities of Genius*, 34. Hereafter cited in text.

6. The reviewer egregiously miscalculated the ages at death for Centlivre, Sheridan, Macaulay, Delany, and possibly Lennox, whose birth year remains uncertain. The *Oxford Dictionary of National Biography* lists the years of birth/baptism and death of the women in this list as follows: Elizabeth, Lady Russell (bap. 1637, d. 1723); Elizabeth Singer Rowe (1674–1737); Lady Mary Wortley Montagu (bap. 1689, d. 1762); Susannah Centlivre (bap. 1669, d. 1723); Mary, Lady Hervey (1699/1700–1768); Henrietta Howard, Lady Suffolk (ca. 1688–1767); Frances Sheridan (1724–66); Hannah Cowley (1743–1809); Catharine Macaulay (1731–91); Elizabeth Montagu (1718–1800); Hester Mulso Chapone (1727–1801); Charlotte Lennox (ca. 1730/31?–1804); Sarah Trimmer (1741–1810); Elizabeth Hamilton (1756?–1816); Ann Radcliffe (1764–1823); Anna Letitia Barbauld (1743–1825); Mary Delany (1700–1788); Elizabeth Inchbald (1753–1821); Hester Lynch Piozzi (1741–1821); and Hannah More (1745–1833).

7. Graves, "Lectures on Medical Statistics," 461–63. My thanks to Andrew Baster for pointing me to this article.

8. For an important study of the aged in eighteenth-century France, see Troyansky, *Old Age in the Old Regime*. For a groundbreaking work on women and old age in the United States, see Premo, *Winter Friends*.

9. Laslett, *Family Life and Illicit Love*, 174.

10. Margaret Morganroth Gullette, "Age (Aging)," in *Encyclopedia of Feminist Literary Theory*, ed. Elizabeth Kowaleski-Wallace (New York: Garland, 1997), 9.

11. Gullette, *Aged by Culture*, 102.

12. Browne, *Women, Feminism, and Aging*, xix.

13. Works such as Betty Friedan's *The Fountain of Age* are eloquent on the "problem" of old age in today's world but do not focus on history. Scholarship in the humanities has primarily attended to classical literature, to canonical writings of the Middle Ages and the Renaissance (especially Shakespeare's *King Lear*), or to recent works, with feminists concentrating primarily on the late twentieth century. Collections such as Wyatt-Brown and Rossen's *Aging and Gender in Literature* (1993) and Woodward's *Figuring Age* (1999) blazed the trail. Important work has appeared on women's aging in national literatures as well; see, e.g., Cavigioli, *Women of a Certain Age*.

14. Laslett, *A Fresh Map of Life*, vi.

15. See Steinem, *Outrageous Acts*, 238–46.

Introduction

1. Woolf, *A Room of One's Own*, 113.

2. For example, Cutting takes Woolf's quotation for her title and echoes the call for a wreath, but she does not remark on the strange impossibility of the request. See "A Wreath for Fanny Burney's Last Novel," 45.

3. Qtd. from Samuel Chew's *The Nineteenth Century and After* (1948), in Newcomer, "Maria Edgeworth and the Critics," 216. Mitzi Myers, after noting Edgeworth's long, successful career, also calls her "the predecessor of Scott and Austen" ("Shot from Canons," 196). Myers's fascinating article exploring Edgeworth's nineteenth-century canonicity and fall from favor does not consider aging as a possible factor.

4. See Botelho and Thane, *Women and Ageing in British Society*. Elisabeth Mignon's is currently the only book-length study of English literary representations of old age in the period; see *Crabbed Age and Youth*. See also Pines, "Past Her Flourishing Time."

5. Ottaway, *The Decline of Life*, 14. Hereafter cited in text.

6. For the aged poor of both sexes, Ottaway demonstrates, "it is impossible to exaggerate the desperate misery" of their conditions (ibid.).

7. Mangum, "Growing Old," 99.

8. Marquise de Lambert, *Advice of a Mother to Her Daughter*, 17.

9. Greene, *Poetical Essays*, 51.

10. On the use of kinship metaphors in literary history, see Spencer, *Literary Relations*. Spencer argues that "metaphors of kinship and family . . . served both to include and subordinate women in the canon" (230).

11. Browning and Browning, *The Brownings' Correspondence*, 10: 14. This quotation first came to my attention in McCarthy, "The Repression of Hester Lynch Piozzi," 103. In a previous letter (3 Jan. 1845), Barrett Browning writes, "Joanna Baillie is the first female poet in all senses, in England" (10: 4).

12. On eighteenth-century women poets, see Backscheider, *Eighteenth-Century Women Poets*.

13. [Maginn], "Miss Jane Porter," 404. On the "Gallery of Illustrious Literary Characters" series, see Fisher, "In the Present Famine of Anything Substantial."

14. Parnell, *Collected Poems*, 161.

15. Erickson, *Mother Midnight*, 148. For a brief feminist history of the "the Wise Crone," see Walker, *The Crone*.

16. Van Tilburg, "Where Has 'the Wise, Old Woman' Gone?," 164.

17. Banner, *In Full Flower*, 17. Hereafter cited in text. Banner's book considers the social and sexual status of older women in Western myth, history, literature, and popular culture from the medieval period to the present. Simone de Beauvoir's flawed but groundbreaking *The Coming of Age* concluded that writing a history of age was impossible and suggested that aging women have no history.

18. On actual grandmothers and their experiences and self-understanding in America, see Premo, *Winter Friends*, 83–102. Hereafter cited in text.

19. See Clifford, *Young Sam Johnson*; Gérin, *The Young Fanny Burney*; Tinker, *Young Boswell*; and Vining, *Young Walter Scott*. Thomas Dormandy, in *Old Masters*, his study of old age and artists, makes a similar point: "No chronological age is probably more creative than any other; but less is known about the creativity of great artists in old age than about their creativity in youth, maturity, or even childhood. Monographs which lovingly explore parents, grandparents, aunts, uncles and second cousins often wrap up their hero's sunset years in a paragraph or two. . . . Hence there are hundreds of books—some excellent—about the childhood and youth of famous artists and virtually none about their old age" (xiv). Dormandy's book covers five centuries of Western artists, including a handful of women.

20. See Laslett, *Family Life and Illicit Love*, 189. Charlotte Lennox may be one such example among women writers.

21. Sontag, "The Double Standard of Aging."

22. Combe and Schmader, "Naturalizing Myths of Aging," 202–3.

23. Terri Premo suggests that the middle of the nineteenth century "signaled the beginning of a new period in age relations" (*Winter Friends*, 2–3). This break seems likely in the British context as well. David Hacker Fischer also argues that a revolution in age relations ought to be dated to the period 1770–1820, but as Premo says, "some instead consider the 1830s as the critical period" in which a cult of youth emerged in America (4), and in any case, aged women may have been left out of this "revolution" (5). Further research is needed on these issues within and across national boundaries. Lynn Bothelo and Susannah Ottaway's multivolume collection of primary documents, *The History of Old Age in England, 1600–1800*, holds much information of great promise for future scholars.

24. Thane, "Social Histories of Old Age and Aging," 93. Hereafter cited in text. That exciting work includes the following: Laslett, *Family Life and Illicit Love*; Quadagno, *Aging in Early Industrial Society*; Stearns, *Old Age in European Society*; Stearns, *Old Age in Preindustrial Society*; Stearns, "Old Women"; Campbell, "Lady Mary Wortley Montagu"; and Thane, *Old Age in English History*. Thane's was the first book-length study on the subject of old age in English history.

25. Thane, *Old Age in English History*, 19. Hereafter cited in text.

26. Troyansky, "The Eighteenth Century," 175.

27. See Botelho, *Old Age and the English Poor Law*, 157.

28. Covey, "The Definitions of the Beginning of Old Age," 328–30.

29. Gordon, *The Plan of a Society*, 2. Though his is an American work, Gordon says he models his proposal on London societies.

30. Stearns, *Old Age in European Society*, 24.

31. Thane, "An Untiring Zest for Life." Hereafter cited in text.

32. Cole and Winkler, *The Oxford Book of Aging*, 8.

33. Sinclair, *The Code of Health and Longevity*.

34. On this problem, see Feinson, "Where Are the Women in the History of Aging?" See also Soland, "Ages of Women." In recent years, it may be that more attention has been paid to women and women's writing and old age in eighteenth-century studies, rather than to men and men's writing. In its special issue, "Aging and Identity: An Eighteenth-Century Perspective," the *Journal of Aging and Identity* 4.2 (1999) includes four essays, three of which deal with women. For an important exception, see Connery, "Self-Representation and Memorials."

35. Stearns, "Old Women," 46.

36. Rousseau, "Towards a Geriatric Enlightenment," 32.

37. Willich, *Lectures on Diet and Regimen*, 170.

38. Hufeland, *The Art of Prolonging Life*. Margaret Morganroth Gullette describes Hufeland's book as "a classic and important statement of the ideology" of late-life virility for men. See "Male Midlife Sexuality," 61.

39. Van Oven, *On the Decline of Life*, 92.

40. Cohausen, *Hermippus Redivivus*, 61. For a nineteenth-century review that pokes fun at the curiosities of this book, see "On the Prolongation of Life."

41. Cohausen, *Hermippus Redivivus*, 38.

42. Cornaro, *Sure Methods of Attaining a Long and Healthful Life*, 50. Hereafter cited in text.

43. Cicero, *Cato maior de senectute*.

44. Godwin, *Enquiry concerning Political Justice*, 2: 520. As Roy Porter notes, Godwin believed prolonged lives would not bring overpopulation because reason would triumph "over the flesh, people would cease to reproduce, and libido would dissolve away"; see *Flesh in the Age of Reason*, 428.

45. Gruman, *A History of Ideas about the Prolongation of Life*, 91. Gruman discussed Godwin and Condorcet alongside Malthus, who wrote a rejoinder to both.

46. MacKenzie, *The History of Health*, 435.

47. Laslett, *Family Life and Illicit Love*, 194.

48. Rousseau, "Towards a Geriatric Enlightenment," 30, 41.

49. Stearns, "Old Women," 47.

50. Honoria, *The Female Mentor*, 86.

51. From the *Rambler* 69 (Nov. 13, 1750), qtd. in Campbell, "Lady Mary Wortley Montagu," 222.

52. De Valangin, *A Treatise on Diet*, 317–18.

53. "Modern Old Age," 582. Even in this shift, there was a skepticism that the studious would enjoy superlongevity. Sir John Sinclair writes, "Those who direct their attention to study, or are engaged in the learned professions, have seldom reached very great longevity, about 80 years of age being their usual highest standard"; see *The Code of Health and Longevity*, 553.

54. Some sources saw women living slightly longer on average though they believed that men lived longest. Consider this source, citing Hufeland: "More women than men become old but men, only, attain to the utmost extent of longevity. The equilibrium and pliability of the female body seem, for a certain time, to give it more durability, and to render it less susceptible of injury from destructive influence. But male strength is, without doubt, necessary to arrive at a very great age. More women, therefore, become old; but fewer very old"; see *An Essay on the Most Rational Means of Preserving Health,* 103–4.

55. *The Female Aegis,* 171–80. As Gina Luria's introduction points out, this text is pirated from Thomas Gisbourne's *Enquiry into the Duties of the Female Sex* (1797), though *The Female Aegis* was more often referred to in bibliographies dealing with the "woman question" (5–6).

56. See Scott, *The Journal of Sir Walter Scott,* 441. I am grateful to Mike Goode, whose work brought this quotation to my attention; see "Drysasdust Antiquarianism and Soppy Masculinity," 61.

57. Mary Wollstonecraft writes of a man in "garrulous old age" (*Historical and Moral View,* 1: 306). Charlotte Smith mentions anecdotes that "garrulous old age loves to repeat" (*Marchmont,* 3: 55). M. G. Lewis also features a "talkative old woman" in his *Ambrosio,* 1: 15. Blair's *The Grave* mentions "garrulous old age" (19). This poem was included in *Elegant Extracts.*

58. More, *Moral Sketches,* xviii.

59. The *OED* notes an exception to this stereotype, the female "old sage," a rare term meaning "midwife," in use in the early nineteenth century. This would be in keeping with Robert Erickson's documentation of the "grandmother wisdom" role; see Erickson, *Mother Midnight.*

60. Klassen, "The Domestic Virtues of Old Age." On the subject of old age in the Revolutionary period, see also Troyansky, "Looking for Grandparents in the French Revolution."

61. David Troyansky has argued that "a major shift" occurred in French attitudes toward aging and the aged in the eighteenth century, moving from "one extreme of ridicule and neglect to another of respect and care"; see *Old Age in the Old Regime,* 6. His view is that "literature replaced a stereotype of resentment with one of honor and respect" in the eighteenth century. I have not located a similar movement to respect the old in a British context— certainly not for individual women writers.

62. Terri Premo put it this way in the American context: "Long before elements of antebellum society attempted to put women 'on a pedestal,' . . . aging women were expected to model their own behavior on a similarly passive version of femininity" (*Winter Friends,* 108).

63. Because much of my argument is based on women writers' receptions, it seems important to target authors who sought print and experienced author as a central identity. Though the term *professional* is a fraught one, and though not all of the women under consideration in this study were able to support themselves through writing, all were selected because they enjoyed a mass readership over a long span of years. This made their late lives more visible than some of their less-often-published contemporaries and therefore makes their late receptions more attributable to ideologies of gender and aging.

64. Turner, *Living by the Pen,* 60. Hereafter cited in text.

65. Bannet, *The Domestic Revolution*, 1.

66. Todd, *Dictionary of British and American Women Writers*; Schleuter and Schleuter, *Encyclopedia of British Women Writers*.

67. The authors included in this sample were Elizabeth Craven, Lady Anspach (1750–1828); Joanna Baillie (1762–1851); Anna Letitia Barbauld (1743–1822); Mary Berry (1763–1852); Elizabeth Bonhote (1744–1818); Frances Burney, Mme d'Arblay (1752–1840); Sarah Harriet Burney (1772–1844); Elizabeth Carter (1717–1806); Maria Edgeworth (1768–1849); Mary Hays (1760–1843); Harriet Lee (1757–1851); Sophia Lee (1750–1824); Charlotte Lennox (1729?–1804); Hannah More (1745–1833); Amelia Opie (1769–1853); Sydney Owenson, Lady Morgan (1776?–1859); Hester Lynch Piozzi (1741–1821); Jane Porter (1776–1850); Clara Reeve (1729–1807); Regina Maria Roche (1764?–1845); Sarah Trimmer (1741–1811); Priscilla Wakefield (1751–1832); and Jane West (1758–1852).

68. Kafker, "La Vieillesse et la productivité intellectuelle."

69. Lehman, *Age and Achievement*, 99. Lehman notes that, though he attempted to prepare a separate chapter on women, he could not proceed, as "the attempt to find sufficient data" was "rather unrewarding" (97).

70. Lehman and his coauthor tried to measure literary quality against age in terms of production. See Lehman and Heidler. "Chronological Age vs. Quality of Literary Output."

71. Heidler and Lehman, "Chronological Age and Productivity."

72. DeMaria, *The Life of Samuel Johnson*, 296.

73. Thomas C. Faulkner, s.v. "Crabbe, George (1754–1832)," *Oxford Dictionary of National Biography*.

74. Lavine, Review of *George Crabbe's Poetry*.

75. Bulstrode goes on to say that his late life poetic talent is a "particular Grace of God, it being very unusual in the Generality, and very hard for Men to seem young when they're old, and much more strange to be so." See *Miscellaneous Essays*, 382.

76. Graves, *Senilities*.

77. See Carlisle, *An Essay on the Disorders of Old Age*, 14.

78. Graves, *The Triflers*.

79. Rogers, "Introductory Note."

80. Kaplan calls the "having-done-this-ness" of second-wave feminists—the having gone through particular historical experiences—a "special quality of aging" ("Introduction 2," 13).

81. Taylor, *Retrospection*. This was not a trope confined to old age or to women writers. Mary Matilda Betham (1776–1852) published a "Retrospect of Youth" in her *Poems* (1808); see Betham, *Poems and Elegies*, 92–93.

82. Retrospection was not always sanguine. A reviewer of D'Israeli's *Calamities of Authors* (1812), e.g., speaks of the "retrospective dissatisfaction" shared by authors and statesmen when looking back on accomplishments from old age; see rev. of *Calamities of Authors*, 8.

83. On literary men and mentors, see Spencer, *Literary Relations*.

84. Anthony Lee is working on the subject of literary mentorship during the eighteenth century, which promises to address these matters.

85. Wood, "*Studious to Please*," 108. The will, reproduced in facsimile in Wood's book, is dated 1824.

86. For information on Lennox's possible year of birth, see Carlile, "Expanding the Feminine."

87. Batchelor, "The Claims of Literature," 519. Batchelor calls Lennox "the exception that proves the rule" of the Fund's poor treatment of women novelist applicants. Royal Literary Fund treatment of women applicants improved from 1840 to 1880, as S. D. Mumm demonstrates; see Mumm, "Writing for Their Lives."

88. Cross, *Archives of the Royal Literary Fund*, reel 1.

89. Blain, Clements, and Grundy, *The Feminist Companion*, 761.

90. E. M. G. Smith, "Hannah More," in *Dictionary of Literary Biography*, 158: 231.

91. Nicholas R. Jones, "Hannah More," in *Dictionary of Literary Biography*, 107: 210.

92. Hester Piozzi, "Lyford Redivivus," Hyde Case 9 (16), Donald and Mary Hyde Collection of Dr. Samuel Johnson, Houghton Library, Harvard College Library. See also Clifford, *Hester Lynch Piozzi*, 436.

93. Mangin, *Piozziana*, 14.

94. Trollope, *An Autobiography*, 28. I thank Tom Lockwood for pointing me to this source.

95. April Alliston, s.v. "Lee, Harriet (1757/8–1851)," *Oxford Dictionary of National Biography*.

96. Gary Kelly, s.v. "Reeve, Clara (1729–1807)," *Oxford Dictionary of National Biography*.

97. Sutherland, "Henry Colburn, Publisher," 59.

98. Vullaimy, *Mrs. Thrale of Streatham*, 319–20.

99. Priscilla Dorr, "Joanna Baillie," in *Encyclopedia of British Women Writers*, 26.

100. Piozzi, *The Piozzi Letters*, 6: 374. I am grateful to Bill McCarthy for this quotation; see his review of *The Piozzi Letters*, 435.

101. Baillie called it her "monster" book. See Slagle, *Joanna Baillie*, 284.

102. Sharon Winn, "Carolina, Baroness Nairne," in *Encyclopedia of British Women Writers*, 473.

103. Kathleen Reuter Chamberlain, "Sydney Owenson, Lady Morgan," in *Dictionary of Literary Biography*, 116: 221.

104. Carol Hart, "Sydney Owenson, Lady Morgan," in *Dictionary of Literary Biography*, 158: 248.

105. See Kittredge, "The Ag'd Dame," 261.

106. Croker, rev. of *The Wanderer*, 125–26. Hereafter cited in text.

107. Quoted in McCarthy and Kraft, *Poems of Anna Letitia Barbauld*, 318. The anecdote is Henry Crabb Robinson's.

One • Past the Period of Choosing to Write a "Love-tale"?

1. Brock, *Feminization of Fame*, 135.

2. Burney, *Evelina*, 275.

3. Qtd. in Bilger, *Laughing Feminism*, 198; Anderson, "Footnotes More Pedestrian Than Sublime," 56. See also Sherbo, "Addenda to 'Footnotes More Pedestrian Than Sublime.' "

4. Brophy, *Women's Lives*, 262; Freedman, "Sufficiently Decayed," 54. See also Eckersley, "The Role of *Evelina*'s 'Worthiest Object.' "

5. Straub, *Divided Fictions,* 46.

6. Burney and Barrett, *Diary and Letters of Madame D'arblay,* 7: 378–85. See also Thaddeus, *Frances Burney,* 4.

7. Burney, Hemlow, and Douglas, *Journals and Letters of Fanny Burney.*

8. Burney and Barrett, *Diary and Letters of Madame D'arblay,* 7: 378, 384.

9. Thomas Babington Macaulay, "Madame D'Arblay," in *Essays,* 5: 13. References to this edition are hereafter cited in text.

10. Burney and Barrett, *Diary and Letters of Madame D'arblay,* 7: 385.

11. Cutting, "A Wreath for Fanny Burney's Last Novel," 47.

12. Hemlow, *The History of Fanny Burney,* 339.

13. Burney, *The Wanderer,* 9. Hereafter cited in text.

14. Burney, Hemlow, and Douglas, *Journals and Letters of Fanny Burney,* 7: 104.

15. On the figure of the wandering Jew, see Anderson, *The Legend of the Wandering Jew.* See also Troyansky, *Old Age in the Old Regime,* 56–57. On women and "painting," see Downing, "Face Painting in Early Modern England," 119–20.

16. Thaddeus describes the "grand climacteric" as the year in which Burney would "by tradition either change greatly or die" (148).

17. Many have speculated that Juliet has biographical resonances with her author. A contemporary anonymous poem identified Burney as a "lonely Wanderer"; see "Addressed to Mrs. D'Arblay," 373.

18. Mrs. Carver, *The Old Woman.*

19. Qtd. in Brightfield, *John Wilson Croker,* 133. Jane Rendall presents a more complicated position on Croker's views of literary women; see "Bluestockings and Reviewers," 367.

20. On Croker and Lady Morgan, see Ferris, *The Achievement of Literary Authority,* 48–51. For an account of Croker as a reviewer, see Morgan, *Literary Critics and Reviewers,* 111–21.

21. Croker, rev. of *The Wanderer,* 123–24. Hereafter cited in text.

22. On this phenomenon and Croker's review, see Ferris, *The Achievement of Literary Authority,* 42.

23. Hazlitt, rev. of *The Wanderer,* 338.

24. Rev. of *The Wanderer, British Critic,* 385. Hereafter cited in text.

25. Rev. of *The Wanderer, Anti-Jacobin Review,* 353. Hereafter cited in text.

26. Rev. of *The Wanderer, Theatrical Inquisitor,* 236–37.

27. Taylor, rev. of *The Wanderer,* 412. Hereafter cited in text.

28. Rev. of *The Wanderer, Gentleman's Magazine,* 579.

29. Rev. of *The Wanderer, European Magazine,* 426.

30. Connery, "Self-Representation and Memorials," 142.

31. For important reassessments of Burney's career and of *The Wanderer,* see Perkins, "Private Men and Public Women," and Justice, *The Manufacturers of Literature.*

32. Maggie Gee, Introduction to *Helen* (1987), ix, xii.

33. Butler, *Maria Edgeworth,* 477–78. Hereafter cited in text.

34. Gonda, *Reading Daughters' Fictions,* 204; for a summary of the father/daughter debates, see 204–7.

35. Jacqueline Pearson suggests that Edgeworth derived the name from Burney's heroine in *Cecilia,* turning her into an antiheroine; see "Arts of Appropriation," 230.

36. Edgeworth, *Novels and Selected Works*, 9: 12. Hereafter cited in text.

37. Ó Gallchoir, *Maria Edgeworth*, 167.

38. Newby, *Maria Edgeworth*, 89.

39. Despite the high price negotiated for *Helen*, Marilyn Butler claims that "Maria probably reached her peak as a selling author in 1812–1814, before her reputation began to suffer from comparison with Scott and Austen" (*Maria Edgeworth*, 491–92).

40. Slade, *Maria Edgeworth*, 199.

41. Lawless, *Maria Edgeworth*, 194.

42. Zimmern, *Maria Edgeworth*, 260.

43. On Gaskell and Edgeworth, see Butler, "The Uniqueness of Cynthia Kirkpatrick."

44. Lockhart, rev. of *Helen*, 483.

45. Rev. of *Helen*. Hereafter cited in text.

46. The attribution to Peabody is made in Butler, *Maria Edgeworth*, 478. On eighteenth-century literature and culture in the nineteenth century, see O'Gorman and Turner, *The Victorians and the Eighteenth Century*.

47. Botkin, "Finding Her Own Voice," 106.

48. Ezell, *Writing Women's Literary History*, 103.

49. Rev. of *The Works of Maria Edgeworth*, 383. Hereafter cited in text.

50. Edgeworth, *Helen*, iii.

51. Ibid., vii.

52. Rev. of *A Memoir of Maria Edgeworth*.

53. Inglis-Jones, *The Great Maria*.

54. Hawthorne, *Doubt and Dogma*, 4.

55. Edgeworth, *Novels and Selected Works*, 1: 46.

56. Edgeworth, *Castle Rackrent*, 1:47.

57. Thomas Babington Macaulay suggests this precise connection for Burney: "She survived her own wake, and overheard the judgment of posterity" (*Essays*, 5: 14). He seems not to draw the conclusion that, like Sir Condy, Burney could have been disappointed.

Two • *Catharine Macaulay's Waning Laurels*

1. Wollstonecraft, *Vindication*, 105. Hereafter cited in text. As is the scholarly tradition, I refer to Catharine Macaulay Graham throughout this essay as "Macaulay."

2. In the wake of her oft-touted revival in the 1990s and afterward, Macaulay is still subject to vituperative response and curious omission, but most signs point to a vigorous reassessment. In a recent article, Philip Hicks refers to *Letters on Education* as a "minor classic of feminist theory"; see "Catharine Macaulay's Civil War," 171, 196.

3. Wollstonecraft, *Works*.

4. J. G. A. Pocock argues, to the contrary, that Wollstonecraft and Macaulay inhabited different worlds: "The mental world of Mary Wollstonecraft is already very different from that of Catharine Macaulay—less classical, less rhetorical, less theatrical. One does not feel that Wollstonecraft wanted to be a Roman matron or a Goddess of Liberty, but Macaulay of course dressed the part; and in Wollstonecraft one finds an authentic feminism, born of Rousseau and her own revolt against Rousseau, which belongs to another world than Macaulay's. The

heirs of the latter were the friends of Mr. Fox and the guardians of his flame, not Godwin's" ("Catharine Macaulay," 257–58). Though Pocock's argument is meticulous and fascinating, I do not think it gives enough credit to the departure evident in Macaulay's last work, *Letters on Education*, particularly as that book seems very much in conversation with Rousseau. Had Macaulay lived, it seems to me that she could have become part of Wollstonecraft's and Godwin's "mental world," despite her generational difference. For an additional comparison of Wollstonecraft to Macaulay, see Sotiropoulos, *Early Feminists*, 131–63. Sotiropoulos finds many commonalities between the two women's educational treatises, though she argues that Macaulay's is "tamer" (137).

5. "Obituary of Considerable Persons," 589.

6. "Catherine Macaulay," *The Times*, no. 551 (10 Oct. 1786): 2C. The entire anecdote reads, "Catherine Macaulay, in the *decline* of *life*, and *heat* of *passion*, took unto herself a juvenile husband, whom she *modestly* calls her *cherisher.*—Every Lady now has her *cherisher*, and as convincing proof of her *piety*, that *cherisher* is a *Bishop*."

7. See Kirkham, *Jane Austen*, 12.

8. Her history is rightly celebrated for its documentary research and strong argumentation.

9. See Boos, "Catherine Macaulay's *Letters on Education* (1790)"; Gardner, "Catharine Macaulay's *Letters on Education*"; and Titone, "Catharine Macaulay's *Letters on Education*."

10. The New York Public Library acquired the letters between Wollstonecraft and Macaulay. See Hill, "The Links between Mary Wollstonecraft and Catharine Macaulay." Hereafter cited in text.

11. Wollstonecraft, rev. of *Letters on Education*.

12. Murch, *Mrs. Barbauld and Her Contemporaries*, 175.

13. Hill, *The Republican Virago*, 1. Hereafter cited in text.

14. On her letters to her daughter, see Hill, "Daughter and Mother." Hereafter cited in text.

15. [Graham], *Letters on Education*; *Observations on the Reflections of the Right Hon. Edmund Burke*. References to both are hereafter cited in text.

16. For an excellent account comparing Macaulay's *Observations* and Wollstonecraft's *Vindication*, see Gunther-Canada, "The Politics of Sense and Sensibility," 126–47. Gunther-Canada argues that "both women turned the tables on Burke by employing a dual strategy of battling his interpretation of the rights of man and belittling his effeminate style of rhetoric" (128).

17. Wordsworth, *The Bright Work Grows*, 49.

18. "Obituary of Considerable Persons," 590.

19. On Macaulay's epistolary history, see Looser, *British Women Writers*. In her *History in Letters*, Macaulay includes several personal asides to her addressee, Dr. Wilson, and she interrupts her history to defend her grandfather from accusations of wrongdoing in the South Sea Bubble episode. See Macaulay, *The History of England from the Revolution to the Present Time*.

20. Macaulay, *A Treatise on the Immutability of Moral Truth*.

21. Badcock, "Original Anecdotes from Mr. Badcock." For another reading of Badcock's letter and Macaulay's citing it, see Brock, *Feminization of Fame*, 55.

22. Wollstonecraft, rev. of *Letters on Education*, 243, 245. Hereafter cited in text. On Wollstonecraft as a reviewer, see Myers, "Sensibility and the 'Walk of Reason.'" Myers notes that Wollstonecraft is "often tart with women writers" in her reviews (126).

23. Rev. of *Letters on Education*. Hereafter cited in text.

24. Griffiths, "Correspondence," 119. Hereafter cited in text.

25. Catharine Macaulay to Ralph Griffiths, Nov. 1790. Catharine Macaulay Papers, GLC 1794.47. The Gilder Lehrman Collection, the Gilder Lehrman Institute of American History, New York City. Hereafter cited in text as GLC 1794.47.

26. Joddrell, *The Female Patriot*, 25. On this era of her life, see Davies, *Catharine Macaulay and Mercy Otis Warren*. See also Davies, "Revolutionary Correspondence."

27. Carter, *Letters*, 3: 98–99. See also Betty Schellenberg's account of Sarah Scott's changing responses to Macaulay in *The Professionalization of Women Writers*, 170–71.

28. See "Account of the Life and Writings," 330, 334. Hereafter cited in text.

29. Bennett, *Strictures on Female Education*, 48, 50.

30. On Macaulay's reception throughout her life and its sexist underpinnings, see Mazzucco-Than, "As Easy As A Chimney Pot to Blacken"; Staves, "The Liberty of a She-Subject"; and Guest, *Small Change*, 195–208.

31. Bridget Hill briefly discusses this passage; see *Republican Virago*, 159–60. See also Brock's long revisionary account of the monument, which also quotes this passage (*Feminization of Fame*, 63–75). Brock's readings of the era's "democratization of fame" in relation to women in general and Macaulay in particular is interesting, but I believe she downplays the extent to which Macaulay seems to have had an eye to posthumous reputation. Furthermore, Macaulay's letter to Griffiths complicates Brock's conclusion that "Macaulay survived to see the benefits of becoming a living monument" (76).

32. Fieser, "Eighteenth-Century British Reviews," 647. Hereafter cited in text.

33. Nangle, *The Monthly Review*, 159. Enfield has been described as "the most feminist of the reviewers" of Mary Wollstonecraft's *Vindication of the Rights of Woman* (Janes, "Reception," 295).

34. [Enfield], Rev. of *Letters on Education*, 309.

35. G. P. Macdonell, rev. Adam I. P. Smith, s.v. "Lolme, John Louis de (1741–1806)," *Oxford Dictionary of National Biography*. Hereafter cited in text.

36. Macaulay expressed concern in her *History in Letters* that she had not provided readers with enough entertainment, but she does not tie it to her sex (*History of England from the Revolution to the Present Time*, 29). In volume 1 of her *History of England*, Macaulay apologizes for her skills and her sex: "The inaccuracies of stile which may be found in this composition, will, I hope, find favour from the candour of the public; and the defects of a female historian, in these points, not weighed in the balance"; see *The History of England from the Accession of James I*, 1: xviii. On women writers and reviewers, see Donoghue, *The Fame Machine*.

37. In her work on reviewing practices, Marilyn Butler concludes that Ralph Griffith's *Monthly Review* was "generally fair" in its judgments and "typically not interested," as its reviewers were "often authorities in their fields"; see "Culture's Medium," 126.

38. W. P. Courtney, "Samuel Badcock," in *Dictionary of National Biography*, ed. Leslie Stephen (London: Smith, Elder, 1885), 2: 382.

39. W. P. Courtney, rev. Antonia Foster, s.v. "Badcock, Samuel (1747–1788)," *Oxford Dictionary of National Biography*. Hereafter cited in text as Courtney, *DNB*.

40. Hawkins, "Some Writers on the *Monthly Review*," 170.

41. Gabriel, *Facts*.

42. Macaulay's name was included in *The Complete Young Man's Companion*, 410.

43. See *Aberdeen Magazine* 64 (1790): 424–27 and 71 (1790): 581–85.

44. See Lickorish, *Sermons*, 218. On Macaulay's inclusion in the "Men of Learning and Genius," see *The Prose Epitome*, 456.

45. Reeve, *Plans of Education*, vii. Hereafter cited in text.

46. "Remarks on Mrs. Macaulay Graham's *Letters on Education*." Hereafter cited in text.

47. D'Israeli, *A Dissertation on Anecdotes*. The story was repeated in a later volume of *Curiosities of Literature*; see D'Israeli, *Curiosities of Literature*, 446. Hereafter cited in text.

48. Rev. of *A Dissertation on Anecdotes*.

49. Richard Gough, rev. of *A Dissertation on Anecdotes*. Even into the twentieth century, critics found D'Israeli's version of events more compelling. Macaulay scholar Robert Pierpont found the "balance of probability" on D'Israeli's side; see *"History."*

50. On D'Israeli's sketches of authors as partial and exaggerated, see rev. of *Calamities of Authors*, 7.

51. Various versions of this text circulated in the periodicals. See D'Israeli, Letter to the Editor. The manuscript itself offers no further clues. There, the text appears as follows:

> Upon examination of this book
> Novr 12, 1764. these four last leaves
> Were torn out   C. Morton
> Mem: Novr 12 sent down to
> Mrs. McCauley. (BL Harley 7379; 3: 529)

A February 1852 annotator (J.M.) questions whether Morton's four is correct and includes an asterisk proposing that three leaves had been cut away, rather than four. There is also some possibility that Morton's note has been dilapidated, as it appears to have been pasted in the volume.

52. "Acknowledgments to Correspondents."

53. D'Israeli, Letter to the Editor; Graham, Letter to the Editor, 907.

54. Graham, Letter to the Editor, 908. On D'Israeli's accusations, see Hill, *Republican Virago*, 242–44. See also Ogden, *Isaac D'Israeli*, 28–29, for a lucid summary of the years of published correspondence on the matter. Ogden deems the evidence "plausible but inconclusive" (28).

55. One respondent ("H. H."), who called himself no friend to D'Israeli, struck back by likening Graham's scolding to that of a "virago," a word that had frequently been used to describe his late wife. H. H., Letter to the Editor, *Gentleman's Magazine* 64 (1794): 1001. For his part, D'Israeli took Graham to task for his "Virulence of Style"; D'Israeli, Letter to the Editor, *British Critic*.

56. D'Israeli, "Advertisement," 225.

57. I am grateful to April London for pointing me to these references. See her essay, "Isaac D'Israeli and Literary History."

58. D'Israeli, *Commentaries on the Life*, 1: xxi. Hereafter cited in text. See also D'Israeli's *Inquiry*, 6–9, 203–14.

59. Hays, *Female Biography*, 292. On Macaulay, Hays, and Wollstonecraft, see Mandell, "Virtue and Evidence."

60. Hays, *Female Biography*, 300.

61. Barbauld, *Works*, 2: 118.

62. Lefanu, *Memoirs*, 234.

63. Polwhele, *Traditions and Recollections*, 1: 98–99. Hereafter cited in text. For the odes, see Graves et al., *Six Odes*. The six odes are attributed, in order, to Richard Graves, E. Rack, Mr. Hinks, Polwhele, and Mr. Meyler (*Traditions*, 43). Polwhele (1760–1838) is best known today as the author of the poem *The Unsex'd Females* (1798), a work that excoriates Wollstonecraft and those in her wake and puts Hannah More and her ilk on a pedestal. Polwhele remains a chivalric friend to Macaulay, noting that "there are few ladies who have written history, with a Macaulay," finding "numerous femalities" in her work (*Unsex'd Females*, 49).

64. On James Graham, see Schnorrenberg, "Medical Men of Bath" See also Altick, *The Shows of London*, 82–84.

65. Another work—Joseph Priestley's *Lectures on History and General Policy* (first published 1783)—went through many editions and lists as its index entry to Macaulay, "Macaulay's (Mrs.), masterly history."

66. Rev. of *History of the Commonwealth*, 59, 60.

67. Lawrence, *The Lives of the British Historians*, 230. Hereafter cited in text.

68. Green, *Woman's Place*. Green's piece was first published in *Nineteenth Century* 41 (1897): 964–74.

69. Stenton, *The English Woman in History*, 311.

70. See Boos, "Catherine Macaulay's *Letters on Education*," 64–78; Boos and Boos, "Catharine Macaulay"; and Hill, *Republican Virago*, 250–51.

Three • *What Is Old in Jane Austen?*

1. Murch, *Mrs. Barbauld and Her Contemporaries*.

2. Woolf, *A Room of One's Own*, 113.

3. Auerbach, *Searching for Jane Austen*, 30.

4. For an account of aunts in eighteenth-century history and literature, see Perry, *Novel Relations*.

5. Lawrence, *A Propos of Lady Chatterly's Lover*, 58. On Lawrence's depreciation of Austen, see Kinkead-Weekes, "This Old Maid."

6. Halperin, *The Life of Jane Austen*.

7. Lee, *Virginia Woolf's Nose*, 69.

8. Fergus, *Jane Austen*, 170.

9. Lamont, "Jane Austen and the Old," 664. Hereafter cited in text. Lamont concludes that in Austen's novels "history [is] being rewritten as heritage" (674).

10. De Rose and McGuire, *Concordance*.

11. Austen, *Sense and Sensibility*, 11. Hereafter cited in text.

12. Austen, *Mansfield Park*, 189. Hereafter cited in text.

13. Austen, *Pride and Prejudice*, 162. Hereafter cited in text.

14. Austen, *Love and Friendship*, 2. Hereafter cited in text.

15. Austen, *Minor Works*, 6: 298. Hereafter cited in text.

16. Sokoloff, *The Margin That Remains*, 17. Hereafter cited in text.

17. Austen, *Emma*, 7. Hereafter cited in text.

18. See Dickens, *Great Expectations*; Gissing, *The Odd Women*. W. R. Greg's essay was first published in the *National Review* 14 (1862) and is included in his essay collection, *Literary and Social Judgments*.

19. On this subject, see Kranidis, *The Victorian Spinster*.

20. Katharine Kittredge argues that "the stereotype which we recognize as the 'Old Maid' came into being during the Eighteenth Century"; see "Tabby Cats Lead Apes in Hell," iv. Hereafter cited in text. Gwendolyn Needham argues, "the old maid did not become a widely recognized social and literary type until the Restoration"; see her "New Light on Old Maids," 116. See also Gwendolyn Bridges Needham, "The 'Old Maid.'" Bridget Hill notes that she chose to study the old maid during the period 1660–1850 because that time frame "sees women beginning to express themselves publicly . . . in the steady growth of writing women." By the end of the period, she notes, "the women's movement had an organized existence and was beginning to address some of the problems faced by spinsters"; see Hill, *Women Alone*, 2001, 4. Hereafter cited in text.

21. For an interesting consideration of this entry and of spinning in the period, see Brophy, *Women's Lives*, 199.

22. Lanser, "Singular Politics," 312. Hereafter cited in text.

23. Murphy, *The Way to Keep Him*, 255. Hereafter cited in text.

24. "Description of a Place."

25. Goldsmith, *The Citizen of the World*, 77.

26. This curious epigram, which has been the subject of scholarly investigations, dates to the sixteenth century and was in use as a folk saying or belief until the early twentieth century. See Whiting, "Old Maids Lead Apes in Hell." Hereafter cited in text. See also Needham, "New Light on Old Maids." Needham notes that the phrase "old maid" (rather than "maid") was first added to the proverb circa 1670 (106).

27. The quotation is from Sarah Hanschurst and appears in Premo, *Winter Friends*, 38.

28. Gregory, *A Father's Legacy to His Daughters*, 105. Hereafter cited in text.

29. *A Poetical Address to the Ladies of Suffolk*, 35–36.

30. *The British Apollo*, 1: 168. Hereafter cited in text.

31. For additional commentary on this periodical, see Larsen, "A Text of Identity."

32. I quote from Anna Letitia Barbauld, "Bouts Rimés," 357. William McCarthy and Elizabeth Kraft offer evidence that this poem was written early in Barbauld's life (before she was married) and discuss its attribution to her; see *Poems of Anna Letitia Barbauld*, 241–42.

33. Katharine Kittredge deems Aunt Patty the most repellent of the dependent spinsters she discusses in her survey of the eighteenth-century old maid, an "extremely negative character" ("Tabby," 273, 289).

34. Staves, "Matrimonial Discord in Fiction and in Court," 169. Hereafter cited in text.

35. Turner, *Living by the Pen*, 63, 80.

36. Mrs. Ross, *The Balance of Comfort*.

37. [Carrington], *Confessions of an Old Maid*, 1: 3. Hereafter cited in text.

38. Rev. of *Confessions of an Old Maid*, *La Belle Assemblée*.

39. Rev. of *Confessions of an Old Maid, Literary Gazette.*

40. The Centre for Editorial and Intertextual Research's "British Fiction 1800–1829" attributes the work to Edmund Frederick John Carrington. See Garside, Belanger, and Ragaz, *British Fiction, 1800–1829.*

41. Carrington also anonymously published *Confessions of an Old Bachelor. Confessions of an Old Maid* purports to be written by the Old Bachelor's sister, whom he mistreats.

42. A lengthy discussion of Hayley's *Essay* may be found in Kittredge, "Tabby." For her brief analysis of Austen and Hayley, see Kittredge, "That Excellent Miss Bates." Hereafter cited in text.

43. Vivienne W. Painting, s.v. "Hayley, William (1745–1820)," *Oxford Dictionary of National Biography.* For the "readable" comment, see "William Hayley," in *Dictionary of National Biography,* ed. Leslie Stephen and Sidney Lee (London: Smith, Elder & Co., 1891), 25: 295–96.

44. "The Life of William Hayley," 504. Hereafter cited in text.

45. This is from a letter to Hester Piozzi. See Seward, *Letters of Anna Seward,* 2: 339–40.

46. Hayley, *A Philosophical, Historical, and Moral Essay,* 1: v–vii. Hereafter cited in text.

47. Pennington, *Memoirs of the Life of Mrs. Elizabeth Carter,* 23.

48. For an account of Hayley's later, successful retirement scheme—an annuity in lieu of a lump payment for his future memoir—see chapter 6.

49. Gilson, *A Bibliography of Jane Austen,* 442.

50. Le Faye, "Jane Austen and William Hayley," 25–26.

51. The Norton Critical Edition of *Persuasion* includes a short excerpt from Hayley's treatise. See Austen, *Persuasion.* See also Teachman, *Understanding Pride and Prejudice.*

52. Rev. of *Philosophical, Historical, and Moral Essay on Old Maids.*

53. The main exceptions to this are Katharine Kittredge's and Jean Kern's essays, discussed below. See Kern, "The Old Maid." Hereafter cited in text. See also Kittredge, "Bates." On *Emma,* age, and patronage, see Hollindale, "Age and Patronage in *Emma.*"

54. Grundy, "Why Do They Talk So Much?," 48.

55. Kittredge, "The Ag'd Dame," 261.

56. Another male champion of old maids was Thomas Malthus, though he takes a different approach. He mentions the "marked inattentions to which many single women of advanced age are exposed" among the "higher classes of people." He laments that the fear of being an old maid and the "silly and unjust ridicule, which folly sometimes attaches to this name, drives many women into the marriage union." See *An Essay on the Principle of Population,* 523–24.

57. Brophy, *Women's Lives,* 232.

58. Utter and Needham, *Pamela's Daughters,* 241.

59. Kaplan, *Jane Austen among Women,* 122. Hereafter cited in text.

60. Austen, *Jane Austen's Letters,* 156–57. Hereafter cited in text.

61. Freeman, *T'Other Miss Austen,* 153. Hereafter cited in text.

62. Moore, "Emma and Miss Bates." 579, 580. Hereafter cited in text.

63. On Austen and feminism, see Looser, *Jane Austen and Discourses of Feminism*; Johnson, *Jane Austen*; and Kirkham, *Jane Austen.*

64. Kittredge, "The Ag'd Dame," 260.

65. It is difficult to imagine an easy way out of this ingrained authorial stereotyping. As Hermione Lee has put it, "If the virtuous and benign—or thwarted and bitter—maiden aunt is refused as the working model, what other shapes can this story [of Austen's life] take?" (*Virginia Woolf's Nose*, 76).

Four • Hester Lynch Piozzi, Antiquity of Bath

1. James Clifford devotes two chapters to the last twenty years of Piozzi's life; see *Hester Lynch Piozzi*. Hereafter cited in text as *HLP*. William McCarthy titles the last chapter of his book on Piozzi "The Farce of Life: Piozzi's After-Career" and covers the years 1801–21; see *Hester Thrale Piozzi*. Hereafter cited in text as *HTP*.

2. Mangin, *Piozziana*, 161. Hereafter cited in text.

3. Vullaimy, *Mrs. Thrale of Streatham*, 319–20.

4. On this subject, see Thaddeus, "Hoards of Sorrow."

5. Piozzi, *Hester Thrale-Piozzi*, reel 25, MS 616. Hereafter cited in text as *H T-P*, followed by reel and manuscript number.

6. Kugler, "Women and Aging in Transatlantic Perspective," 80.

7. Rodriguez, "A Story of Her Own," 128.

8. Spacks, "Scrapbook of a Self," 222. Hereafter cited in text.

9. Piozzi, *The Piozzi Letters*, 6: 482. Hereafter cited in text as *Piozzi Letters*.

10. [Piozzi], "Old England to Her Daughters," 79.

11. Piozzi, *Retrospection*, 1:, vii. Hereafter cited in text.

12. Orianne Smith argues persuasively that we should understand *Retrospection* through the lens of millenarianism and female prophecy; see "Unlearned & Ill-Qualified Pokers into Prophecy."

13. Hester Piozzi, "Lyford Redivivus," Hyde Case 9 (16), Donald and Mary Hyde Collection of Dr. Samuel Johnson, Houghton Library, Harvard College Library. Hereafter cited in text as Hyde Case 9 (16).

14. Rev. of *Retrospection, Critical Review*, 28–29.

15. Rev. of *Retrospection, London Review*, 188.

16. Campbell, "Lady Mary Wortley Montagu," 213.

17. Tearle, *Mrs. Piozzi's Tall Young Beau*, 21–22. Hereafter cited in text.

18. Ripley and Dana, *The American Cyclopedia*, 13: 535.

19. Jane Porter to Robert Ker Porter, 26 Sept. 1838, KU MS 197.

20. *Love Letters of Mrs. Piozzi*.

21. Chapman, "A Literary Fraud."

22. Rev. of *Love Letters of Mrs. Piozzi*, 259. Hereafter cited in text.

23. Hayward, *Autobiography*.

24. Ellet, "Mrs. Piozzi's Love-Letters," 50. Hereafter cited in text.

25. Rev. of *Autobiography, Letters, and Literary Remains of Mrs. Piozzi (Thrale), Knickerbocker*.

26. Rev. of *Autobiography, Letters, and Literary Remains of Mrs. Piozzi (Thrale), Edinburgh Review*.

27. "The Lives of Two Ladies."

28. "Memoirs of Mrs. Piozzi."

29. "Hayward's Mrs. Piozzi," 121. Hereafter cited in text.

30. Cook, "Mr. Conway and Mrs. Piozzi."

31. Merritt, *The So-Called Love Letters*, 85.

32. Ryskamp, *Mrs. Piozzi to Mr. Conway*. On the selection of letters to publish in *The Piozzi Letters* and its problematic partiality, see McCarthy, "Review Essay: *The Piozzi Letters*."

33. McCarthy, rev. of *The Piozzi Letters*.

34. See Knapp, *Intimate Letters of Hester Piozzi and Penelope Pennington*, 290–93. Pennington reports that her husband, too, was captivated by Conway (294). The two women refer to Conway as "our Chevalier" (298, 313). On Pennington as a potential biographer, see 374–75.

35. Francis, *Old New York*, 248. Hereafter cited in text.

36. "Original Memorials of Mrs. Piozzi." Hereafter cited in text.

37. Premo, *Winter Friends*, 7. Premo's impressive study draws on private letters and life writing from 160 women.

38. On the practice of marginalia in the period, see Jackson, *Marginalia*, and Jackson, *Romantic Readers*. Hereafter cited in text as *Readers*.

39. Piozzi, *The Imperial Family Bible*.

40. For information on Mrs. Rudd's will and speculations on Conway's son, see Tearle, *Mrs. Piozzi's Tall Young Beau*, 225. Tearle is himself a descendant of William Augustus Conway, through Frederick Bartlett Conway.

41. "Review of Current Literature."

42. "Dr. Johnson and Mrs. Thrale."

43. Rev. of *Autobiography, Letters, and Literary Remains of Mrs. Piozzi (Thrale)*.

44. Clifford, "Hester Thrale-Piozzi," 16.

Five • *"One generation passeth away, and another cometh"*

1. "Mrs. Barbauld."

2. "Reminiscences for the Week."

3. McCarthy and Kraft, *Poems of Anna Letitia Barbauld*, xxxv, 318. For the original anecdote, see Robinson, *Diary, Reminiscences, and Correspondence*, 1: 226–27.

4. On the publication history of "Life," as well as Barbauld's other works, throughout the nineteenth century, see Watson, "When Flattery Kills."

5. See Le Breton, *Correspondence of William Ellery Channing and Lucy Aikin*, 5.

6. See also Barbauld's poem "A Thought on Death," which takes on different meanings depending on the order in which its stanzas are arranged. It is printed in McCarthy and Kraft, *Poems of Anna Letitia Barbauld*, with notes about the variations in stanza order (168, 320).

7. These choices may also have to do with how Barbauld has been placed in relation to feminism—an issue that remains fraught. See Bradshaw, "The Limits of Barbauld's Feminism."

8. See Johnson, "Let Me Make the Novels of a Country"; Moore, "Ladies. Taking the Pen in Hand"; and Rogers, "Anna Barbauld's Criticism of Fiction." References to Johnson hereafter cited in text.

9. See, e.g., Keach, "A Regency Prophecy," and Favretti, "The Politics of Vision." Hereafter cited in text.

10. Folger Collective on Early Women Critics, *Women Critics 1660–1820*, 174.

11. Wakefield, *Anna Laetitia Barbauld*, 80.

12. McKillop, *Samuel Richardson*, 285.

13. Richardson, *Selected Letters*, 7.

14. Sabor, "Publishing Richardson's Correspondence," 248. See also Zircker, "Richardson's Correspondence."

15. For an exception, see Warner, *Licensing Entertainment*, 16–17. Warner's discussion of Barbauld's editing *The British Novelists* notes the "special privilege" she gives to Richardson in that collection (17).

16. McCarthy, "What Did Anna Barbauld Do to Samuel Richardson's Correspondence?" 208. Hereafter cited in text.

17. Richardson, *Correspondence of Samuel Richardson*, 1: iv. Hereafter cited in text.

18. Rev. of *Correspondence of Samuel Richardson, Critical Review*, 287. Hereafter cited in text.

19. Sabor, "Publishing Richardson's Correspondence," 243.

20. [Moody], Rev. of *Correspondence of Samuel Richardson*, 29. Hereafter cited in text.

21. Rev. of *Correspondence of Samuel Richardson, Imperial Review*. Hereafter cited in text.

22. Rev. of *Correspondence of Samuel Richardson, Eclectic Review*, 122–23. Hereafter cited in text.

23. "European Literary Intelligence" Hereafter cited in text.

24. The *Critical Review*'s review of the letters finds them "seldom containing any particular subject of inquiry or discussion," with "little that is particularly interesting" on literary information of the era (284, 285). After its warm praise, the *Eclectic Review*, too, turns sour: "But after every exertion of candour, we must avow, that in reading these letters, we have betrayed symptoms of weariness, and even of disgust" (123). Because of the repetition of subject and the frequent idolizing of Richardson in the letters, the reviewer proclaims, "we cannot wholly suppress emotions of mingled pity and contempt" (123). Many of the reviews spent little space on volumes two through six—the letters themselves.

25. Rev. of *Correspondence of Samuel Richardson, Anti-Jacobin Review*. Hereafter cited in text.

26. On this issue, see McCarthy, "What Did Anna Barbauld Do."

27. The portion of her commentary that gets the most positive attention is her work on *Clarissa*. Francis Jeffrey considers her commentary on *Clarissa* "equally judicious and refined; and we could easily prolong this extract." See rev. by Jeffrey of the *Correspondence of Samuel Richardson, Edinburgh Review*. Hereafter cited in text.

28. Rickards, "Mrs. Barbauld and Her Pupil," 712.

29. Le Breton, *Memoir of Mrs. Barbauld*, 106.

30. Barbauld, *Selections from the "Spectator,"* 1: v. Hereafter cited in text.

31. In Barbauld's essay on Akenside, she again invokes the term "classic": "We may venture to predict that his work, which is not formed on any local or temporary subject, will continue to be a classic in our language" (Akenside 36). One of her main criticisms of Akenside is

that he continued to revise the poem written in his youth into his late middle age: "It betrays a mind rather brooding with fond affection over old productions, than inspired by a fresh stream of new ideas. The flowers of fancy are apt to lose their odour by much handling" (32). See Akenside, *The Pleasures of Imagination.*

32. Lucy Aikin believes that there "were many striking points of resemblance between [Barbauld's] genius and that of Addison"; see Barbauld, *Works,* 1: xl. Hereafter cited in text. Later, Aikin herself would write the first full-length biography of Addison, not well received by the critics. See Aikin, *The Life of Joseph Addison.* An 1826 review of Barbauld's *Works* also considers her "the Female Addison," noting "the style of Addison is less perfect than hers." See "Works for Young Persons."

33. Barbauld, *The Female Speaker,* vi. Hereafter cited in text.

34. Lucy Aikin does not speak so dismissively of edited and compiled work in her memoir of her author-father, John Aikin (Barbauld's brother and sometime coauthor). Lucy Aikin does, however, downplay his important translations on occasion. She writes, "Literary occupation had now become to Mr. Aikin one of the habits, and almost the wants, of daily life; and no plan of original composition at this time suggesting itself, he undertook the translation of Tacitus's *Life of Agricola*" (*Memoir of John Aiken* 1: 22). In Lucy Aikin's terms, translating the writings of others is something an author would undertake only when at a loss for "original" ideas.

35. For further information, see McCarthy, "A 'High-Minded Christian Lady,' " 181–82.

36. John Keats, too, might be added to this list, as his work prompted a venomous review from Croker.

37. Newlyn, *Reading, Writing, and Romanticism,* 168.

38. Birns, "Thy World, Columbus!," 556.

39. [Moody], Rev. of *Eighteen Hundred and Eleven, Monthly Review.* Hereafter cited in text.

40. Rev. of *Eighteen Hundred and Eleven, Anti-Jacobin Review,* 204. Hereafter cited in text.

41. In his 1995 introduction to a facsimile reprint of the book, Jonathan Wordsworth repeats this rhetoric, claiming that "*Eighteen Hundred and Eleven* has an old-fashioned air" though an "up-to-date" message. See Jonathan Wordsworth, Introduction to *Eighteen Hundred and Eleven.* Hereafter cited in text.

42. Rev. of *Eighteen Hundred and Eleven, Eclectic Review,* 478. Hereafter cited in text. This review has been attributed to James Montgomery (Wordsworth, n.p.).

43. Scott, *Letters of Sir Walter Scott,* 3: 173. This letter, dated 11 Oct. 1812, is addressed to Joanna Baillie.

44. Smith, *Memoir and Correspondence,* 2: 175. Hereafter cited in text.

45. Edgeworth believed that the public would do Barbauld justice. For Edgeworth's comments, see Rodgers, *Georgian Chronicle,* 142. According to Barbauld's great niece, Edgeworth's letter went on to suggest that " 'dear Mrs. Barbauld' write '1812' in a more hopeful strain and commemorate the victories and death of the great Nelson"; see Le Breton, *Memories of Seventy Years,* 47, and Croker, rev. of *Eighteen Hundred and Eleven.* Hereafter cited in text.

46. Claudia Johnson notes that "Croker in fact has nothing to say about Barbauld's edition of the novels and indeed mockingly enjoins her to return to the busy work of editing or writing children's tales, as though these were contemptible tasks, by implication appropriate to the abilities of fussy old women" ("Let," 173).

47. In his review, Croker refers to Barbauld as a "fatidical spinster." As William Keach points out, this is either a "coarse mistake" or "deliberate slur" as Barbauld had been widowed less than four years earlier ("Regency Prophecy," 569).

48. Aikin remained infuriated about the review of *Eighteen Hundred and Eleven* throughout her own long life. Twenty-five years after Barbauld's death, Aikin concluded (mistakenly, as it turns out) that the damning review had been written by Robert Southey (Ellis, *Memoir,* 274–75).

49. For the story of this poem's publication, see McCarthy and Kraft, *Poems of Anna Letitia Barbauld,* 320. The poem was first published in England in the *Monthly Repository* 17 (Oct. 1822): 636, and a letter with corrections appeared in 17 *Monthly Repository* (Nov. 1822): 679.

50. Estlin, *Familiar Lectures.* For the poems, see McCarthy and Kraft, *Poems of Anna Letitia Barbauld,* 362–63.

51. Nangle, *The Monthly Review,* 5–6.

52. On the review allegedly prompting a total cessation of publication for Barbauld, see, e.g., Chandler, *England in 1819,* 115. Norma Clarke, too, suggests that Croker's review "marked the end of [Barbauld's] public career"; see *The Rise and Fall of the Woman of Letters,* 317.

53. The "other" previously published poem has been identified by McCarthy and Kraft as probably being her "On the Death of the Princess Charlotte," printed in the *Annual Register for the Year 1818* (323–24). It was not included in Baillie's *Collection.* The "trifle" McCarthy and Kraft identify as "To Mrs. H——, on Returning a Fine Hyacinth Plant" (*Poems of Anna Letitia Barbauld,* 327). It was printed in Baillie's *Collection,* with an attribution to Barbauld, but did not appear in the 1825 *Works;* see Baillie, *A Collection of Poems.*

54. McCarthy and Kraft find no reason to believe that Barbauld had a role in the 1825 *Works* (*Poems of Anna Letitia Barbauld,* xxxviii).

55. Murch, *Mrs. Barbauld and Her Contemporaries,* 82–83. Hereafter cited in text.

56. Sarah Hale, *Biography of Distinguished Women,* 197.

57. On Barbauld and old maids, see the discussion of her poem on the subject in chapter three.

58. Child, *Looking toward Sunset,* 68. On Child's own apparently difficult old age, see Cole, *The Journey of Life.* For important commentary on Cole's conclusions, see Woodward, "Age-Work in American Culture."

Six • Jane Porter and the Old Woman Writer's Quest for Financial Independence

1. References to "Porter" in this chapter are to Jane Porter. When Porter is discussed alongside her siblings, their first names are employed for clarity.

2. Botelho, *Old Age and the English Poor Law,* 158.

3. Austen, *Jane Austen's Letters,* 312. Hereafter cited in text.

4. Porter, *The Scottish Chiefs,* 1: 39. Hereafter cited in text. Porter's story was also repeated during her lifetime, in a chapter on her sister, the novelist Anna Maria Porter, featured in Elwood, *Memoirs of the Literary Ladies of England,* 2: 290.

5. Jones, *Ideas and Innovation,* 136. Hereafter cited in text.

6. Price, "Biography of Jane Porter."

7. Wilson, *These Were Muses*, 137. Hereafter cited in text.

8. Tytler [Henrietta Keddie], *Jane Austen and Her Works*, 28. Hereafter cited in text.

9. Jane Porter to Robert Ker Porter, 20 Nov. 1823, Jane Porter Papers, Huntington Library, San Marino, CA, POR 2067. Hereafter cited as HL, followed by collection abbreviation (POR) and item number.

10. Jane Porter's own political and military interests (and ambitions) may have played a role in this episode, but that speculation deserves more space than I am able to provide here.

11. Gary Kelly, Introduction to *The Scottish Chiefs*, ed. Kelly, vii.

12. Critic Ann Jones is skeptical of the Porters' claims to financial difficulty, calling them "nonsense" and saying they "lived well" (*Ideas*, 114). But one typical letter gives a sense of the state of that family's finances in disarray. Anna Maria Porter writes to her sister Jane, on 31 March 1804, upon the receipt of two pounds, from their publishers: "The difficulties . . . render us at this period, almost insanely happy at the sight of 2 pounds—such is our real situation, while the world considers us rolling in riches" (HL, POR 442). The reasons for the Porter family's indebtedness are varied and complicated. They were not "poor," but it is sufficient to say here that the women lived anxiously and modestly.

13. See Foster, *The Duke of Clarence* and *Jaquelina of Hainault*; *Charles Dacres*, 1: xi.

14. See *The Count de Rethel*; De Castera, *The Lady's Philosopher's Stone*, and De Tencin, *The Siege of Calais*.

15. On the eighteenth-century novel, genre, and historical change, see Hunter, *Before Novels*, and Davis, *Factual Fictions*.

16. Garside, "Walter Scott and the 'Common' Novel."

17. *Reginald Dalton*, the novel under review, was published anonymously but written by Scott's son-in-law, John Gibson Lockhart. See rev. of *Reginald Dalton*, 200. Hereafter cited in text.

18. Some writers in the reviewer's list had taken a hiatus from publication. Jane West brought out no new novels between 1816 and 1827, but Edgeworth had brought forward several works of fiction after *Patronage* (1814).

19. See Ferris, *The Achievement of Literary Authority*; Gamer, *Romanticism and the Gothic*; and London, *Women and Property*.

20. See Scott, *Prefaces to the Waverley Novels*, 5. Hereafter cited in text.

21. Porter claims, plausibly, that their mothers were "intimate friends" in Edinburgh. She writes of Scott as her childhood playmate, with whom she rekindled a friendship in adulthood ("Recollective Preface," 39).

22. "Countess of Blessington."

23. Thomas McLean is working on Porter and Scott, and I thank him for sharing his work in progress. See "Nobody's Argument." His article discusses an anonymous periodical essay, recently attributed to Porter by McLean, that makes public Porter's boiling frustrations with Scott. On Scott and Porter, see also Price, "Resisting 'the Spirit of Innovation.' "

24. Rev. of *Duke Christian of Luneburg, La Belle Assemblée*. Because Porter herself contributed to *La Belle Assemblée*, it seems possible that its review of her novel was not a disinterested one. See Thomas McLean, "Newly Attributed Works by Jane Porter, and the Identity of a Reclusive Author," unpublished manuscript.

25. Porter, *Thaddeus of Warsaw, Revised*, vi. Hereafter cited in text.

26. Puff, "Letters to Certain Persons," 552. Hereafter cited in text. I thank Thomas McLean for bringing this piece to my attention.

27. Sir Robert Ker Porter was knighted multiple times by several sovereigns, first by the King of Sweden in 1808 (Armstrong, "Many-Sided World," 43–45). According to the *DNB*, Porter had been knighted by the Prince Regent in 1813.

28. Porter, *Duke Christian of Luneburg*, vi. Hereafter cited in text.

29. See Garside, Belanger, and Ragaz, *British Fiction, 1800–1829: A Database of Production, Circulation, and Reception*, designer A. A. Mandal, www.british-fiction.cf.ac.uk: 1824A078. The Longman's ledger book and letters, as transcribed, indicate that Porter earned £630 for *Duke Christian* but that her terms with them were not renewed for future productions because of that novel's nonsuccess.

30. Rev. of *Duke Christian of Luneburg*, *New Monthly Magazine*.

31. Longman & Co to Miss Jane Porter, 17 May 1825, Longman Archives, Longman I, 101, no. 507B (draft).

32. "Miss Jane Porter," letter to the *Edinburgh Literary Gazette*, 28 Aug. 1829, ACC 9856/18, National Library of Scotland, Edinburgh.

33. She subsequently published, with her sister, two collections of short stories / novellas: *Tales Round a Winter Hearth* and *Coming Out*.

34. "Memoir of Miss Jane Porter," *Edinburgh Literary Gazette* 1.18 (1829): 273–74.

35. This figure is likely underestimated, as Porter cites it as a "not large" amount in a begging letter to Peel. She claims that the indebtedness resulted from a bank failure that affected her brother, from his funeral expenses abroad, and from her own living and travel expenses until she was able to return from Russia. See BL Add. 40522 f. 187. In actuality, Robert had many other private debts, some dating back more than twenty years.

36. Jane Porter to John Shepherd, 22 Apr. 1850, KU MS 197.

37. Lord Skelmersdale to Sir Robert Peel, 21 Dec. 1842. See BL Add 40520 ff. 161.

38. In the first decades of the eighteenth century, less than 10 percent of the aged used parish relief under the Old Poor Law, but by the 1790s, this number had grown to one-quarter to one-third of those over 60 years old, according to Susannah Ottaway. The old were also increasingly defined as a recognizable subset of the population. Both of these factors, Ottaway theorizes, led to the surge in age-based pension schemes in the late eighteenth century; See *The Decline of Life*, 10, 13.

39. Thomson, "I Am Not My Father's Keeper," 267. Hereafter cited in text. For a full-length study on the subject, see Botelho, *Old Age and the English Poor Law*.

40. Porchaska, *Royal Bounty*. Hereafter cited in text.

41. May, *Constitutional History*, 1: 166. Hereafter cited in text.

42. Gary Kelly, "Elizabeth Hamilton." In *Dictionary of Literary Biography*, 115: 122; Barbara Brandon Schnorrenberg, s.v. "Delany, Mary (1700–1788)," *Oxford Dictionary of National Biography*.

43. Marie-Jeanne Colombani, s.v. "Paoli (Filippo Antonio), Pasquale (1725–1807)," *Oxford Dictionary of National Biography*.

44. The king proposes offering O'Keeffe "a moderate annual stipend, as will enable him

to close his hitherto long life in comfort"; Fitzgerald, *Life of George the Fourth* (830).

45. Grant, *Memoir and Correspondence*, 1: 29. Hereafter cited in text.

46. Anne Grant to George IV, 1825, BL, Add. 38300.

47. See Scott, *Journal*, 30. See 21–22 for Grant's alleged comments about the sum she would receive.

48. This was not the only sum that Grant was awarded. According to her son, "Her distinguished friend the late Sir William Grant, Master of the Rolls, left her an annuity of similar amount; and these sums, added to some other bequests by friends, and the emoluments of her writings, rendered Mrs. Grant, with her simple tastes and habits of self-denial, not only in easy circumstances in her latter days, but also enabled her to gratify the generosity of her nature by giving to others" (Grant 1: 30).

49. See Lady Morgan (Sydney Owneson), *Lady Morgan's Memoirs*, 2: 419. Hereafter cited in text. Mary Campbell, recent biographer of Lady Morgan, mistakenly refers to this pension as "the very first literary pension ever offered to a woman" (226). Campbell notes that the pension "caused a lot of resentment, for it was bigger than most given to other writers in much more straitened circumstances. By the standards of her day, Lady Morgan was very well off. She was reported to have £1,000 a year of her own money coming in, as well as her husband's income"; see *Lady Morgan*, 227. She died leaving an estate of £16,000 to her nieces, according to Dennis Dean, s.v. "Morgan, Sydney, Lady Morgan (bap. 1783, d. 1859)," *Oxford Dictionary of National Biography*.

50. Qtd. in Campbell, *Lady Morgan*, 231. The source cited is the *Dublin Review*.

51. Jane Porter to John Shephard, 22 April 1850, PC/NYPL.

52. Jane Porter to Prince Albert, with Petition to Queen Victoria. 15 Apr. 1844, BL, Add. 40542 ff. 253, 254.

53. Sir Robert Peel to Jane Porter, ca. May 1846; BL, Add. 40592 f. 44.

54. Deborah Manley, s.v. "Belzoni, Sarah (1783–1870)," *Oxford Dictionary of National Biography*.

55. Jane Porter to Robert Ker Porter, 24–30 May 1838, KU MS 197.

56. Among Jane Porter's correspondence from 1844 is a clipping identified as being from *The Arithmetic of Annuities*, by Edward Baylis. It reads, "The aged sister of the celebrated Sir Sidney Smith, the hero of Acre, having been reduced by a long series of misfortunes to poverty and destitution, a few generous friends undertook to raise a subscription for her relief. Amongst others, the accomplished Jane Porter pleaded urgently and successfully in her favor. Her most gracious Majesty Queen Victoria, her Royal Highness the Duchess of Kent, and many of the nobility and gentry, contributed liberally to this benevolent fund, which ultimately amounted to £370 9s. This sum was immediately invested in the purchase of an annuity, payable quarterly, to this unfortunate lady, who was in the sixty-sixth year of her age, during the remainder of her life. What amount of the annuity was thus obtained, reckoning at the rate of 5 per cent, per annum for the interest of money? Answer, £50 per annum, payable quarterly."

57. Select Committee on Pensions, *First Report*, 26. The report claims that Smith spent between £8,000 and £9,000 "from his private resources for public service" (27). Hereafter cited in text as SCP.

58. Jane Porter to Sir Robert Peel, 10 June 1842, BL Add. 40510 ff. 75–76.

59. Somerville published new work at age 89, with her memoirs published posthumously. See Mary R. S. Creese, s.v. "Somerville, Mary (1780–1872)," *Oxford Dictionary of National Biography*.

60. Geoffrey Carnall, s.v. "Moore, Thomas (1779–1852)," *Oxford Dictionary of National Biography*.

61. Jane Porter to J. Emerson Tennant, 20 June 1844, BL, Add. 40547 f. 147.

62. Ibid.

63. Geoffrey Carnall, s.v. "Campbell, Thomas (1777–1844)," *Oxford Dictionary of National Biography*.

64. Jane Porter to J. Emerson Tennant, 7 Jan. 1843, HL POR 2171. Hereafter cited in text.

65. Jane Porter to Robert Ker Porter, 30 Dec. 1839, KU MS 197. Hereafter cited in text.

66. Jane Porter to Robert Ker Porter, 27 Nov. 1840, KU MS 197.

67. Thomas Longman to Sir Robert Peel, 8 Dec. 1842, BL, Add. 40520 f. 159.

68. Sir Robert Peel to John Shepard, 30 Aug. 1845, PC/NYPL.

69. Lord Russell to Jane Porter, 16 Oct. 1846, PC/NYPL.

70. William Law to Jane Porter, 26 May 1848, PC/NYPL.

71. Jane Porter to Leopold I, King of the Belgians, ca. 1843, HL POR 1375.

72. Jane Porter, untitled memorandum, 19 Feb. 1850, KU MS 197.

73. She may have chosen this in lieu of trusting her small capital to banks, because she had previously experienced losses when they failed.

74. Turner, *Living by the Pen*, 107–8.

75. Austen, *Sense and Sensibility*, 93.

76. Bishop, *Blake's Hayley*, 327.

77. Olive Baldwin and Thelma Wilson, s.v. "O'Keeffe, John (1747–1833)," *Oxford Dictionary of National Biography*.

78. Jane Porter to Robert Ker Porter, 13 May 1840, KU MS 197.

79. Jane Porter to George Virtue, 14 Sept. 1844, PC/NYPL.

80. Ibid.

81. See Genette, *Paratexts*. On Porter's claiming that her prefaces and postscripts would serve as sufficient biographical material, see Jane Porter to Robert Ker Porter, HL POR 2110.

82. For information about Porter's collapsed lung, see Jane Porter, untitled memorandum describing a letter to Lady Clarendon, 26 Apr. 1850, KU MS 197. Porter spent three months in Clifton in late 1849 and recovered, staying at No. 4 Sion Row, Clifton, the basement story of Mrs. Chaplin's rooming house. See Jane Porter, untitled memorandum, 4 Oct. 1849, KU MS 197. In a strange coincidence, Porter successfully convalesced very near the apartment where Hester Lynch Piozzi had died in 1821, No. 10 Sion Row, Clifton.

83. Ina Mary White, "The Diary of Jane Porter," *Scottish Review* 29 (1897): 322.

84. Porter, *Thaddeus of Warsaw*, ed. Baker. Not a decade earlier, the novel had been featured in an American series called "Famous Books by Famous Authors." See Porter, *Thaddeus of Warsaw [by] Jane Porter*.

85. Wilson, *These Were Muses*, vii. Hereafter cited in text.

86. Vaughan, *From Anne to Victoria*, 123.

87. Philoscotus, "Scott and Jane Porter," 408.

88. Porter et al., *The Scottish Chiefs*.

89. Porter, *The Scottish Chiefs*, adapted by O'Rourke.

90. Mel Gibson, *Braveheart*, produced by Bruce Davey, Alan Ladd Jr., and Mel Gibson, directed by Mel Gibson, 177 min, Paramount Pictures, 1995.

91. Porter, *The Scottish Chiefs*, ed. Kelly.

92. Porter, *The Scottish Chiefs*, ed. Price.

Conclusion

1. Siskin, *The Work of Writing*, 225. For more on the "great forgetting," see Schellenberg, *The Professionalization of Women Writers*, 162–82.

2. This is not a problem limited to biographies of early modern British figures; see Ross, "Bertrand Russell in His Nineties," 67.

3. Staves, *Women's Writing in Britain*, 10–11. Hereafter cited in text.

4. Friedan, *The Fountain of Age*, 62–63.

5. Davis, *Age Rage and Going Gently*.

6. On widowhood in eighteenth-century British literature, see Gevirtz, *Life afer Death*.

7. Pat Thane has commented on how death in childbirth affected the population of old women: "It is sometimes thought that before at least the nineteenth century female life expectancy must have been sharply reduced by the ravages of death in childbirth. But . . . childbirth was never a mass killer of women in western societies. It was not comparable with the ravages of work, war and everyday violence on the lives of men"; see "Social Histories of Old Age and Aging," 95. Hereafter cited in text.

8. On the Bluestockings, see Pohl and Schellenberg, *Reconsidering the Bluestockings*. None of the work in this collection considers old age directly, though many essays touch on these women's late lives.

9. I am grateful to Deborah Heller for this material. See Elizabeth Montagu to Elizabeth Vesey: 17 May [1780], MO 6539, Huntington Library, San Marino, CA.

10. Heller, "A Friend Is the Medicine of Life."

11. Some details on her late life, in which she had to "limit her participation in society because of her narrow means," are found in Myers, *The Bluestocking Circle*, 229–39.

12. Seward, *Letters*, v–vi.

13. West, *Ringrove*, 2: 427.

14. Pamela Lloyd, "Jane West," in *An Encyclopedia of British Women Writers*, 669–70. Hereafter cited in text.

15. Marilyn L. Brooks, Foreword to *The Correspondence (1779–1843) of Mary Hays*, ix. Hereafter cited in text.

16. Hays, *Memoirs of Queens*, v. Hereafter cited in text.

17. Eleanor Ty, "Mary Hays," in *Dictionary of Literary Biography*, 142: 160. Hereafter cited in text.

18. Gary Kelly, "Mary Hays," in *Dictionary of Literary Biography*, 158: 124–30.

19. Walker, *Mary Hays (1759–1843)*, 236–37.

20. Knight, *Autobiography of Miss Cornelia Knight*, x. Hereafter cited in text.

21. Knight, *Sir Guy De Lusignan*.

22. Luttrell, *The Prim Romantic*, 217–18. Luttrell's biography provides a chapter on Knight's late life, but the tone is melodramatic and the conclusions she reaches are often suspect.

23. Ferrier, *Destiny*.

24. David E. Latané Jr., "Susan Ferrier," in *Dictionary of Literary Biography*, 116: 100.

25. B. E. Schneller, "Susan Ferrier," in *British Women Writers: A Critical Reference Guide*, ed. Janet Todd (New York: Continuum, 1989), 243.

26. Parker, *Susan Ferrier and John Galt*, 19. Parker concludes that Ferrier "wisely decided that she would write no more fiction" after the "artistic disappointment" of *Destiny*.

27. Lynda Thompson, "Susan Ferrier," *The Cambridge Guide to Women's Writing in English*, ed. Lorna Sage (Cambridge: Cambridge University Press, 1999), 241.

28. For all of these facts, see Grundy, Introduction to *Secresy*, 20.

29. Michael Skakun and Natalie Joy Woddall, "Amelia Opie," in *Encyclopedia of British Women Writers*, 491–92.

30. Somerville, *Personal Recollections*, 364.

31. Mary R. S. Creese, s.v. "Somerville, Mary (1780–1872)," *Oxford Dictionary of National Biography*.

32. Sylvia Bowerbank, s.v. "Southcott, Joanna (1750–1814)," *Oxford Dictionary of National Biography*.

33. This quotation is attributed to D. Hughson, LlD, and appears in the introduction to Joanna Southcott's *Dispute between the Woman and the Powers of Darkness*, i.

34. Ann Radcliffe, *The Italian*, ed. Frederick Garber (Oxford: Oxford University Press, 1998), 373.

Manuscript Sources

Department of Manuscripts. British Library

Donald and Mary Hyde Collection of Dr. Samuel Johnson. Houghton Library. Harvard College Library

Jane Porter Papers. Huntington Library. San Marino, CA

Jane Porter Papers. Pforzheimer Collection. New York Public Library

National Library of Scotland. Edinburgh

Porter Papers. Department of Special Collections. Kenneth Spencer Research Library. University of Kansas. Lawrence

Printed Sources

"Account of the Life and Writings of Mrs. Catherine Macauley [sic] Graham." *European Magazine and Monthly Review* (1783): 330–34.

"Acknowledgments to Correspondents." *British Critic* 4 (1794): 219.

"Addressed to Mrs. D'Arblay, on Reading Her 'Wanderer.'" *Gentleman's Magazine* 84 (1814): 373.

"Ages of Women: Age as a Category of Analysis in Women's History." Ed. Birgitte Soland. *Journal of Women's History* 12.4 (2001).

Aikin, Lucy. *The Life of Joseph Addison.* 2 vols. London: Longman, Brown, Green & Longmans, 1843.

———. *Memoir of John Aikin, M.D.: With a Selection of His Miscellaneous Pieces, Biographical, Moral, and Critical.* 2 vols. London: Baldwin, Cradock & Joy, 1823.

Akenside, Mark. *The Pleasures of Imagination.* New ed. London: T. Cadell & W. Davies, 1810.

Altick, Richard D. *The Shows of London.* Cambridge, MA: Harvard UP, 1978.

Anderson, Earl R. "Footnotes More Pedestrian Than Sublime: A Historical Background for the Foot-Races in Evelina and Humphry Clinker." *Eighteenth-Century Studies* 14.1 (1980): 56–68.

Anderson, George Kumler. *The Legend of the Wandering Jew.* Providence, RI: Brown UP, 1965.

Armstrong, W. M. "The Many-Sided World of Sir Robert Kerr Porter." *Historian* 25.1 (1962): 36–58.

Auerbach, Emily. *Searching for Jane Austen*. Madison: U of Wisconsin P, 2004.

Austen, Jane. *Emma*. Ed. R. W. Chapman. 3rd ed. Vol. 4. Oxford: Oxford UP, 1966.

———. *Jane Austen's Letters*. Ed. Deirdre Le Faye. New ed. Oxford: Oxford UP, 1995.

———. *Love and Friendship and Other Early Works*. New York: Harmony, 1981.

———. *Mansfield Park*. Ed. R. W. Chapman. 3rd ed. Vol. 3. Oxford: Oxford UP, 1966.

———. *Minor Works*. Ed. R. W. Chapman. Rev. ed. Vol. 6. Oxford: Oxford UP, 1967.

———. *Persuasion*. Ed. Patricia Meyer Spacks. New York: W. W. Norton, 1995.

———. *Pride and Prejudice*. Ed. R. W. Chapman. 3rd ed. Vol. 1. Oxford: Oxford UP, 1966.

———. *Sense and Sensibility*. Ed. R. W. Chapman. 3rd ed. Vol. 1. Oxford: Oxford UP, 1966.

Rev. of *Autobiography, Letters, and Literary Remains of Mrs. Piozzi (Thrale)*, by A. Hayward. *Knickerbocker* 57.6 (1861): 655–56.

Rev. of *Autobiography, Letters, and Literary Remains of Mrs. Piozzi (Thrale)*, by A. Hayward. *Edinburgh Review* 113 (1861): 501–23.

Rev. of *Autobiography, Letters, and Literary Remains of Mrs. Piozzi (Thrale)*, by A. Hayward. *New Monthly Magazine* 121 (1861): 440–54.

Backscheider, Paula. *Eighteenth-Century Women Poets and Their Poetry: Inventing Agency, Inventing Genre*. Baltimore: Johns Hopkins UP, 2005.

Badcock, Samuel. "Original Anecdotes from Mr. Badcock, from His Own Letters." *Gentleman's Magazine* 66 (1789): 776–78.

Baillie, Joanna, ed. *A Collection of Poems, Chiefly Manuscript, and from Living Authors*. London: Longman, Hurst, Rees, Orme & Brown, 1823.

Banner, Lois. *In Full Flower: Aging Women, Power, and Sexuality*. New York: Knopf, 1992.

Bannet, Eve Tavor. *The Domestic Revolution: Enlightenment Feminisms and the Novel*. Baltimore: Johns Hopkins UP, 2000.

Barbauld, Anna Letitia. "Bouts Rimés, in Praise of Old Maids." *Amulet* 3 (1828): 357.

———. *Eighteen Hundred and Eleven*. 1812. New York: Woodstock, 1995.

———. *The Female Speaker; or, Miscellaneous Pieces in Prose and Verse, Selected from the Best Writers, and Adapted to the Use of Young Women*. London: J. Johnson & Co., 1811.

———. *The Poems of Anna Letitia Barbauld*, Ed. William McCarthy and Elizabeth Kraft. Athens: U of Georgia P, 1994.

———. *Selections from the "Spectator," "Tatler," "Guardian," and "Freeholder."* 2 vols. London: Edward Moxon, 1849.

———. "A Thought on Death." *Monthly Repository* 17 (Oct. 1822): 636.

———. *The Works of Anna Laetitia Barbauld, with a Memoir by Lucy Aikin*. 2 vols. London: Routledge/Thoemmes Press, 1996.

Batchelor, Jennie. "The Claims of Literature: Women Applicants to the Royal Literary Fund, 1790–1810." *Women's Writing* 12.3 (2005): 505–21.

Baylis, Edward. *The Arithmetic of Annuities and Life Assurance; or, Compound Interest Simplified*. London: Longman, Brown, Green & Longmans, 1844.

Bennett, John. *Strictures on Female Education*. London: T. Cadell, 1787.

Betham, Matilda. *Poems and Elegies*. Ed. Donald H. Reiman. New York: Garland, 1978.

Bilger, Audrey. *Laughing Feminism: Subversive Comedy in Frances Burney, Maria Edgeworth, and Jane Austen.* Detroit: Wayne State UP, 1998.

Birns, Nicholas. " 'Thy World, Columbus!' Barbauld and Global Space, 1803, '1811,' 1812, 2003." *European Romantic Review* 16.5 (2005): 545–62.

Bishop, Morchard. *Blake's Hayley: The Life, Works, and Friendship of William Hayley.* London: Victor Gollancz, 1951.

Blain, Virginia, Patricia Clements, and Isobel Grundy, eds. *The Feminist Companion to Literature in English: Women Writers from the Middle Ages to the Present.* New Haven: Yale UP, 1990.

Blair, Robert. *The Grave: A Poem.* Perth: H. Fry, 1799.

Boos, Florence. "Catherine Macaulay's *Letters on Education* (1790): An Early Feminist Polemic." *University of Michigan Papers in Women's Studies* 2.2 (1976): 64–78.

Boos, Florence, and William Boos. "Catharine Macaulay: Historian and Political Reformer," *International Journal of Women's Studies* 3.1 (1980): 49–65.

Botelho, L. A. *Old Age and the English Poor Law, 1500–1700.* Woodbridge, UK: Boydell & Brewer, 2004.

Botelho, Lynn, and Susannah R. Ottaway, eds. *The History of Old Age in England, 1600–1800.* 8 vols. London: Pickering & Chatto, 2008–9.

Botelho, Lynn, and Pat Thane, eds. *Women and Ageing in British Society since 1500.* Harlow, UK: Longman, 2001.

Botkin, Frances R. "Finding Her Own Voice or 'Being on Her Own Bottom': A Community of Women in Maria Edgeworth's *Helen,*" 93–108. In *New Essays on Maria Edgeworth,* ed. Julie Nash. Aldershot, UK: Ashgate, 2006.

Bradshaw, Penny. "The Limits of Barbauld's Feminism: Re-reading 'The Rights of Woman.' " *European Romantic Review* 16.1 (2004): 23–37.

"Brainwork and Longevity." *Scientific American* 10.15 (1864): 226.

Brightfield, Myron F. *John Wilson Croker.* Berkeley, U of California P, 1940.

The British Apollo: Containing Two Thousand Answers to Curious Questions in Most Arts and Sciences, . . . Approved of by Many of the Most Learned . . . 3rd ed. 3 vols. London: Theodore Sanders, 1726.

Brock, Claire. *The Feminization of Fame, 1750–1830.* Houndsmills, UK: Palgrave Macmillan, 2006.

Brooks, Marilyn L., ed. *The Correspondence (1779–1843) of Mary Hays, British Novelist.* Lewiston, NY: Edwin Mellen, 2004.

Brophy, Elizabeth Bergen. *Women's Lives and the Eighteenth-Century English Novel.* Tampa: U of South Florida P, 1991.

Browne, Colette. *Women, Feminism, and Aging.* New York: Springer, 1998.

Browning, Elizabeth Barrett, and Robert Browning. *The Brownings' Correspondence.* Ed. Philip Kelley and Scott Lewis. 12 vols. Winfield, KS: Wedgestone Press, 1984.

Bulstrode, Sir Richard. *Miscellaneous Essays.* 2nd ed. London: Whitlocke Bulstrode, 1724.

Burney, Frances. *Evelina; or, The History of a Young Lady's Entrance into the World.* New York: Oxford UP, 1982.

———. *Memoirs of Dr. Burney, Arr. from His Own Manuscripts, from Family Papers, and from Personal Recollections. By His Daughter, Madame d'Arblay.* London: E. Moxon, 1832.

————. *The Wanderer; or, Female Difficulties.* Ed. Margaret Anne Doody, Robert L. Mack, and Peter Sabor. Oxford: Oxford UP, 1991.

Burney, Frances, and Charlotte Barrett. *Diary and Letters of Madame D'arblay.* 7 vols. London: H. Colburn, 1842–46.

Burney, Frances, Joyce Hemlow, and Althea Douglas. *The Journals and Letters of Fanny Burney (Madame D'arblay).* Vols. 7–12. Oxford: Clarendon, 1972.

Butler, Marilyn. "Culture's Medium: The Role of the Review." In *Cambridge Companion to British Romanticism,* ed. Stuart Curran, 120–47. Cambridge: Cambridge UP, 1993.

————. *Maria Edgeworth: A Literary Biography.* Oxford: Clarendon, 1972.

————. "The Uniqueness of Cynthia Kirkpatrick: Elizabeth Gaskell's *Wives and Daughters* and Maria Edgeworth's *Helen.*" *Review of English Studies* 23 (1972): 278–90.

Rev. of *Calamities of Authors,* by Isaac D'israeli. *Scourge* 4 (1 July 1812): 3–8.

Campbell, Jill. "Lady Mary Wortley Montagu and the 'Glass Revers'd' of Female Old Age." In *"Defects": Engendering the Modern Body,* ed. Helen Deutsch and Felicity Nussbaum, 213–51. Ann Arbor: U of Michigan P, 2000.

Campbell, Mary. *Lady Morgan: The Life and Times of Sydney Owenson.* London: Pandora, 1988.

Carlile, Susan. "Expanding the Feminine: Reconsidering Charlotte Lennox's Age and *The Life of Harriot Stuart.*" *Eighteenth-Century Novel* 4 (2005): 103–37.

Carlisle, Sir Anthony. *An Essay on the Disorders of Old Age and on the Means for Preserving Human Life.* 2nd ed. London: Longman, Hurst, Rees, Orme & Brown, 1818.

[Carrington, Edmund Frederick John.] *Confessions of an Old Bachelor.* London: Henry Colburn, 1827.

————. *Confessions of an Old Maid.* 3 vols. London: Henry Colburn, 1828.

Carter, Elizabeth. *Letters from Mrs. Elizabeth Carter to Mrs. Montagu, Between the Years 1755 and 1800. Chiefly Upon Literary and Moral Subjects.* Ed. Montagu Pennington. 3 vols. London: F. C. & J. Rivington, 1817.

Carver, Mrs. *The Old Woman: A Novel.* 2 vols. London: Minerva, 1800.

Casler, Jeanine. "Aging and Opportunity: Growing Older in Clara Reeve's *School for Widows.*" *Journal of Aging and Identity* 4. 2 (1999): 111–26.

"Catherine Macaulay," *The Times,* no. 551 (10 Oct. 1786): 2C.

Cavigioli, Rita. *Women of a Certain Age: Contemporary Italian Fictions of Female Aging.* Madison, NJ: Fairleigh Dickinson UP, 2005.

Chandler, James. *England in 1819: The Politics of Literary Culture and the Case of Romantic Historicism.* Chicago: U of Chicago P, 1998.

Chapman, R. W. "A Literary Fraud." *London Mercury* 22 (1930): 154–56.

Charles Dacres: or, The Voluntary Exile. An Historical Novel, Founded on Facts. 2 vols. Edinburgh: John Moir, 1797.

Child, Lydia Maria. *Looking toward Sunset: From Sources Old and New, Original and Selected.* 9th ed. Boston: James R. Osgood, 1871.

Cicero, Marcus Tullius. *Cato maior de senectute.* Ed. J. G. F. Powell. Cambridge: Cambridge UP, 1988.

Clarke, Norma. *The Rise and Fall of the Woman of Letters.* London: Pimlico, 2004.

Clifford, James L. *Hester Lynch Piozzi (Mrs. Thrale),* 2nd ed. Oxford: Clarendon, 1952.

————. "Hester Thrale-Piozzi." *Bath Weekly Chronicle and Herald* (17 June 1950): 16.

————. *Young Sam Johnson.* New York: Oxford UP, 1955.

Cohausen, Johann Heinrich. *Hermippus Redivivus; or, the Sage's Triumph over Old Age and the Grave. Wherein a Method Is Laid Down for Prolonging the Life and Vigour of Man,* 2nd ed. Trans. John Campbell. London: J. Nourse, 1749.

Cole, Thomas R. *The Journey of Life: A Cultural History of Aging in America.* Cambridge: Cambridge UP, 1992.

Cole, Thomas R., and Mary G. Winkler, eds. *The Oxford Book of Aging.* Oxford: Oxford UP, 1994.

Combe, Kirk, and Kenneth Schmader. "Naturalizing Myths of Aging: A Cautionary Tale." In *Power and Poverty: Old Age in the Pre-Industrial Past,* ed. Susannah R. Ottaway, L. A. Botelho, and Katharine Kittredge, 187–205. Westport, CT: Greenwood Press, 2002.

The Complete Young Man's Companion or Self-Instructer: Being an Introduction to All the Various Branches of Useful Learning and Knowledge. Manchester: Sowler & Russell, 1800.

Rev. of *Confessions of an Old Maid. La Belle Assemblée,* 3rd ser. 7 (1828): 301.

Rev. of *Confessions of an Old Maid. Literary Gazette,* 572 (1828): 8.

Connery, Brian A. "Self-Representation and Memorials in the Late Poetry of Swift." In *Aging and Gender in Literature: Studies in Creativity,* ed. Anne M. Wyatt-Brown and Janice Rossen, 141–63. Charlottesville: UP of Virginia, 1993.

Cook, Dutton. "Mr. Conway and Mrs. Piozzi." *Gentleman's Magazine* 251 (1881): 547–48.

Cornaro, Luigi. *Sure Methods of Attaining a Long and Healthful Life,* 25th ed. Trans. W. Jones. Edinburgh: A. Donaldson, 1777.

Rev. of *The Correspondence of Samuel Richardson. Anti-Jacobin Review* 18 (1804): 176.

Rev. of *The Correspondence of Samuel Richardson. Critical Review* 3 (1804): 155–65, 276–87.

Rev. of *The Correspondence of Samuel Richardson. Eclectic Review* 1 (1805): 122–28.

Rev. of *The Correspondence of Samuel Richardson. Imperial Review* 2 (1804): 415.

Coster, Will. *Family and Kinship in England, 1450–1800.* Harlow, UK: Longman, 2001.

The Count de Rethel: An Historical Novel. Taken from the French. 3 vols. London: T. Hookham, 1779.

"Countess of Blessington," *North American and Daily Advertiser,* no. 1830 (13 Feb. 1845): G.

Covey, H. C. "The Definitions of the Beginning of Old Age in History." *International Journal of Aging and Human Development* 34 (1992): 325–37.

Croker, John Wilson. Rev. of *Eighteen Hundred and Eleven,* by Anna Laetitia Barbauld. *Quarterly Review* 7 (1812): 309–13.

————. Rev. of *The Wanderer,* by Frances Burney. *Quarterly Review* 11 (1814): 123–30.

Cross, Nigel., ed. *Archives of the Royal Literary Fund, 1790–1918.* London: World Microfilms Publications, 1982.

Cutting, Rose Marie. "A Wreath for Fanny Burney's Last Novel: *The Wanderer*'s Contribution to Women's Studies." *Illinois Quarterly* 37. 3 (1975): 45–64.

Davies, Kate. *Catharine Macaulay and Mercy Otis Warren: The Revolutionary Atlantic and the Politics of Gender.* Oxford: Oxford UP, 2005.

————. "Revolutionary Correspondence: Reading Catharine Macaulay and Mercy Otis Warren." *Women's Writing* 13. 1 (2006): 62–82.

Davis, Lennard J. *Factual Fictions: The Origins of the English Novel.* New York: Columbia UP, 1983.

Davis, Oliver. *Age Rage and Going Gently: Stories of the Senescent Subject in Twentieth-Century French Writing.* Amsterdam: Rodopi, 2006.

De Beauvoir, Simone. *The Coming of Age.* Tran. P. O'Brien. New York: G. P. Putnam's, 1972.

De Castera, Louis-Adrien Du Perron. *The Lady's Philosopher's Stone; or, The Caprices of Love and Destiny: An Historical Novel.* Trans. from French. London: D. Browne, Junr. & S. Chapman, 1725.

De Lambert, Marquise Anne Thérèse de Marguenat de Courcelles. *Advice of a Mother to Her Daughter.* Poughnill, UK: G. Nicholson, 1801.

DeMaria, Robert, Jr. *The Life of Samuel Johnson.* Oxford: Blackwell, 1993.

De Rose, Peter L., and S. W. McGuire. *A Concordance to the Works of Jane Austen.* New York: Garland, 1982.

"Description of a Place in the Infernal Regions Allotted to Old Maids." *Gentleman's Magazine* 19 (1749): 131–32.

De Tencin, Claudine Alexandrine Guérin. *The Siege of Calais by Edward of England: An Historical Novel.* Trans. from the French. London: T. Woodward & Paul Vaillant, 1740.

de Valangin, Francis. *A Treatise on Diet; or, The Management of Human Life: By Physicians Called the Six Non-Naturals, Viz. I. The Air. Ii. Food. Iii. Excretions and Retentions. Iv. Motion and Rest. V. Sleep and Watching. Vi. The Affections of the Mind. . . . Addressed to the Inhabitants of This Metropolis.* London: J. & W. Oliver, 1768.

Dickens, Charles. *Great Expectations.* Ed. Margaret Cardwell. New York: Oxford UP, 1993.

Dictionary of Literary Biography, Vol. 107, *British Romantic Prose Writers, 1789–1832.* Ed. John R. Greenfield. Detroit: Gale Research, 1991.

———. Vol. 116, *British Romantic Novelists, 1789–1832.* Ed. Bradford K. Mudge. Detroit: Gale Research, 1992.

———. Vol. 142, *Eighteenth-Century British Literary Biographers.* Ed. Steven Serafin. Detroit: Gale Research, 1994.

———. Vol. 158. *British Reform Writers, 1789–1832.* Ed. Gary Kelly and Edd Applegate. Detroit: Gale Research, 1996.

D'Israeli, Isaac. "Advertisement." *An Essay on the Manners and Genius of the Literary Character.* London: T. Cadell, 1795.

———. *Commentaries on the Life and Reign of Charles the First, King of England.* London: Henry Colburn, 1828.

———. *Curiosities of Literature.* New York, Garland, 1971.

———. *A Dissertation on Anecdotes.* London: C. & G. Kearsley, 1793.

———. *An Inquiry into the Literary and Political Character of James the First.* London: John Murray, 1816.

———. Letter to the Editor. *British Critic* 4 (1794): 338.

———. Letter to the Editor. *Gentleman's Magazine* 64 (1794): 816.

Rev. of *A Dissertation on Anecdotes,* by Isaac D'Israeli. *British Critic* 3 (1794): 40.

Donoghue, Frank. *The Fame Machine: Book Reviewing and Eighteenth-Century Literary Careers.* Stanford: Stanford UP, 1996.

Dormandy, Thomas. *Old Masters: Great Artists in Old Age.* London: Hambledon, 2000.

Downing, C. "Face Painting in Early Modern England." *PMLA* 109 (1994): 119–20.

"Dr. Johnson and Mrs. Thrale." *St. James' Magazine* 1 (1861): 245.

Rev. of *Duke Christian of Luneburg*, by Jane Porter. *La Belle Assemblée*, n.s. 29 (Apr. 1824): 170–71.

Rev. of *Duke Christian of Luneburg*, by Jane Porter. *New Monthly Magazine* 12 (1824): 220.

Eckersley, L. Lynette. "The Role of *Evelina*'s 'Worthiest Object' in Frances Burney's Resistance to Eighteenth-Century Gender Ideology." *Eighteenth-Century Novel* 2 (2002): 192–213.

Edgeworth, Maria. *Helen*. London: J. M. Dent, 1893.

———. *Helen*. London: Macmillan, 1903.

———. *Helen*. London: Pandora, 1987.

———. *The Novels and Selected Works of Maria Edgeworth*. Vol. 1, *General Introduction, Castle Rackrent, Irish Bulls, Ennui*. Ed. Jane Desmarais, Tim McLoughlin, and Marilyn Butler. London: Pickering & Chatto, 1999.

———. *The Novels and Selected Works of Maria Edgeworth*. Vol. 9, *Helen*. Ed. Susan Manly and Cliona Ó Gallchoir. London: Pickering & Chatto, 1999.

———. *Orlandino*. Edinburgh: William & Robert Chambers, 1848.

Rev. of *Eighteen Hundred and Eleven*, by Anna Letitia Barbauld. *Anti-Jacobin Review* 42 (1812): 203–9.

Rev. of *Eighteen Hundred and Eleven*, by Anna Letitia Barbauld. *Eclectic Review* 8 (1812): 474–78.

Ellet, E. F. "Mrs. Piozzi's Love-Letters." *Athenaeum* 1811 (12 July 1862): 50.

Ellis, Grace A. *A Memoir of Mrs. Anna Laetitia Barbauld, with Many of Her Letters*. 2 vols. Boston: James R. Osgood, 1874.

Elwood, Anne. *Memoirs of the Literary Ladies of England from the Commencement of the Last Century*, 2 vols. London: Henry Colburn, 1843.

An Encyclopedia of British Women Writers. See Schleuter, Paul, and June Schleuter.

[Enfield, William]. Rev. of *Letters on Education*, by Catharine Macaulay Graham. *Monthly Review* 3 (1790): 309.

Erickson, Robert A. *Mother Midnight: Birth, Sex, and Fate in Eighteenth-Century Fiction*. New York: AMS, 1986.

An Essay on the Most Rational Means of Preserving Health and of Attaining to an Advanced Age. To Which Are Added, Anecdotes of Longevity. London: James Wallis, 1799.

Estlin, J. P. *Familiar Lectures on Moral Philosophy*. London: Longman, Hurst, Rees, Orme & Brown, 1818.

"European Literary Intelligence." *Literary Magazine* 2 (1804): 532–33.

Ezell, Margaret J. M. *Writing Women's Literary History*. Baltimore: Johns Hopkins UP, 1992.

Favretti, Maggie. "The Politics of Vision: Anna Barbauld's 'Eighteen Hundred and Eleven.'" In *Women's Poetry in the Enlightenment: The Making of a Canon 1730–1820*. Ed. Isobel Armstrong and Virginia Blain. New York: St. Martin's, 1999.

Feinson, Marjorie Chary. "Where Are the Women in the History of Aging?" *Social Science History* 9.4 (1985): 429–52.

The Female Aegis; or, The Duties of Women New York: Garland, 1974.

Fergus, Jan. *Jane Austen: A Literary Life*. New York: St. Martin's, 1991.

Ferrier, Susan. *Destiny; or, The Chief's Daughter.* 3 vols. Edinburgh: Robert Caddell, 1831.

Ferris, Ina. *The Achievement of Literary Authority: Gender, History, and the Waverley Novels.* Ithaca, NY: Cornell UP, 1991.

Fieser, James. "The Eighteenth-Century British Reviews of Hume's Writings." *Journal of the History of Ideas* 57. 4 (1996): 645–57.

Fischer, David Hackett. *Growing Old in America.* 2nd ed. New York: Oxford UP, 1978.

Fisher, Judith L. " 'In the Present Famine of Anything Substantial': Fraser's 'Portraits' and the Construction of Literary Celebrity; or, 'Personality, Personality Is the Appetite of the Age.' " *Victorian Periodicals Review* 39.2 (2006): 97–135.

Fisher, Judith W. "Creating Another Identity: Aging Actresses in the Eighteenth Century." *Journal of Aging and Identity* 4.2 (1999): 57–78.

Fitzgerald, Percy. *The Life of George the Fourth.* New York: Harper & Bros., 1881.

Folger Collective on Early Women Critics. *Women Critics 1660–1820: An Anthology.* Bloomington: Indiana UP, 1995.

Fortescue-Brickdale, Charles. "Dr. Johnson and Mrs. Macaulay: The Credibility of Boswell." *Notes & Queries* 159 (1930): 111–12.

Foster, E. M. *The Duke of Clarence. An Historical Novel.* 4 vols. London: William Lane, at the Minerva-Press, 1795.

———. *Jaquelina of Hainault: An Historical Novel.* 3 vols. London: J. Bell, 1798.

Francis, John W. *Old New York; or, Reminiscences of the Past Sixty Years. Being an Enlarged and Revised Edition of the Anniversary Discourse Delivered before the New York Historical Society (November 17, 1857).* New York: C. Roe, 1858.

Freedman, Richard. "Sufficiently Decayed: Gerontophobia in English Literature." In *Aging and the Elderly: Humanistic Perspectives in Gerontology.* Ed. Stuart F. Spicker, Kathleen M. Woodward, and David D. Van Tassel. Atlantic Highlands, NJ: Humanities Press, 1978.

Freeman, Kathleen. *T'Other Miss Austen.* London: Macdonald, 1956.

Friedan, Betty. *The Fountain of Age.* New York: Simon & Schuster, 1993.

Gamer, Michael. *Romanticism and the Gothic: Genre, Reception, and Canon Formation.* Cambridge: Cambridge UP, 2000.

Gardner, Catherine. "Catharine Macaulay's *Letters on Education:* Odd But Equal." *Hypatia* 13.1 (1998): 118–37.

Garside, P. D. "Walter Scott and the 'Common' Novel, 1808–1819," *Cardiff Corvey: Reading the Romantic Text.* 3 (Sept. 1999). www.cf.ac.uk/encap/corvey/articles/cc03_n02.html (accessed 11 Oct. 2004).

Garside, P. D., J. E. Belanger, and S. A. Ragaz, *British Fiction, 1800–1829: A Database of Production, Circulation, and Reception,* designer A. A. Mandal. 2004. www.british-fiction.cf.ac.uk (accessed 13 Sept. 2005).

Gee, Maggie. Introduction to *Helen* by Maria Edgeworth. London: Pandora, 1987.

Gérin, Winifred. *The Young Fanny Burney.* London: T. Nelson, 1961.

Gevirtz, Karen Bloom. *Life after Death: Widows and the English Novel, Defoe to Austen.* Newark: U of Delaware P, 2006.

Gilson, David. *A Bibliography of Jane Austen.* Oxford: Clarendon, 1982.

Gissing, George. *The Odd Women.* Ed. Patricia Ingham. Oxford: Oxford UP, 2000.

Godwin, William. *Enquiry Concerning Political Justice, and Its Influence on Morals and Happiness.* 2nd ed. 2 vols. London: G. G. & J. Robinson, 1796.

Goldsmith, Oliver. *The Citizen of the World and the Bee.* London: J. M. Dent, 1934.

Gonda, Caroline. *Reading Daughters' Fictions, 1709–1834: Novels and Society from Manley to Edgeworth.* Cambridge: Cambridge UP, 1996.

Goode, Mike. "Drysasdust Antiquarianism and Soppy Masculinity: The Waverley Novels and the Gender of History." *Representations* 82 (2003): 52–86.

Gordon, William. *The Plan of a Society for Making Provision for Widows, by Annuities for the Remainder of Life; and for Granting Annuities to Persons after Certain Ages.* Boston: Joseph Edwards & John Fleeming, 1772.

Gough, Richard. Rev. of *A Dissertation on Anecdotes,* by Isaac D'Israeli. *Gentleman's Magazine* 63 (1793): 1121.

Graham, James J. G. "Mrs. Catherine [sic] Macaulay." *Notes & Queries,* 9th ser., 4 (1899): 238.

Graham, William. Letter to the Editor. *Gentleman's Magazine* 64 (1794): 907–8.

Grant, Anne. *Memoir and Correspondence of Mrs. Grant of Laggan.* Ed. J. P. Grant. 3 vols. London: Longman, Brown, Green & Longmans, 1844.

Graves, Richard. *The Invalid: With the Obvious Means of Enjoying Health and Long Life, by a Nonagenarian.* London: Phillips, 1804.

———. *Senilities; or, Solitary Amusements in Prose and Verse.* London: Longman & Rees, 1801.

———. *The Triflers; Consisting of Trifling Essays, Trifling Anecdotes, and a Few Poetical Trifles.* London: H. D. Symonds, 1805.

Graves, Richard, E. Rack, Mr. Hinks, Polwhele, and Mr. Meyler. *Six Odes, Presented to That Justly-Celebrated Historian, Mrs. Catharine Macaulay, on Her Birth-Day, and Publicly Read to a Polite and Brilliant Audience, Assembled April the Second, at Alfred House, Bath, to Congratulate That Lady of the Happy Occasion.* Bath: R. Crutwell, 1777.

Graves, Robert. "Lectures on Medical Statistics by Robert Graves, M D." *Medical and Chirurgical Review* 24.1 (1836): 461–63.

Green, Alice Stopford. *Woman's Place in the World of Letters.* London: Macmillan, 1913.

Greene, Edward Burnaby. *Poetical Essays.* London: J. Ridley, 1772.

Greg, William Rathbone. *Literary and Social Judgments.* London: Trubner & Co, 1880.

Gregory, John. *A Father's Legacy to His Daughters.* New ed. London: W. Strahan, 1775.

Griffiths, Ralph. "Correspondence." *Monthly Review* 4 (1791): 119.

Gruman, Gerald J. *A History of Ideas about the Prolongation of Life: The Evolution of the Prolongevity Hypotheses to 1800.* Transactions of the American Philosophical Society 56.9 (1966).

Grundy, Isobel. Introduction to *Secresy; or, The Ruin on the Rock,* by Eliza Fenwick. Peterborough, ON: Broadview, 1994.

———. "Why Do They Talk So Much? How Can We Stand It? John Thorpe and Miss Bates." In *The Talk in Jane Austen,* ed. Bruce Stovel and Lynn Weinlos Gregg, 41–56. Edmonton: U of Alberta P, 2002.

Guest, Harriet. *Small Change: Women, Learning, Patriotism, 1750–1810.* Chicago: U of Chicago P, 2000.

Gullette, Margaret Morganroth. *Aged by Culture.* Chicago: U of Chicago P, 2004.

————. "Male Midlife Sexuality in a Gerontocratic Economy: The Privileged Stage of the Long Midlife in Nineteenth-Century Age Ideology." *Journal of the History of Sexuality* 5.1 (1994): 58–89.

Gunther-Canada, Wendy. "The Politics of Sense and Sensibility: Mary Wollstonecraft's and Catharine Macaulay Graham on Edmund Burke's *Reflections on the Revolution in France.*" In *Women Writers and the Early Modern British Political Tradition*, ed. Hilda L. Smith, 126–47. Cambridge: Cambridge UP, 1998.

H. H., Letter to the Editor. *Gentleman's Magazine* 64 (1794): 1001.

Hale, Sarah Josepha. *Biography of Distinguished Women; or, Woman's Record from the Creation to A. D. 1869.* 3rd ed. New York: Harper & Bros, 1876.

Halperin, John. *The Life of Jane Austen.* Baltimore: Johns Hopkins UP, 1984.

Hawkins, Aubrey. "Some Writers on the *Monthly Review.*" *Review of English Studies* 7. 26 (1931): 168–81.

Hawthorne, Mark D. *Doubt and Dogma in Maria Edgeworth.* Gainesville: U of Florida P, 1967.

Hayley, William. *A Philosophical, Historical, and Moral Essay upon Old Maids.* 3 vols. London: T. Cadell, 1785.

Hays, Mary. *Female Biography: or Memoirs of Illustrious and Celebrated Women . . . Alphabetically Arranged.* London: R. Phillips, 1803.

————. *Memoirs of Queens: Illustrated and Celebrated.* London: T. & J. Allman, 1821.

Hayward, A. *Autobiography, Letters, and Literary Remains of Mrs. Piozzi (Thrale), Edited with Notes and an Introductory Account of Her Life and Writings.* Boston: Ticknor & Fields, 1861.

"Hayward's Mrs. Piozzi." *Littell's Living Age* 69 (1861): 120–24.

Hazlitt, William. Rev. of *The Wanderer,* by Frances Burney. *Edinburgh Review* 76 (1815): 320–38.

Heidler, Joseph B., and Harvey C. Lehman. "Chronological Age and Productivity: Various Types of Literature." *English Journal (College Edition)* 26 (1937): 294–304.

Heilbrun, Carolyn. *Writing a Woman's Life.* New York: W. W. Norton, 1988.

Rev. of *Helen,* by Maria Edgeworth. *North American Review* 39.84 (1834): 167.

Heller, Deborah. "'A Friend Is the Medicine of Life': Doctoring Body and Mind in Bluestocking Correspondence." Paper presented at the Western Society for Eighteenth-Century Studies meeting, Tempe, Arizona, Feb. 17–18, 2006.

Hemlow, Joyce. *The History of Fanny Burney.* Oxford: Clarendon, 1958.

Hicks, Phillip. "Catharine Macaulay's Civil War: Gender, History, and Republicanism in Georgian Britain." *Journal of British Studies* 41 (Apr. 2002): 170–98.

Hill, Bridget. "Daughter and Mother: Some New Light on Catharine Macaulay and Her Family." *British Journal for Eighteenth-Century Studies* 22.1 (2000): 35–49.

————. "The Links between Mary Wollstonecraft and Catharine Macaulay: New Evidence." *Women's History Review* 4.2 (1995): 177–92.

————. *The Republican Virago: The Life and Times of Catharine Macaulay, Historian.* Oxford: Clarendon, 1992.

————. *Women Alone: Spinsters in England 1660–1850.* New Haven: Yale UP, 2001.

Rev. of *History of the Commonwealth*, by William Godwin. *London Magazine* 10 (1824): 57–60.

Hollindale, Peter. "Age and Patronage in *Emma*." In *Critical Essays on Emma*, ed. Linda Cookson and Bryan Loughrey, 105–14. Harlow, UK: Longman, 1988.

Honoria. *The Female Mentor; or, Select Conversations*, 2 vols, 2nd ed. London: T. Cadell, 1798.

Hunter, J. Paul. *Before Novels: The Cultural Contexts of Eighteenth-Century English Fiction.* New York: W. W. Norton, 1990.

Rev. of *The Infirmities of Genius Illustrated by Referring the Anomalies of the Literary Character to the Habits and Constitutional Peculiarities of Men of Genius*, by R. R. Madden. *Quarterly Review* 50.99 (1834): 34–56.

Inglis-Jones, Elisabeth. *The Great Maria.* London: Faber & Faber, 1959.

Jackson, H. J. *Marginalia: Readers Writing in Books.* New Haven: Yale UP, 2001.

———. *Romantic Readers: The Evidence of Marginalia.* New Haven: Yale UP, 2005.

Janes, R. M. "On the Reception of Mary Wollstonecraft's *A Vindication of the Rights of Woman*." *Journal of the History of Ideas* 39.2 (1978): 293–302.

Jeffrey, Francis. Rev. of the *Correspondence of Samuel Richardson*, *Edinburgh Review* 5 (1804): 23–44.

Joddrell, Richard. *The Female Patriot: An Epistle from C-t-e M-c-y to the Rev. Dr. W-l-n on Her Late Marriage.* London: J. Bew, 1779.

Johnson, Claudia L. *Jane Austen: Women, Politics, and the Novel.* Chicago: U of Chicago P, 1988.

———. " 'Let Me Make the Novels of Country': Barbauld's *The British Novelists* (1810/1820)." *Novel* 34.2 (2001): 163–79.

Jones, Ann H. *Ideas and Innovation: Best Sellers of Jane Austen's Age.* New York: AMS Press, 1986.

Justice, George. *The Manufacturers of Literature: Writing and the Literary Marketplace in Eighteenth-Century England.* Newark: U of Delaware P, 2002.

Kafker, Frank A. "La Vieillesse et la Productivité intellectuelle chez les Encyclopédistes [Old Age and the Intellectual Productivity of the Encyclopedists]." *Revue d'Histoire Moderne et Contemporaine* 28 (1981): 304–27.

Kaplan, Deborah. *Jane Austen among Women.* Baltimore: Johns Hopkins UP, 1992.

Kaplan, E. Ann. "Introduction 2: Feminism, Aging, and Changing Paradigms." In *Generations: Academic Feminists in Dialogue*, ed. Devoney Looser and E. Ann Kaplan, 13–29. Minneapolis: U of Minnesota P, 1997.

Keach, William "A Regency Prophecy and the End of Anna Barbauld's Career." *Studies in Romanticism* 33 (1994): 569–77.

Kern, Jean B. "The Old Maid, or, 'to Grow Old, and Be Poor, and Laughed at.' " In *Fetter'd or Free? British Women Novelists 1670–1815*, ed. Mary Anne Schofield and Cecilia Macheski. Athens: Ohio UP, 1986.

Kinkead-Weekes, Mark. "This Old Maid: Jane Austen Replies to Charlotte Brontë and D. H. Lawrence." *Nineteenth-Century Fiction* 30.3 (1975): 399–419.

Kirkham, Margaret. *Jane Austen, Feminism, and Fiction.* Sussex: Harvester, 1983.

———. *Jane Austen, Feminism, and Fiction.* 2nd ed. London: Athlone, 1997.

Kittredge, Katharine. " 'The Ag'd Dame to Venery Inclin'd': Images of Sexual Older Women in Eighteenth-Century Britain." In *Power and Poverty: Old Age in the Pre-Industrial Past*, ed. Susannah R. Ottaway, L. A. Botelho, and Katharine Kittredge, 247–64. Westport, CT: Greenwood Press, 2002.

———. " 'Tabby Cats Lead Apes in Hell': Spinsters in Eighteenth-Century Life and Fiction." PhD diss., State University of New York–Binghamton, 1992.

———. "That Excellent Miss Bates." *Persuasions* 17 (1995): 26–30.

Klassen, Sherri. "The Domestic Virtues of Old Age: Gendered Rites in the Fête De La Vieillesse." *Canadian Journal of History* 32 (1997): 393–403.

Knapp, Oswald G., ed. *The Intimate Letters of Hester Piozzi and Penelope Pennington, 1788–1821.* London: John Lane, 1914.

Knight, Ellis Cornelia. *Autobiography of Cornelia Ellis Knight, Lady Companion to the Princess Charlotte of Wales: With Extracts from Her Journals and Anecdote Books.* 2 vols. 4th ed. London: W. H. Allen, 1861.

———. *Sir Guy De Lusignan: A Tale of Italy.* 2 vols. London: Saunders & Otley, 1833.

Kranidis, Rita. *The Victorian Spinster and Colonial Emigration: Contested Subjects.* New York: St. Martin's, 1999.

Lamont, Claire. "Jane Austen and the Old." *Review of English Studies* 54 (2003): 661–74.

Lanser, Susan S. "Singular Politics: The British Nation and the Old Maid." In *Singlewomen in the European Past, 1250–1800*, ed. Judith M. Bennett and Amy M. Froide, 297–323. Philadelphia: U of Pennsylvania P, 1999.

Larsen, Elizabeth. "A Text of Identity: Frances Brooke and the Rhetoric of the Aging Spinster." *Journal of Aging and Identity* 4.4 (1999): 255–68.

Laslett, Peter. *Family Life and Illicit Love in Earlier Generations.* Cambridge: Cambridge UP, 1977.

———. *A Fresh Map of Life: The Emergence of the Third Age.* London: Weidenfeld & Nicolson, 1989.

Lavine, Steven David. Review of *George Crabbe's Poetry* by Peter New. *Modern Philology* 76.4 (1979): 416.

Lawless, Emily. *Maria Edgeworth.* New York: Macmillan, 1905.

Lawrence, D. H. *A Propos of Lady Chatterly's Lover.* New York: Haskell House, 1973.

Lawrence, Eugene. *The Lives of the British Historians.* 2 vols. New York: C. Scribner, 1855.

Le Breton, Anna Laetitia. *Memoir of Mrs. Barbauld, Including Letters and Notices of Her Family and Friends.* London: George Bell, 1874.

———. *Memories of Seventy Years.* Ed. Mrs. Herbert Martin. London: Griffith & Farran, 1883.

Le Breton, Anna Laetitia, ed. *Correspondence of William Ellery Channing and Lucy Aikin from 1826 to 1842.* London: Williams & Norgate, 1874.

Lecky, William Edward Hartpole. *A History of England in the Eighteenth Century.* 3 vols. New York: D. Appleton, 1891.

Lee, Hermione. *Virginia Woolf's Nose: Essays on Biography.* Princeton: Princeton UP, 2005.

Lefanu, Alicia. *Memoirs of the Life and Writings of Mrs. Frances Sheridan, Mother of the Late Right Hon. Richard Brinsley Sheridan.* London: G. & W. B. Whittaker, 1824.

Le Faye, Deirdre. "Jane Austen and William Hayley." *Notes & Queries* 34 (1987): 25–26.

Lehman, Harvey C. *Age and Achievement.* Philadelphia: American Philosophical Society, 1953.

Lehman, Harvey C., and Joseph B. Heidler. "Chronological Age vs. Quality of Literary Output." *American Journal of Psychology* 62.1 (1949): 75–89.

Rev. of *Letters on Education*, by Catharine Macaulay Graham. *European Magazine* 19 (1791): 269–72; 20 (1791): 45–48.

Lewis, M. G. *Ambrosio; or, The Monk.* 3 vols. 5th ed. London: J. Bell, 1800.

Lickorish, Richard. *Sermons and Tracts upon Various Subjects; Literary, Critical, and Political.* Coventry: N. Rollason, 1793.

"The Life of William Hayley." *London Magazine* 10 (1824): 504.

"The Lives of Two Ladies." *Blackwood's Edinburgh Review* 81 (1862): 423.

Lloyd, Pamela. "Jane West: A Critical Biography." PhD diss., Brandeis U, 1997.

Lockhart, J. G. Rev. of *Helen*, by Maria Edgeworth. *Quarterly Review* 51 (1834): 483.

London, April. "Isaac D'Israeli and Literary History: Opinion, Anecdote, and Secret History in the Early Nineteenth Century." *Poetics Today* 26 (2005): 351–86.

———. *Women and Property in the Eighteenth-Century English Novel.* Cambridge: Cambridge UP, 1999.

Looser, Devoney. *British Women Writers and the Writing of History, 1670–1820.* Baltimore: Johns Hopkins UP, 2000.

———. "'What the Devil a Woman Lives for After 30': The Late Careers of Late Eighteenth-Century British Women Writers." *Journal of Aging and Identity* 4.1 (1999): 3–11.

Looser, Devoney, ed. *Jane Austen and Discourses of Feminism.* New York: St. Martin's, 1995.

Love Letters of Mrs. Piozzi, Written When She Was Eighty to William Augustus Conway. London: John Russell Smith, 1843.

Rev. of *Love Letters of Mrs. Piozzi. Athenaeum* 803 (18 Mar. 1843): 259.

Luttrell, B. *The Prim Romantic: A Biography of Ellis Cornelia Knight, 1758–1837.* London: Chatto & Windus, 1965.

Macaulay, Catharine. *The History of England from the Accession of James I, to That of the Brunswick Line.* 8 vols. London: J. Nourse, 1763.

———. *The History of England from the Revolution to the Present Time: In a Series of Letters to a Friend.* Vol. 1. Bath: R. Crutwell, 1778.

———. *Letters on Education: With Observations on Religious and Metaphysical Subjects.* London: C. Dilly, 1790.

———. *Observations on the Reflections of the Right Hon. Edmund Burke, on the Revolution in France, in a Letter to the Right Hon. the Earl of Stanhope On Burke's Reflections on the French Revolution.* New York: Woodstock, 1997.

———. "On the Idea of a Sexual Difference in the Human Character" *Aberdeen Magazine* 66 (1790): 424–27.

———. *A Treatise on the Immutability of Moral Truth.* London: A. Hamilton, 1783.

———. "Various Interesting Observations on Women." *Aberdeen Magazine* 71 (1790): 581–85.

Macaulay, Thomas Babington. "Madame D'Arblay." In *Critical and Miscellaneous Essays.* 7 vols. New York: Dodd, Mead, 1880.

MacKenzie, James. *The History of Health, and the Art of Preserving It, or, an Account of All That Has Been Recommended by Physicians and Philosophers, Towards the Preser-*

vation of Health, from the Most Remote Antiquity to This Time . . . 2nd ed. Edinburgh: W. Gordon, 1759.

Madden, R. R. *Infirmities of Genius Illustrated by Referring the Anomalies in the Literary Character to the Habits and Constitutional Peculiarities in Men of Genius.* 2 vols. London: Saunders & Otley, 1833.

[Maginn, William]. "Miss Jane Porter." *Fraser's Magazine* 11 (1835): 404.

Malthus, Thomas R. *An Essay on the Principle of Population; or, A View of Its Past and Present Effects on Human Happiness; with an Inquiry into Our Prospects Respecting the Future Removal or Mitigation of the Evils Which It Occasions.* London: J. Johnson, 1803.

Mandell, Laura. "Virtue and Evidence: Catharine Macaulay's Historical Realism." *Journal for Early Modern Cultural Studies* 4.1 (2004): 127–57.

Mangin, Edward. *Piozziana; or, Recollections of the Late Mrs. Piozzi, with Remarks.* London: E. Moxon, 1833.

Mangum, Teresa. "Growing Old: Age." In *Companion to Victorian Literature and Culture.* ed. Herbert F. Tucker, 97–109. Oxford: Blackwell, 1999.

May, Thomas Erskine. *The Constitutional History of England: Since the Accession of George the Third.* 3 vols. London: Longmans, Green, 1912.

Mazzucco-Than, Cecile. "'As Easy As A Chimney Pot to Blacken': Catharine Macaulay 'the Celebrated Female Historian.'" *Prose Studies: History, Theory, and Criticism* 18.3 (1995): 78–104.

McCarthy, William. *Hester Thrale Piozzi: Portrait of a Literary Woman.* Chapel Hill: U of North Carolina P, 1985.

———. "A 'High-Minded Christian Lady': The Posthumous Reception of Anna Laetitia Barbauld." In *Romanticism and Women Poets: Opening the Doors of Reception,* ed. Harriet Kramer Linkin and Stephen C. Behrendt, 165–91. Lexington: UP of Kentucky, 1999.

———. Rev. of *The Piozzi Letters,* by Hester Lynch Piozzi. *Age of Johnson* 15 (2004): 434–38.

———. "The Repression of Hester Lynch Piozzi; or, How We Forgot a Revolution in Authorship." *Modern Language Studies* 18.1 (1988): 99–111.

———. "Review Essay: *The Piozzi Letters.*" *Age of Johnson* 12 (2001): 399–420.

———. "What Did Anna Barbauld Do to Samuel Richardson's Correspondence? A Study of Her Editing." *Studies in Bibliography* 54 (2001): 191–224.

McCarthy, William, and Elizabeth Kraft. *The Poems of Anna Letitia Barbauld.* Athens: U of Georgia P, 1994.

McDonald, Lynn. *The Women Founders of the Social Sciences.* Ottawa: Carleton UP, 1994.

McKillop, Alan Dugald. *Samuel Richardson, Printer and Novelist.* Chapel Hill: U of North Carolina P, 1936.

McLean, Thomas. "Nobody's Argument: Jane Porter and the Historical Novel." *Journal for Early Modern Cultural* Studies 7.2 (2007): 88–103.

Rev. of *A Memoir of Maria Edgeworth, with a Selection from Her Letters,* by Maria Edgeworth. *Edinburgh Review* 126 (1867): 458–98.

"Memoir of Miss Jane Porter." *Edinburgh Literary Gazette* 1.18 (1829): 273–74.

"Memoirs of Mrs. Piozzi." *National Review* 12 (1861): 390–91.

"Men of Learning and Genius." *The Prose Epitome: Elegant Extracts Abridged.* London: C. Dilly, 1791.

Merritt, Percival, ed. *The True Story of the So-Called Love Letters of Mrs. Piozzi: "In Defense of an Elderly Lady."* Cambridge, MA: Harvard UP, 1927.

Mignon, Elisabeth. *Crabbed Age and Youth: The Old Man and Woman in the Restoration Comedy of Manners.* Durham, NC: Duke UP, 1947.

Minois, Georges. *The History of Old Age: From Antiquity to the Renaissance.* Trans. Sarah Hanbury Tenison. Chicago: U of Chicago P, 1987.

"Modern Old Age." *Once a Week* 9 (1863) 581–84.

[Moody, Christopher], Rev. of *The Correspondence of Samuel Richardson. Monthly Review* 46 (1805): 29–48.

[————]. Rev. of *Eighteen Hundred and Eleven*, by Anna Letitia Barbauld. *Monthly Review* 67 (1812): 428–32.

Moore, Catherine E. " 'Ladies. Taking the Pen in Hand': Mrs. Barbauld's Criticism of Eighteenth-Century Women Novelists." In *Fetter'd or Free? British Women Novelists 1670–1815*, ed. Mary Anne Schofield and Cecilia Macheski, 383–97. Athens: Ohio UP, 1986.

Moore, E. Margaret. "Emma and Miss Bates: Early Experiences of Separation and the Theme of Dependency in Jane Austen's Novels." *Studies in English Literature, 1500–1900* 9.4 (1969): 573–85.

Morgan, Lady [Sydney Owenson]. *Lady Morgan's Memoirs: Autobiography, Diaries, and Correspondence.* 2 vols. London: Wm. H. Allen, 1862.

Morgan, Peter F. *Literary Critics and Reviewers in Early Nineteenth-Century Britain.* London: Croom Helm, 1983.

"Mrs. Barbauld." *Gentleman's Magazine* 95 (1825): 281–82.

Mumm, S. D. "Writing for Their Lives: Women Applicants to the Royal Literary Fund, 1840–1880." *Publishing History* 27 (1990): 27–48.

Murch, Jerom. *Mrs. Barbauld and Her Contemporaries: Sketches of Some Eminent Literary and Scientific Englishwomen.* London: Longmans, Green, 1877.

Murphy, Arthur. *The Way to Keep Him and Five Other Plays.* New York: New York UP, 1956.

Myers, Mitzi. "Sensibility and the 'Walk of Reason': Mary Wollstonecraft's Literary Reviews as Cultural Critique." In *Sensibility in Transformation: Creative Resistance to Sentiment from the Augustans to the Romantics*, ed. Syndy McMillen Conger, 120–45. Rutherford, NJ: Fairleigh Dickinson UP, 1990.

————. "Shot from Canons; or, Maria Edgeworth and the Culture Production and Consumption of the Late Eighteenth-Century Woman Writer." In *The Consumption of Culture, 1600–1800: Image, Object, Text*, ed. Ann Bermingham and John Brewer, 193–216. London: Routledge, 1997.

Myers, Sylvia Harcstark. *The Bluestocking Circle: Women, Friendship, and the Life of the Mind in Eighteenth-Century England.* Oxford: Clarendon, 1990.

Nangle, Benjamin Christie. *The Monthly Review Second Series, 1790–1815.* Oxford: Clarendon, 1955.

Needham, Gwendolyn Bridges. "New Light on Old Maids 'Leading Apes in Hell.' " *Journal of American Folklore* 75.296 (1962): 106–19.

————. "The 'Old Maid' in the Life and the Fiction of Eighteenth-Century England." PhD diss., University of California–Berkeley, 1937.

Newby, P. H. *Maria Edgeworth.* Denver: A. Swallow, 1950.

Newcomer, James. "Maria Edgeworth and the Critics." *College English* 26.3 (1964): 214–18.

Newlyn, Lucy. *Reading, Writing, and Romanticism: The Anxiety of Reception.* Oxford: Oxford UP, 2000.

"Obituary of Considerable Persons; with Biographical Anecdotes." *Gentleman's Magazine* 61 (1791): 589–90.

Ó Gallchoir, Cliona. "Gender, Nation, and Revolution: Maria Edgeworth and Stéphanie Félicité-De Genlis." In *Women, Writing, and the Public Sphere: 1700–1830,* ed. Elizabeth Eger, Charlotte Grant, Cliona Ó Gallchoir, and Penny Warburton, 200–216. Cambridge: Cambridge UP, 2001.

——. *Maria Edgeworth: Women, Enlightenment and Nation.* Dublin: U College Dublin P, 2005.

Ogden, James. *Isaac D'Israeli.* Oxford: Clarendon, 1969.

O'Gorman, Frances, and Katherine Turner, eds. *The Victorians and the Eighteenth Century: Reassessing the Tradition.* Burlington, VT: Ashgate, 2003.

"On the Prolongation of Life." *Retrospective Review* 7.1 (1823): 64–87.

"Original Memorials of Mrs. Piozzi." *Atlantic Monthly* 7 (1861): 616.

Ottaway, Susannah R. *The Decline of Life: Old Age in Eighteenth-Century England.* Cambridge: Cambridge UP, 2004.

Oxford Dictionary of National Biography. Multiple vols. Prepared under various editors. Oxford: Oxford UP, 2004. Also available online at www.oxforddnb.com/.

Parker, W. M. *Susan Ferrier and John Galt.* London: Longmans, Green, 1965.

Parnell, Thomas. *Collected Poems of Thomas Parnell.* Ed. Claude Rawson and F. P. Lock. Newark: U of Delaware P, 1989.

Pearson, Jacqueline. "'Arts of Appropriation': Language, Circulation, and Appropriation in the Work of Maria Edgeworth." *Yearbook of English Studies* 28 (1998): 230.

Pennington, Montagu. *Memoirs of the Life of Mrs. Elizabeth Carter.* London: F. & C. Rivington, 1807.

Perkins, Pam. "Private Men and Public Women: Social Criticism in Fanny Burney's *'The Wanderer.'" Essays in Literature* 23.1 (1996): 69–84.

Perrakis, Phyllis Sternberg, ed. *Adventures of the Spirit: The Older Woman in the Works of Doris Lessing, Margaret Atwood, and Other Contemporary Women Writers.* Columbus: Ohio State UP, 2007.

Perry, Ruth. *Novel Relations: The Transformation of Kinship in English Literature and Culture, 1748–1818.* Cambridge: Cambridge UP, 2005.

Philoscotus. "Scott and Jane Porter." *Notes & Queries* 178 (Jan.–June 1940): 408.

Rev. of *Philosophical, Historical, and Moral Essay on Old Maids,* by William Hayley. *Gentleman's Magazine* 56 (1786): 241.

Pierpont, Robert. *"History." The Marble Statue (of Mrs. Catharine Macaulay) in the Entrance Hall of Warrington Town Hall.* (Reprinted from the *Warrington Guardian.*) MS. corrections and additions [by the Author]. For Private Circulation. (1908). BL 10803.f.10.(2.)

Pines, Irene. "'Past Her Flourishing Time': The Older Woman in Restoration and Eighteenth-Century English Literature." PhD diss., U of Miami, 1995.

Piozzi, Hester Lynch. *Hester Thrale-Piozzi, Samuel Johnson, and Literary Society, 1755–1821.* Microfilm. Research Publications, Reading / John Rylands Library, Manchester, 1989.

————. *The Imperial Family Bible. Illustrated with Explanations. The Whole Embellished with Engravings. Copious Ms. Notes [by Mrs. Piozzi].* Stourbridge: J. Heming, 1811. BL C.61.f.3.

————. "Old England to Her Daughters." In *The Warning Drum: The British Home Front Faces Napoleon: Broadsides of 1803,* ed. F. J. Klingberg and S. B. Hustvedt, 76–79. Berkeley: U of California P, 1944.

————. *The Piozzi Letters.* Ed. Edward A. Bloom, Lillian Bloom, and O. M. Brack. 6 vols. Newark: U of Delaware P, 2002.

————. *Retrospection; or, A Review of the Most Striking and Important Events, Characters, Situations and Their Consequences, Which the Last Eighteen Hundred Years Have Presented to the View of Mankind.* 2 vols. London: Stockdale, 1801.

Pocock, J. G. A. "Catharine Macaulay: Patriot Historian." In *Women Writers and the Early Modern British Political Tradition,* ed. Hilda L. Smith, 243–58. Cambridge: Cambridge UP, 1998.

A Poetical Address to the Ladies of Suffolk. London: S. Neele, 1785.

Pohl, Nicole, and Betty Schellenberg, eds. *Reconsidering the Bluestockings.* San Marino, CA: Huntington Library, 2003.

Polwhele, Richard. *Traditions and Recollections; Domestic, Clerical, and Literary; in Which Are Included Letters of Charles II, Cromwell, Wolcot, Edgecumbe, Macaulay, Wolcot. And Other Distinguished Characters.* 2 vols. London: John Nichols, 1826.

————. *The Unsex'd Females; a Poem, Addressed to the Author of The Pursuits of Literature. By the Rev. Richard Polwhele. To which is Added, a Sketch of the Private and Public Character of P. Pindar.* New York: Wm. Cobbett, 1800.

Porchaska, Frank. *Royal Bounty: The Making of a Welfare Monarchy.* New Haven: Yale UP, 1995.

Porter, Jane. *Duke Christian of Luneburg; or, Tradition from the Hartz.* 3 vols. London: Longman, Hurst, Rees, Orme, Brown & Green, 1824.

————. *The Scottish Chiefs.* New rev. ed. 2 vols. London: George Virtue, 1840.

————. *The Scottish Chiefs.* Adapted by John H. O'Rourke. Illustrated by Alex A. Blum. *Classics Illustrated.* No. 67. New York: Gilberton, 1950.

————. *The Scottish Chiefs.* Ed. Gary Kelly. Vol. 4 of *The Varieties of Female Gothic.* London: Pickering & Chatto, 2002.

————. *The Scottish Chiefs.* Ed. Fiona Price. Peterborough, ON: Broadview Press, 2007.

————. *Thaddeus of Warsaw, Revised, Corrected, and Illustrated with a New Introduction, Notes, Etc., by the Author.* London: Colburn & Bentley, 1831.

————. *Thaddeus of Warsaw [by] Jane Porter, Library of Famous Books by Famous Authors,* 241. New York: H. M. Caldwell, 1898.

————. *Thaddeus of Warsaw.* Ed. Ernest A. Baker. Half-Forgotten Books. London: George Routledge, 1905.

[Porter, Jane?]. "Memoir of Miss Jane Porter." *Edinburgh Literary Gazette* 1.18 (1829): 273–74.

Porter, Jane, and Anna Maria Porter. *Coming Out; and The Field of Forty Footsteps,* London: Longman, 1828.

————. *Tales Round a Winter Hearth,* London: Longman, 1826.

Porter, Jane, Kate Douglas Smith Wiggin, Nora Archibald Smith, and N. C. Wyeth. *The Scottish Chiefs. Scribner Illustrated Classics for Younger Readers.* New York: Scribner, 1921.

Porter, Roy. *Flesh in the Age of Reason: The Modern Foundations of Body and Soul.* New York: W. W. Norton, 2003.

Premo, Terri L. *Winter Friends: Women Growing Old in the New Republic, 1785–1835.* Urbana: U of Illinois P, 1990.

Price, Fiona. "Biography of Jane Porter." *Corvey Women Writers on the Web (CW3): An Electronic Guide to Literature 1796–1834* (Feb. 2000), www2.shu.ac.uk/corvey/cw3/ContribPage.cfm?Contrib=405.

———. "Resisting 'the Spirit of Innovation': The Other Historical Novel and Jane Porter." *Modern Language Review* 101.3 (2006): 638–51.

Priestley, Joseph. *Lectures on History and General Policy; to which Is Prefixed an Essay on a Course of Liberal Education for Civil and Active Life.* Birmingham: J. Johnson, 1788.

Puff, Peter. "Letters to Certain Persons: Epistle I: To Miss Jane Porter." *Aberdeen Magazine.* (Oct. 1831): 552.

Quadagno, Jill S. *Aging in Early Industrial Society: Work, Family, and Social Policy in Nineteenth-Century England.* New York: Academic Press, 1982.

Reeve, Clara. *Plans of Education, with Remarks on the Systems of Other Writers in a Series of Letters between Mrs. Darnford and Her Friends.* London: T. Hookham, 1792.

Rev. of *Reginald Dalton* [by John Gibson Lockhart]. *Monthly Review,* 2nd ser., 103 (Feb. 1824): 199–208.

"Remarks on Mrs. Macaulay Graham's *Letters on Education.*" *Literary and Critical Remarks, on Sundry Eminent Divines and Philosophers of the Last and Present Age.* London: B. Crosby, 1794.

"Reminiscences for the Week." *Halfpenny Magazine* 7 (1832): 60.

Rendall, Jane. "Bluestockings and Reviewers: Gender, Power, and Culture in Britain, c. 1800–1830." *Nineteenth-Century Contexts* 26.4 (2004): 355–74.

Rev. of *Retrospection,* by Hester Lynch Piozzi. *Critical Review* 32 (1801): 28–35.

Rev. of *Retrospection,* by Hester Lynch Piozzi. *London Review and Literary Journal* 39 (1801): 188–93+.

"Review of Current Literature." *Christian Examiner* 70.3 (1861): 458–59.

Richardson, Samuel. *The Correspondence of Samuel Richardson. Selected from the Original Manuscripts, Bequeathed by Him to His Family, to Which Are Prefixed, a Biographical Account of the Author, and Observations on His Writings.* Ed. Anna Letitia Barbauld. 6 vols. London: R. Phillips, 1804.

———. *Selected Letters of Samuel Richardson.* Ed. John Carroll Oxford: Clarendon, 1964.

Rickards, E. C. "Mrs. Barbauld and Her Pupil." *Murray's Magazine* 10 (1891): 706–26.

Ripley, George, and Charles Dana, eds. *The American Cyclopedia: A Popular Dictionary of General Knowledge.* Vol. 13. New York: D. Appleton, 1875.

Robinson, Henry Crabb. *Diary, Reminiscences, and Correspondence of Henry Crabb Robinson.* 3 vols. London: Macmillan, 1869.

Rodgers, Betsy. *Georgian Chronicle: Mrs Barbauld and Her Family.* London: Methuen, 1958.

Rodriguez, Catherine. "A Story of Her Own: Hester Lynch Piozzi's Autobiography." *Journal of Aging and Identity* 4.2 (1999): 127–38.

Rogers, Katharine M. "Anna Barbauld's Criticism of Fiction—Johnsonian Mode, Female Vision." *Studies in Eighteenth-Century Culture* 21 (1991): 27–41.

Rogers, Pat. "Introductory Note." *Journal of Aging and Identity* 4.2 (1999): 55.

Ross, Mrs. *The Balance of Comfort; or, The Old Maid and the Married Woman: A Novel.* 4 vols. London: Minerva, 1817.

Ross, William T. "Bertrand Russell in His Nineties: Aging and the Problem of Biography." *Journal of Aging and Identity* 6.2 (2001): 67–76.

Rousseau, George. "Towards a Geriatric Enlightenment." *1650–1850: Ideas, Aesthetics, and Inquiries in the Early Modern Era* 6 (2000): 3–43.

Ryskamp, Charles. *Mrs. Piozzi to Mr. Conway.* New York: Stinehour, 1981.

Sabor, Peter. "Publishing Richardson's Correspondence: The 'Necessary Office of Selection,' " In *Samuel Richardson: Tercentenary Essays,* ed. Margaret Doody and Peter Sabor, 237–50. Cambridge: Cambridge UP, 1989.

Schellenberg, Betty. *The Professionalization of Women Writers in Eighteenth-Century Britain.* Cambridge: Cambridge UP, 2005.

Schleuter, Paul, and June Schleuter, eds. *An Encyclopedia of British Women Writers.* Rev. ed. New Brunswick, NJ: Rutgers UP, 1998.

Schnorrenberg, Barbara Brandon. "Medical Men of Bath." *Studies in Eighteenth-Century Culture* 13 (1984): 189–203.

Scott, Sir Walter. *The Journal of Sir Walter Scott.* Ed. W. E. K. Anderson. Oxford: Clarendon, 1972.

———. *Letters of Sir Walter Scott.* Ed. Herbert Grierson. 12 vols. London: Constable & Co., 1937.

———. *The Prefaces to the Waverley Novels.* Ed. Mark A. Weinstein. Lincoln: U of Nebraska P, 1978.

Select Committee on Pensions. *First Report from the Select Committee on Pensions.* London: House of Commons, 1838.

Seward, Anna. *Letters of Anna Seward: Written Between the Years 1784–1807.* Edinbugh: A. Constable, 1811.

Sherbo, Arthur. "Addenda to 'Footnotes More Pedestrian Than Sublime.' " *Eighteenth-Century Studies* 14.3 (1981): 313–16.

Sinclair, Sir John. *The Code of Health and Longevity.* 4 vols. 2nd ed. London: T. Cadell, W. Davies & J. Murray, 1807.

———. *The Code of Health and Longevity.* 3rd ed. London: M'Millan, 1816.

Siskin, Clifford. *The Work of Writing: Literature and Social Change in Britain, 1700–1830.* Baltimore: Johns Hopkins UP, 1998.

Slade, Bertha Coolidge. *Maria Edgeworth, 1767–1849: A Bibliographical Tribute.* London: Constable, 1937.

Slagle, Judith Bailey. *Joanna Baillie: A Literary Life.* Madison, NJ: Fairleigh Dickinson UP, 2002.

Smith, Charlotte. *Marchmont: A Novel.* 4 vols. London: S. Low, 1796.

Smith, James Edward. *Memoir and Correspondence of the Late Sir James Edward Smith, M.D.* Ed. Lady Smith. 2 vols. London: Longman, Rees, Orme, Brown, Green & Longman, 1832.

Smith, Orianne. "'Unlearned & Ill-Qualified Pokers into Prophecy': Hester Lynch Piozzi and the Female Prophetic Tradition." *Eighteenth-Century Life* 28.2 (2004): 87–112.

Sokoloff, Janice. *The Margin That Remains: A Study of Aging in Literature.* New York: Peter Lang, 1987.

Soland, Birgitte, ed. "Ages of Women: Age as a Category of Analysis in Women's History." *Journal of Women's History* 12.4 (2001).

Somerville, Martha. *Personal Recollections, from Early Life to Old Age, of Mary Somerville: With Selections from Her Correspondence.* Boston: Roberts Bros., 1874.

Sontag, Susan. "The Double Standard of Aging." *Saturday Review of the Society* 55 (1972): 29–38.

Sotiropoulos, Carol Strauss. *Early Feminists and the Education Debates: England, France, Germany, 1760–1810.* Madison, NJ: Fairleigh Dickinson UP, 2007.

Southcott, Joanna. *A Dispute between the Woman and the Powers of Darkness.* Ed. Jonathan Wordsworth. Poole, UK: Woodstock, 1995.

Spacks, Patricia Meyer. "Scrapbook of a Self: Mrs. Piozzi's Late Journals." *Harvard Library Bulletin* 18 (1970): 221–47.

Spencer, Jane. *Literary Relations: Kinship and the Canon, 1660–1830.* Oxford: Oxford UP, 2005.

Staves, Susan. "'The Liberty of a She-Subject of England': Rights Rhetoric and the Female Thucydides." *Cardozo Studies in Law and Literature* 1.2 (1989): 161–83.

———. *A Literary History of Women's Writing in Britain, 1660–1789.* Cambridge: Cambridge UP, 2006.

———. "Matrimonial Discord in Fiction and in Court: The Case of Ann Masterman." In *Fetter'd or Free? British Women Novelists, 1670–1815,* ed. Mary Anne Schofield and Cecilia Macheski, 169–87. Athens: Ohio UP, 1986.

Stearns, Peter N. *Old Age in European Society: The Case of France.* New York: Holmes & Meier, 1978.

———. "Old Women: Some Historical Observations." *Family History* 5 (1980): 44–57.

Stearns, Peter N., ed., *Old Age in Preindustrial Society.* New York: Holmes and Meier, 1982.

Steinem, Gloria. *Outrageous Acts and Everyday Rebellions.* New York: Signet, 1983.

Stenton, Doris Mary. *The English Woman in History.* London: George Allen & Unwin, 1957.

Straub, Kristina. *Divided Fictions: Fanny Burney and Feminine Strategy.* Lexington: UP of Kentucky, 1987.

Sutherland, John. "Henry Colburn, Publisher." *Publishing History* 19 (1986): 59–84.

Taylor, Ann Martin. *Retrospection: A Tale.* London: Taylor & Hessey, 1821.

Taylor, William. Rev. of *The Wanderer,* by Frances Burney. *Monthly Review* 76 (1815): 412–19.

Teachman, Debra. *Understanding Pride and Prejudice: A Student Casebook to Issues, Sources, and Historical Documents.* Westport, CT: Greenwood, 1997.

Tearle, John. *Mrs. Piozzi's Tall Young Beau: William Augustus Conway.* Rutherford, NJ: Associated UP, 1991.

Thaddeus, Janice Farrar. *Frances Burney: A Literary Life.* New York: St. Martin's, 2000.

———. "Hoards of Sorrow: Hester Lynch Piozzi, Frances Burney D'Arblay, and Intimate Death." *Eighteenth-Century Life* 14.3 (1990): 108–29.

Thane, Pat. *Old Age in English History: Past Experiences, Present Issues.* New York: Oxford UP, 2000.

————. "Social Histories of Old Age and Aging." *Journal of Social History* 37.1 (2003): 93–111.

————. "'An Untiring Zest for Life': Images and Self-Images of Old Women in England." *Journal of Family History* 25.2 (2000): 235–47.

Thomson, David. "'I Am Not My Father's Keeper': Families and the Elderly in Nineteenth-Century England." *Law and History Review* 2.2 (1984): 265–86.

Tinker, Chauncey Brewster. *Young Boswell: Chapters on James Boswell the Biographer Based Largely on New Material.* Boston: Atlantic Monthly, 1922.

Titone, Connie. "Catharine Macaulay's *Letters on Education.*" *Teacher's College Record* 99.1 (1997): 179–208.

Todd, Janet, ed. *A Dictionary of British and American Women Writers, 1660–1800.* Totowa, NJ: Rowman & Littlefield, 1985.

Trollope, Anthony. *An Autobiography.* Berkeley: U of California P, 1947.

————. *The Fixed Period.* Oxford: Oxford UP, 1993.

Troyansky, David G. "The Eighteenth Century." In *A History of Old Age*, ed. Pat Thane. Los Angeles: Paul Getty, 2005.

————. "Looking for Grandparents in the French Revolution." *Annales de Démographie Historique* (1991): 127–31.

————. *Old Age in the Old Regime: Image and Experience in Eighteenth-Century France.* Ithaca: Cornell UP, 1989.

Turner, Cheryl. *Living by the Pen: Women Writers in the Eighteenth Century.* London: Routledge, 1992.

Tytler, Sarah [Henrietta Keddie]. *Jane Austen and Her Works.* New York: Cassell, Petter, Galpin, 1880.

Utter, Robert Palfrey, and Gwendolyn Bridges Needham. *Pamela's Daughters.* New York, Macmillan, 1936.

Van Oven, Barnard. *On the Decline of Life in Health and Disease, Being an Attempt to Investigate the Causes of Longevity; and the Best Means of Attaining a Healthful Old Age.* London: John Churchill, 1853.

Van Tilburg, Marja. "Where Has 'the Wise, Old Woman' Gone? Gender and Age in Early Modern and Modern Advice Literature." In *The Prime of Their Lives: Wise Old Women in Pre-Industrial Europe*, ed. Anneke B. Mulder-Bakker and Renée Nip, 149–65. Leuven: Peeters, 2004.

Vining, Elizabeth Gray. *Young Walter Scott.* New York: Viking Press, 1935.

Vullaimy, C. E. *Mrs. Thrale of Streatham.* London: Cape, 1936.

Walker, Barbara G. *The Crone: Woman of Age, Wisdom, and Power.* San Francisco: Harper & Row, 1985.

Walker, Gina Luria. *Mary Hays (1759–1843): The Growth of a Woman's Mind.* Aldershot, UK: Ashgate, 2006.

Wakefield, Dick. *Anna Laetitia Barbauld.* London: Centaur, 2001.

Rev. of *The Wanderer*, by Frances Burney. *Anti-Jacobin Review* 46 (1814): 347–54.

Rev. of *The Wanderer*, by Frances Burney. *British Critic*, n.s. 1 (1814): 374–86.

Rev. of *The Wanderer*, by Frances Burney. *European Magazine and London Review* 66 (1814): 424–27.

Rev. of *The Wanderer,* by Frances Burney. *Gentleman's Magazine* 84 (1814): 579–81.

Rev. of *The Wanderer,* by Frances Burney. *Theatrical Inquisitor and Monthly Mirror* 4 (1814): 234–37.

Warner, William. *Licensing Entertainment: The Elevation of Novel Reading in Britain, 1684–1750.* Berkeley: U of California P, 1998.

Watson, Mary Sidney. "When Flattery Kills: The Silencing of Anna Laetitia Barbauld." *Women's Studies* 28 (1999): 617–43.

West, Jane. *Ringrove; or, Old Fashioned Notions.* London: Longman, Rees, Orme, Brown & Green, 1827.

White, Ina Mary. "The Diary of Jane Porter." *Scottish Review* 29 (1897): 321–37.

Whiting, B. J. "Old Maids Lead Apes in Hell." *Englische Studien* 70 (1935/36): 337–51.

Willich, A. F. M. *Lectures on Diet and Regimen: Being a Systematic Inquiry into the Most Rational Means of Preserving Health and Prolonging Life,* 2nd ed. London: T. N. Longman & O. Rees, 1799.

Wilson, Mona. *These Were Muses.* London: Sidgwick & Jackson, 1924.

Wollstonecraft, Mary. *An Historical and Moral View of the Origin and Progress of the French Revolution.* London, 1794.

———. Rev. of *Letters on Education,* by Catharine Macaulay Graham. *Analytical Review* 8 (1790): 241–54.

———. *A Vindication of the Rights of Woman.* Ed. Carol Poston. 2nd ed. New York: W. W. Norton, 1988.

———. *The Works of Mary Wollstonecraft.* Ed. Janet Todd and Marilyn Butler. 7 vols. New York: New York UP, 1989.

Wood, Marilyn. *"Studious to Please": A Profile of Jane West, an Eighteenth-Century Author.* Donington, UK: Shaun Tyas, 2003.

Woodward, Kathleen. "Age-Work in American Culture." *American Literary History* 6.4 (1994): 779–91.

Woodward, Kathleen, ed. *Figuring Age: Women, Bodies, Generations.* Bloomington: Indiana UP, 1999.

Woolf, Virginia. *A Room of One's Own.* New York: Harcourt, Brace, 1929.

Wordsworth, Jonathan. *The Bright Work Grows: Women Writers of the Romantic Age.* Poole, UK: Woodstock, 1997.

"Works for Young Persons." *Eclectic Review,* n.s. 25 (1826): 79.

Rev. of *The Works of Maria Edgeworth, in Six Volumes,* by Maria Edgeworth. *North American Review* 17.41 (1823): 383–89.

Wyatt-Brown, Anne M., and Janice Rossen. *Aging and Gender in Literature: Studies in Creativity.* Charlottesville: UP of Virginia, 1993.

Yahnke, Robert. *Aging in Literature: A Reader's Guide.* New York: American Library Association, 1990.

Zimmern, Helen. *Maria Edgeworth.* Boston: Roberts Bros., 1883.

Zircker, Malvin R., Jr. "Richardson's Correspondence: The Personal Letter as Private Experience." In *The Familiar Letter in the Eighteenth Century,* ed. Howard Anderson, Philip B. Daghlian, and Irvin Ehrenpreis, 71–91. Lawrence: U of Kansas P, 1966.